DAHLIAS

SEED TO BLOOM

The Dahlia Grower's Companion

Kristine Albrecht

Brion Sprinsock

ISBN: 9798391379737

..

At left: unnamed 'KA's' seedling.

My home garden.

ACKNOWLEDGMENTS

This book is the collective effort of many people who must be thanked. My husband and co-author, Brion Sprinsock, has his fingerprints all over this book. He wore many hats including writer, editor, graphic designer, interviewer, photographer, researcher, and cheerleader.

When I first discovered dahlias two generous people took me under their wing and taught me many of the techniques in this book. Special thanks to Karen Zydner and Kevin Larkin for their kindness, generosity, and patience.

Nine friends generously read the first drafts and offered helpful edits. Thanks to Art Lewis, Sybil Albrecht Lewis, Patricia Santana, Lee Kavaljian, Eben Sprinsock, Janet Egger, Dr. Virginia Walbot, and Dr. Keith Hammett. Special thanks to Missy Foran who took on the responsibility of chief editor. Her red pen and her gracious nudging transformed this effort from a manuscript into a book.

My small farm is the laboratory for the techniques described in this book. I have the best farm crew that includes Jan Palia, Iris Wallace, Brittany Nielsen, and Narcizo Solorio Lopez.

Finally, I wish to thank and celebrate Erin Benzakein of Floret Farm for supporting and inspiring me throughout my dahlia journey. Erin has been the standard-bearer for flower farmers and farmer-florists, and the path I am on now owes much to her encouragement and generosity.

'KA's Mocha Katie (left) and 'KA's Mocha Maya' (center).

CONTENTS

Author Kristine Albrecht with 'Pam Howden' dahlias.

INTRODUCTION

FIRST THINGS FIRST. I have grown and hybridized dahlias for 18 years, and if I have learned anything in that time, it is that there is no single way to grow them. This book is based on my hands-on experience, and in the hope of giving you growing advice from multiple perspectives, I have gathered a group of nine dahlia growers to add their voices to this book.

I am so grateful for the contributions of Gabriela Salazar of la Musa de las Flores in Valle de Bravo, Mexico, Heather Henson of Boreal Blooms in Alberta, Canada; Lorelie Merton of Florelie Seasonal Flowers in Bungaree, Victoria, Australia; Galena Berkompas of Micro Flower Farm in Vancouver, Washington; David Hall of Halls of Heddon in Northumberland, England; Emily Avenson of Fleuropean in eastern Belgium; Philippa Stewart of Justdahlias in Cheshire, England; Melissa Smith of Fraylick Farm in Traveler's Rest, South Carolina; and Dr. Keith Hammett, QSM in Auckland, New Zealand.

They have experiences in different climates and with different growing goals than mine. I will introduce each contributor within these pages and share some of their methods. The idea of including advice from other growers was not mine. I came across it when my son was preparing to hike the 2,650-mile Pacific Crest Trail. He and I were reading a trail handbook written by Jackie McDonnell. She included several contributors to weigh in on their preferred equipment, favorite foods, and functional hiking clothes. It was so useful for us to read advice from a variety of experienced hikers. I knew then that if I ever wrote a book on growing dahlias I would follow Jackie's lead and include information from others.

I describe here everything I do to care for my dahlias on the central coast of California. My farm duties take many hours of work every day. I don't expect every reader to commit the same amount of time to their dahlias as I do. So, please take what you can use from this book, experiment, and find what works for you.

Finally, throughout this book, I mention tools and products that I like. Everything I recommend I use on my farm. I don't accept payment or free products from companies in exchange for promotion.

WHY DAHLIAS?

MY PATH TO GROWING DAHLIAS WAS NOT DIRECT OR DELIBERATE. The groundwork was laid in my 40s when my neighbor Sheryl was given an 80-pound pumpkin for Halloween. It was a marvel, but sadly vandals smashed it in the street. I decided to gather a few seeds, hoping they would grow another large pumpkin the following year. They did, leading me down a rabbit hole of giant pumpkin genetics and cross-breeding. At the time, my son was in elementary school and he was my enthusiastic pumpkin partner (see photo on page 268). Eventually, the two of us grew a giant weighing 876 pounds (396 kg)!

When my son reached his teen years, he began new pursuits and lost interest in our pumpkin project. About this time, a friend gave me a dahlia tuber she purchased at a large retailer. I don't remember what variety it was; however, those blooms caught my imagination. Even though these were my first dahlia plants, the blooms were big, beautiful, and prolific. My husband was running a bed and breakfast inn at the time. He put my dahlias on display, and they caused a minor stir. He suggested I plant more the following year, so we could put dahlia arrangements in the guest rooms. That was the inspiration I needed to dive in.

We owned a weed-choked quarter-acre (2,023 sq m) of land near our home that had occasionally beckoned me over the years. My interest in dahlias led me to transform this plot into a proper suburban farm. The first task was to remove the overgrown blackberries and dead pine trees and battle the established weeds. At the time the plot was called Blackbird Farm after the high number of resident crows. I planted half vegetables and half dahlias.

That original half-acre is now Santa Cruz Dahlias, where I grow most of my dahlias today. In 2006 I started breeding dahlias. It was a natural transition for me based on my experience from hand-pollinating pumpkins. For me, dahlia breeding is so rewarding, partly because it plays to my natural strengths. Since childhood, I have been drawn to the arts. In high school I made pottery and in college I majored in ceramic sculpture. I consider flower breeding to be another visual art. Selective breeding involves decisions about color, hue, shape, and form. Hand pollination reminds me of glazing ceramic sculptures, layering two or three glazes on top of each other without a guaranteed result. I only saw the final color for the first time when the piece came out of the kiln. Today, I hand-pollinate dahlias without a guarantee of what the resulting flowers will be. However, instead of waiting a few days for the kiln to fire, I now wait eleven months from pollination to the resulting new blooms. For most of my life, I have been a pretty impetuous person. Breeding dahlias has taught me a whole new level of patience.

In my opinion, dahlias are the most giving plants for the amount of work we put in. When planted in a sunny spot of fertile soil with adequate water, they reward us with months of cut-and-come-again blooms. They are so diverse that one can choose to grow varieties of many colors, flower forms, or bloom sizes. Even a pocket garden with room for only a few dahlia plants will give a gardener enough blooms to share with friends and neighbors. The icing on the cake is that at the end of each year, the tubers can be dug up and divided for more plants the following year, or given to others as gifts. I encourage you to dive in if you are new to growing dahlias. A good place to start is with some attention to your soil.

1. Soil

THE FIRST STEP: A SOIL TEST

THE EARTH IS A BIG PLANET, AND THE essential elements in its soil are not distributed evenly across its surface. Over time, erosion, sea level changes, glaciation, volcanism, and tectonic uplift have left a varied pattern of soil fertility across the globe. Depending on where we are, the soil we start with may need some work before we plant our dahlias.

I highly recommend starting with a soil test. Testing involves sending away a few cups of soil (gathered from various locations in your planting beds) to an agricultural lab for analysis. The results will quantify your soil's pH level, organic matter content, levels of many essential nutrients, and more. Most soil tests return a list of numerical results for each nutrient and a chart showing each element as very low, low, medium, high, or very high. The lab report will recommend amendments you can add to your soil to bring it into balance and help your plants thrive.

Before we dive into the world of soil tests, there is one situation where they are not needed: growing dahlias in containers. When growing a dahlia in a pot or other container, it is customary to use fresh potting soil each year. I don't recommend growing dahlias in containers with soil from your yard. High-quality potting soil is typically mixed and balanced for the benefit of plants. Soil tests are for gardeners and farmers who will be growing their plants in native soil.

You can find a soil testing lab near you in the U.S. by contacting the USDA extension office in your area. Once you find a lab, they will instruct you on how to take a sample and how to ship it to them. For example, I use A & L Laboratories which has offices in Modesto, California, and Portland, Oregon. For the first several years that I was growing dahlias on my new

plot, I did a soil test every year. Now that I've been growing on the same plot for 18 years, I do a soil test every few years.

I typically send in my soil sample in the fall and I let the lab know I am an organic gardener and that I grow dahlias. I also let them know the size of my plot so I get amendment recommendations listed in pounds per 1,000 square feet (93 sq m) instead of pounds per acre. Because they know I am an organic gardener, they recommend natural products that benefit dahlias, instead of a list of synthetic fertilizers. I can usually purchase locally everything they recommend.

SOIL PREPARATION

Soil is the foundation of quality gardening. The perfect soil for dahlias is easy to dig, gets lots of sun, has nutrients and organic matter, and holds moisture, yet has adequate drainage. Dahlias grow in many kinds of soil, but the more you can improve it, the happier your plants will be. Dahlias prefer soil that is slightly acidic,

Unnamed 'KA's' seedlings.

between pH 6.5 and 7. They grow well in soil that is covered with mulch, which helps retain moisture and discourages weed growth. A high-quality mulch will also add organic matter to the soil.

Most garden soil has about 2% organic matter; however, if you can bring this up to 4 or 5%, your dahlia plants will be healthier. I recommend a fall soil test so you can add any amendments before winter. However, don't let the calendar stop you. A soil test can be done and amendments can be added any time of year.

Applying a layer of compost on the ground in late fall will feed the living bacteria and fungi in the soil over the winter. I am a no-till gardener, so after digging up my tubers in the fall I plant a cover crop that grows through the winter. I then chop it down six weeks before planting time and cover it with a tarp. The organisms in the soil consume the green cuttings. A little bit of love for your beds in the fall will make springtime planting easier.

Gabriela Salazar, Mexico
Gabriela Salazar of la Musa de las Flores in the mountains near Mexico City has soil with a high clay content. For this reason, she has installed raised beds for her dahlias. The 16-inch (40 cm) wooden walls on the edge of her beds hold good quality soil she has installed on top of her native clay soil. The paths between her beds are covered with crushed gravel.

CROP ROTATION
Good farming practices call for crop rotation–planting different plants sequentially every year or at different times on a plot of land. On large farms with movable irrigation and mechanized tilling, this is relatively simple. An entire field can be tilled and quickly replanted with another crop. For the home gardener or farmer-florist, crop rotation is more challenging.

In my dahlia plots, the paths between my beds are fixed. Some of my paths are permanently covered in black weed cloth. The soil in my paths is compacted because I walk on them constantly. My planting beds are in the same place each year. My irrigation system is firmly in place and is not easily moved. For me, crop rotation occurs after I dig my dahlias out and plant my winter cover crop, which I discuss starting on page 19.

Heather Henson, Canada
Heather Henson of Boreal Blooms in Cold Lake, Alberta has three 14-by-80 foot (4.2 by 24 m) tunnels on her half-acre farm. Because her growing season is short, she plants her dahlias inside her tunnels to keep them blooming through September. Each season only a single tunnel is planted with dahlias. The other two hold fall crops like stock, zinnias, marigolds, and late sunflowers. Therefore, each year the dahlias are planted in a different tunnel. This rotation system provides Heather's soil a two-year rest between each dahlia crop.

Lorelie Merton, Australia
Lorelie Merton of Florelie Seasonal Flowers in Bungaree, Victoria does not plant dahlias in the same beds year after year. With her abundant available land, she plants dahlias in each bed every other year. In the intervening years, beds are planted for pasture that she will use to graze her flock of sheep.

THE BENEFITS OF NO-TILL GARDENING
When I first started growing dahlias, I tilled my soil. There was satisfaction that all the weeds were tilled under and I loved how my freshly tilled fields looked. Planting into a tilled field was so easy with loosened soil. But once I began researching no-till practices my thoughts changed. I learned that feeding the life in the soil was better for my plants than disrupting that

Hand watering young dahlia plants.

life. My focus quickly shifted to preserving and enhancing the organisms in the soil.

As written in Jesse Frost's book *The Living Soil Handbook*, no-till gardening is based on three fundamental ideas.

-First, disturb the soil as little as possible.

-Second, keep the soil covered as much as possible.

-Third, keep the soil planted as much as possible.

The more consistently I can put these three ideas into practice, the better my soil and the healthier my plants will be with the fewest weeds.

THE LIVING SOIL

We tend to think of our plants as alive and the soil as inert. However, soil is a living web of billions of organisms. The more we care for it, the more it cares for our plants. There are 17 essential nutrients that plants need from the soil to thrive. They can only get a few of these on their own. For the rest, our plants are involved in a complex exchange with soil bacteria, microbes, and fungi. The roots of our plants release sugars and vitamin C that are consumed by organisms in the soil. In return, these organisms bring the plant important nutrients. All the interactions of water, sugars, and nutrients occur in the tiny root hairs underground. When taken care of, the life in our soil will provide optimal conditions for the growth of our plants.

Although we can't easily observe it, the soil is like a complex underground city. It is full of bacteria and fungi. One tablespoon of soil contains more organisms than there are people on Earth! They are breathing, growing, competing, and excreting wastes and other compounds that feed our plants. Without soil organisms, our plants would not grow. Eighty percent of the nitrogen a plant requires comes from waste produced by bacteria and other soil organisms. Since these organisms are attracted to the plant's root exudates (sugars), this nitrogen source is delivered right in the root zone where it is needed most.

Healthy soil is also full of microbes that perform another service: decomposition. Without bacteria and fungi, we would be living in mounds of waste. These invisible organisms are vital for plant nutrition. They break down and ingest complex plant materials such as stems and roots, then release nitrogen, carbon, and other nutrients that would otherwise leach away from the soil and be unavailable to our plants.

Mycorrhizal fungi build networks in soil with threads branching out in all directions. These threads (called hyphae) surround plant roots and bring them nutrients (mainly nitrogen and phosphorus). Fungal networks extend the effective root system of our plants by a factor of 100. The root hairs on our plants are woefully inefficient in absorbing water and most nutrients, compared to fungi. Our plants produce carbohydrates at their roots that fungi use to expand their hypha network. The fungi

ESSENTIAL NUTRIENTS

The 17 essential nutrients plants need are hydrogen, oxygen, carbon, nitrogen, phosphorus, potassium, calcium, magnesium, sulfur, chloride, iron, boron, manganese, zinc, copper, molybdenum and nickel.

pump moisture into the roots of our plants that they could not reach on their own. In exchange, our plants supply the fungi with sugars.

While most fungi help our plants, some species bring harm. Powdery mildew, root rot, botrytis, and rust are examples of fungi that damage our plants. These typically don't kill host plants, but they can weaken them. Fortunately, there are more good guys in the soil than bad guys. The best way to increase the good guys is to enhance and maintain soil health through added organic matter and mulching.

Earthworms play an essential role in soil health. As impossible as it sounds, an acre of good soil typically holds over two million earthworms that move 18 tons of soil each year in search of food. As they forage, they shred organic matter, aerate the soil, and excrete mucus-coated particles. Vermicastings (worm poop) enrich the soil and are 50% richer in organic matter than the surrounding soil. In addition, they have seven times the total amount of phosphate, ten times the amount of potash (soluble phosphate), five times the nitrogen, and three times more magnesium than the surrounding soil.

Worms transform our soil with the help of bacteria that live in their intestines. The bacteria and grit in their intestines are required to break down organic matter. Worms will eat their weight in decaying plant matter every day. The waste they leave behind includes organic matter broken down into particles small enough that bacteria and fungi can take them up, transform them, and make them chemically available to our plants.

As worms move, they make tunnels that increase the porosity of our soil and increase its capacity to hold water. Their burrows become pathways for air and water. Like us, earthworms breathe air. Their tunnels create gaps in the soil so they can breathe. After a big rainstorm, we often find earthworms above ground because their burrows fill with water forcing them to the surface to breathe. Earthworm burrows are also the pathways that our plant roots use to extend their reach for water and nutrients. While most worms spend their lives underground, night crawlers live up to their name. After dark, they emerge out of their burrows to find plant matter on the surface and pull it underground.

Learning about the value of earthworms, and the fact that they can live up to eight years, I switched to no-till gardening. Tiller blades kill earthworms, reducing their population and contributing to a loss of soil health. When we rototill or use other mechanical methods to break open our soil, we destroy the earthworm burrows and tunnels that our plant roots utilize. Tilling rips through the below-ground infrastructure and turns it upside down. The threaded hyphae networks are severed. Nematodes and other arthropods are killed, and those that survive lose the habitat they built and the organic matter they need for food. Tilling also changes the soil structure in favor of weed growth by bringing weed seeds from deep in the cold soil to the warm surface, where they can germinate.

Tilling introduces air into the top layer of the soil and pulls organic matter in the soil up to the surface, where the sun burns it off. That new rush of air stimulates microbial activity that rapidly depletes organic matter. As a result, tilled agricultural fields are typically deficient in organic matter. Tilling speeds up the

Unnamed 'KA's' seedling.

decomposition of organic matter so much that even if organic matter is added while tilling, the result is still a net loss. Organic matter in soil needs to be processed by worms and digested by bacteria before it is small enough to be chemically available to our plants.

One long-term effect of tilling is compaction. It is difficult or impossible to till soil without standing on it or driving a tractor over it, compacting the soil, and collapsing the networks of tunnels and air pockets in healthy soil. It is true that immediately after tilling, the soil will be lighter and less compact, but that is transient. With the first rains, the soil will become more compact than before tilling as the soil has lost its web of underground tunnels and fungal structures that give air and water places to go.

I don't walk on my planting beds. I have paths for walking on either side of my beds. These paths allow me to add or remove plants, lay drip lines, set stakes, disbud my plants, cut my blooms, and spray my plants, all while standing or kneeling outside my beds. As a result, my dahlia beds remain undisturbed, with one necessary exception. Every fall I dig out my tubers while trying to disturb the soil as little as possible. There are several additional benefits from no-till gardening. Here are a few.

EXTENDING THE GROWING SEASON

In the early days, I started the growing season every year by tilling my land. I believed it was necessary. In one of those early years, my plants went in the ground late because a poorly timed rain made the ground too wet to till. As the days and weeks passed, I waited impatiently for my soil to become dry enough to till. Now that I am no longer tilling, I can plant on my schedule rather than a schedule dictated by the weather. Instead of waiting for the soil to dry up, I pull the mulch aside, dig a small hole with my hands, and plant: no

tilling, no noise, no exhaust, and no delays. Not having to wait for the weather or the tiller contractor is a welcome feeling of freedom and independence. It also gives my florists and designers dahlia blooms weeks earlier.

REDUCING WEEDS

Weeds are nature's way of covering bare soil with living plants. They germinate fast, cover the soil, and go to seed quickly to cover even more soil. Nature's preference is for roots in the soil to feed the organisms below, hold the soil from washing away, and provide ground cover, cooling shade, and insect habitats. By keeping my soil covered with plants or mulch all year, I eliminate the majority of weeds on my farm.

REDUCED CARBON DIOXIDE EMISSIONS

Tilling our soil releases carbon dioxide that is held in the soil. This greenhouse gas contributes to climate change. By not tilling our soil, we sequester carbon dioxide underground and reduce our garden's carbon footprint.

QUICK CROP TURNOVER

One benefit of a no-till practice is the ability to plant a new crop immediately after the previous crop has been harvested. In the fall, I dig and divide my tubers. As each row of tubers is removed, I immediately broadcast my cover crop seeds. It might take me six weeks to dig and divide all my tubers. Starting the cover crop seeds row by row allows me to keep my soil covered and planted at all times. In my climate, I have to water the seeds for a month until our rains start falling.

PLANTING A COVER CROP

After digging my tubers, I rake my mulch to the edges of my beds for future use and rake the soil flat, removing any weeds. Next, I broadcast cover crop seeds onto the soil, using roughly seven pounds

Planting into no-till soil.

(3.2kg) per 100 square feet (30 sq m). I then rake the seeds into the soil to a depth of one-half inch (1.3 cm), water the seeds in, and cover the ground with Agribon row cover weighed down with bricks or rocks. Hiding the seeds under a row cover protects them from hungry birds and provides extra warmth to get them off to a good start in the fall. Agribon is permeable, so rain and irrigation water go through it. If rain has not started falling, I will water the seeds daily for a week until they sprout and once or twice a week after that. Once our rainy season begins, the cover crop will grow without added water. Agribon row cover is sold in several thicknesses, allowing varying amounts of light to pass through. I use AG-19 which blocks 15% of the sunlight. Once the seeds sprout and reach a height of 3-4 inches (7.5-10 cm), I remove the row cover since the seeds are no longer vulnerable to birds.

There are several seed mixes one can use for a cover crop. These usually include a blend of legumes, vetch, clovers, peas, and winter grains. The organic seed mix I use is popular with farmers in my area and consists of:

-Bell Beans: 30%
-Dundale Peas: 25%
-Cayuse Oats: 15%
-Hairy Vetch: 15%
-Common Vetch: 15%

Each seed in the mix benefits the soil in its own way. The beans and peas have bacterial partners that fix nitrogen into the ground that the roots of my dahlias can take up. They also support microbial life in the soil. Oats are frost tolerant and grow tall quickly, out-competing any weeds. Oats also improve the productivity of bell beans and peas when planted together. Vetch, another legume, has bacterial nitrogen fixation and is a prolific weed suppressor. Vetch is also cold tolerant, even growing when covered in snow. If you are interested in planting a cover crop, your local farm bureau may have a list of grasses, legumes, and other seeds recommended for your climate.

I plant my cover crop in September or October and let it grow. In Santa Cruz this means it can typically reach 3 to 5 feet (1 to 1.5 m) in height. In colder climates cover crops may not grow as tall before being killed by frost. I terminate my cover crop six weeks before my dahlia planting date. I use a weed whacker to cut it down to within 1 inch (2.4 cm) of the ground. I don't cut the growth down all at once, leaving long green stalks on the ground. Instead, I cut it in layers, trimming off the greenery from top to bottom about every six inches (15 cm). This way, I end up with small pieces of vegetation rather than large intact plants lying on the ground.

It is best to terminate a cover crop before the flowers go to seed. Plants give first priority to flowers when distributing sugars. These nutrients are what you want to transfer from the crop into your soil. If the flowers are allowed to mature and go to seed, the sugars turn to starch, and you will lose some nutritional benefits to the soil. In addition, the older a cover crop gets, the woodier the stalks will become, making it harder to terminate them.

Once cut, I don't rake the mass of greenery; instead, I leave it lying on top of the soil. I give the soil a good soaking if the weather has been dry. I then use an opaque silage tarp or weed cloth to cover the plot for a minimum of six weeks. The tarps block the sun, killing off the cover crop, and halting weed germination. They also create a warm moist environment where worms, sow bugs, bacteria, fungi, nematodes, and other organisms can devour the cut stalks and roots. When I'm ready to plant my dahlias I roll back the

Cover crop seeds.

Agribon row cover protecting the seeds from birds.

tarps and, depending on the moisture level, the remains of the cover crop are gone, or if it has been a dry winter, 90% of the cover crop is gone with 10% straw-like stalks remaining. The organisms in and on the soil have eaten it or pulled it underground. Every year it amazes me how quickly and completely this "green manure" is processed by the organisms in the soil.

The bonus is that breaking down the terminated cover crop took no effort on my part. It was done by a host of organisms working day and night while I worked on other tasks. After removing the tarp, I plant my young dahlia plants right into the soil, which will be rich and loose; I can typically dig the planting holes with a gloved hand. My friend Iris rolls her silage tarp back one row at a time during planting. This keeps moisture in the soil on the rows that are still covered. As a one-person operation, planting her garden may take several weeks, and keeping the unplanted rows covered ensures she won't stimulate weed growth as she's working her way across the rows. You can see a short video of my cover crop on the Kristine Albrecht YouTube channel. Look for video 93.

Cover crop growing across an entire plot, both beds and paths.

Galena Berkompas, Washington

Galena Berkompas of Micro Flower Farm in Vancouver, Washington plants a cover crop at two different times of the year. After her tubers are dug out in the fall, she plants a combination of buckwheat, peas, and oats. These crops grow through the winter and typically get killed by a hard frost. She then lays down tarps to retard weeds and ensure the cover crop will not resprout. However, in some winters, her farm does not get a killing frost. In that event, she will terminate the crop with a weed whacker and cover the remains with a tarp.

Her second cover crop grows over the summer when her spring flowers have finished blooming and are removed. Where the spring flowers were, she grows buckwheat and mustard. The buckwheat grows quickly, suppresses weeds, and makes phosphorus available to her plants. Mustard is a natural fumigant and can suppress soil pathogens like Pythium and Fusarium.

Cover crop after termination with a weed-whacker.

HOW TO START A NO-TILL GARDEN

If you are interested in no-till gardening, I recommend three books that have been a big help to me. First, *The Organic No-Till Farming Revolution* by Andrew Mefferd. In its pages, you will find there is not one way to start no-till gardening. I love this book because of his examples that show how to transition to no-till in different situations. The second recommendation is *Teaming with Microbes, The Organic Gardener's Guide to* *the Soil Food Web*, by Jeff Lowenfels. This book helped me understand what happens underground and how vital the soil food web is to our plants. The third book is *The Living Soil Handbook* by Jesse Frost. This book is filled with examples of no-till gardens and allows us to tailor techniques to our individual needs.

I grow dahlias on two separate plots in two different locations. The first plot I transitioned to no-till is my seedling patch, a 40 by 40 foot (12 x 12 m) plot in my

A silage tarp covering the garden bed after cover crop termination.

front yard. It had a suburban lawn that I wanted to convert to dahlia beds. Without removing any existing grass, I spread about two inches (5 cm) of quality compost over the entire lawn. After leveling it out as much as possible, I covered the compost with a layer of cardboard. The cardboard I used was not fancy. It was just flattened color-free and wax-free corrugated boxes laid out across the entire plot. One benefit of using cardboard is that worms love it. Make sure to remove the plastic tape that might be on the cardboard. I learned this the hard way. Ten years later I still find

small bits of packing tape in my soil. Next, I made sure that there were no gaps in the cardboard where I could see the compost underneath. I used a six-inch (15 cm) overlap where the cardboard pieces met and added strips where needed to cover voids.

Next, I brought in another load of quality compost and spread it evenly on top of the cardboard. Instead of two inches (5 cm), I laid it down six inches (15 cm) thick. Finally, I placed a light-proof tarp on top of this "lasagna" and weighed it down with

No-till soil after six weeks under the silage tarp.

bricks. Many no-till gardeners use silage tarps made from black polypropylene. Silage tarps come in various sizes and allow a gardener to cover an entire plot with one large cover. I use both silage tarps and six-foot (1.8 m) wide weed cloth; my favorite is weed cloth for a few reasons. First, it is lightweight and rolls up into small rolls that I can handle by myself. A silage tarp to cover my entire 40 by 40 foot (12 x 12 m) plot would be very heavy, unwieldy, and require two helpers to move and later store.

Second, although I put bricks down on the edges of my cover, there are times when a strong wind can lift the cloth. If the wind gets under a 40-by-40 foot (12 x 12 m) silage tarp, it could be a significant job to get it back in place. However, if one of my six-foot (1.8 m) wide strips of weed cloth gets loose, I can single-handedly get it back where it belongs.

Third, when I am not covering my cardboard and compost lasagna, the weed cloth strips have other uses as path covers in my garden. A large silage tarp is only suitable for one thing: covering an entire plot. Finally, silage tarps are not permeable. Rain falling on them puddles up in the low spots or floods the outside edges of the tarp. Weed cloth is woven and allows the rain to flow through.

Choose the type of tarp that makes sense for your garden. In dry climates, a silage tarp helps trap moisture, giving the organisms in the soil much-needed hydration; weed cloth allows for airflow so soil will dry out more quickly.

After tarping my plot, I left it in place for three months. During this time, the lawn on the surface of the soil died. Without sunlight, it no longer grew. The worms, arthropods, and other organisms in the soil broke down the cardboard and decomposed the old lawn. The addition of

*Early season dahlias growing under rice straw
mulch in no-till beds.*

accessible organic matter in the compost and cardboard stimulated a buzz of activity under the tarp. After three months, I removed the tarp, and my plot was ready for spring planting. The cardboard and lawn had disappeared, and I laid out my rows and paths without tilling.

The second plot where I grow dahlias is my suburban Santa Cruz farm. It's a one-quarter acre (5,058 sq m) plot about a mile (1.6 km) from my home. When I decided to go no-till, I had already been growing dahlias and tilling the soil for about four years. Because this plot was already in use and did not have an existing lawn, the transition was more straightforward. In the fall of my transition year, I dug and divided

my tubers and then grew a cover crop; see the section starting on page 19 for a complete discussion of how to plant, grow, and harvest cover crops. By the time my last frost date passed, I was able to plant my dahlias into beautiful, organically enhanced soil without tilling or turning.

Six weeks before my last frost date, I used a weed whacker to terminate the cover crop, water it, if the weather was dry, cover it with weed cloth, and let the soil organisms process the organic matter. After six weeks, I removed the weed cloth to find that 95% of the cover crop was gone. Almost all organic matter had been chewed up, decomposed, or pulled underground. I was then able to plant my dahlias without tilling or turning the soil.

Gabriela Salazar of la Musa de las Flores. Photo by Laura May Grogan.

Gabriela Salazar, Mexico

Two hours west of Mexico City sits Valle de Bravo, a small town a mile high in the mountains. There you will find Gabriela Salazar's garden and design studio, la Musa de las Flores. Gabriela grows 600 to 700 dahlias on her one-third acre (1,350 sq m) property. She uses her blooms for her floral designs and leads design workshops. She also has an active wedding and event business, primarily serving Americans at Mexican resorts. In 2020 international travel decreased, and Gabriela moved her workshops online. Those workshops made her instruction more accessible, and have blossomed into a worldwide community passionate about working with flowers. Gabriela believes strongly in the sustainability of local flowers. She teaches farmer-florists to focus on design to increase the value of their own harvest.

The rainy season in the mountains runs the length of her growing season, from May to October. Gabriela protects her dahlia plants with a canopy that lets in light but keeps the punishing rain and hail from damaging her plants. Her location also receives strong winds blocked by walls on all four sides of her dahlia garden. Finally, the sun returns in November, and the Mexican highlands have a second spring bloom.

Dahlias are the national flower of Mexico, and species dahlias grow wild in the mountains around Gabriela's home. However, rather than blooming in late summer and early fall, like Gabriela's protected dahlia plants, wild species dahlias bloom in November after the rainy season has ended.

Gabriela grew up in northern Mexico in a hot desert climate. It was in England that she discovered cut flowers. She was in London working on a master's degree in architectural interiors and would occasionally buy and arrange flowers for her architecture projects. She loved going to the flower market, even when no arrangements were needed. Her neighborhood had a bookstore with a bouquet of fresh flowers every week. She approached the owner to see if she could provide the store's arrangements. They said yes. This gave Gabriela a reason to go to the flower market every week. It was there she developed her passion for flowers.

Gabriela's Website: lamusadelasflores.com
Gabriela's Instagram: @lamusadelasflores

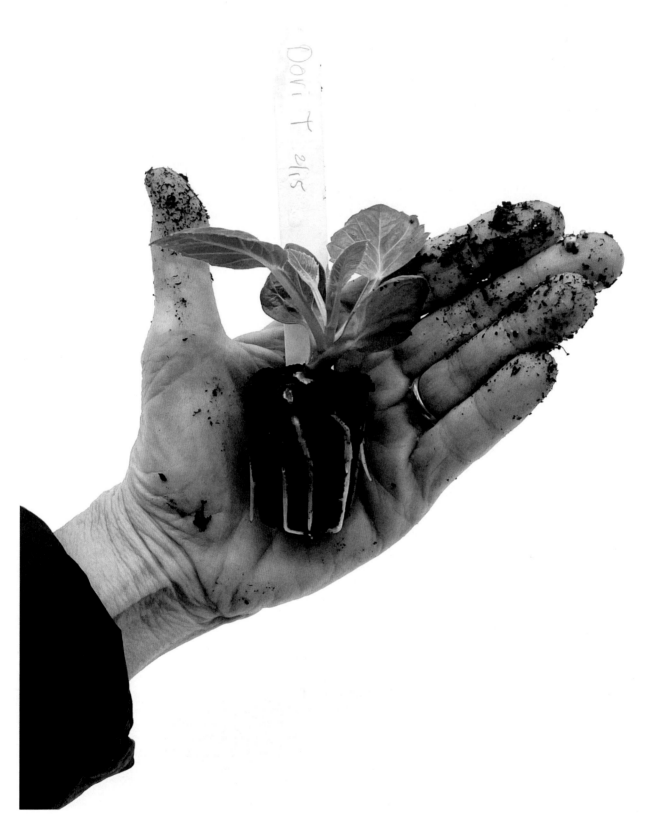

A rooted dahlia cutting.

30

2. Propagating Dahlias

TUBERS

Dahlia plants typically produce between two and twenty tubers underground throughout the growing season. Tubers are swollen root tissue and have four parts: a body, a neck, a crown, and an eye. The crown is where the growth buds (called eyes) of the tuber are and where it will develop sprouts that grow into a plant. Without an eye, a dahlia tuber will not grow a plant.

After a tuber clump is dug up, divided into individual tubers, and stored in a cold environment over the winter, in the spring the individual tubers are warmed up and sprout from an eye growing into a clone of

the plant they came from. They will produce blooms that are exactly like the parent plant. Depending on the latitude, growers typically plant them after the last frost date, between April and late May (in the northern hemisphere).

Dahlia tubers.

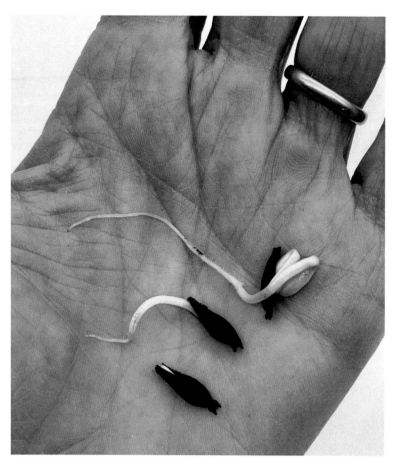

Germinating dahlia seeds.

produce blooms in their first year. They will also produce tubers underground that can be dug up and divided in the fall (See page 37 for step-by-step instructions on making cuttings).

SEEDS

Propagating dahlias with tubers and cuttings will produce healthy, productive plants, but it will not fulfill the plant's fundamental need to produce seeds. Seeds result when the pollen from one dahlia bloom fertilizes the ovule of another dahlia bloom. The genetic variation from this random blending of genes ensures that the species will evolve and produce varieties that are unique.

If left on the plant to fully mature, dahlia blooms can be pollinated by insects or by humans. If a pollinated flower remains on the plant, it will develop a seed head. Dahlias, like their close relatives the sunflowers, have many ovules and require each one to be fertilized by an individual pollen grain. The result is that each seed is genetically different from its "seed-mates." Dahlia seed heads can hold as few as one or as many as 100 or more seeds. Unlike tubers or cuttings, dahlia seeds grow into plants that are not clones. Each seed's genetic code is unique.

CUTTINGS

Dahlias can also be propagated from cuttings. An individual tuber, tuber clump, or pot root (miniature tuber clump) brought indoors and placed in potting soil with a source of heat, light, and moisture will produce multiple green sprouts. These sprouts, or cuttings, can be removed from the tuber crown and placed into a rooting medium. If kept warm and moist, cuttings will produce roots and grow into full-size plants.

Using this technique, a grower can multiply the stock of favorite varieties because each individual tuber in a cutting bed will typically produce five to ten cuttings. Pot roots and tuber clumps will produce many more. Cuttings, like tubers, are clones. They produce blooms that are exactly like the parent plant. Plants grown from cuttings will grow to full height and

Every named dahlia variety that we grow in our gardens started out as a single plant grown from one unique seed. A dahlia plant grown from a seed is called a seedling. Growing dahlia seedlings can be rewarding if you appreciate surprises. Some dahlia growers compare the blooming season in their seedling garden to Christmas because every day reveals another surprise bloom. After growing from seed for 18 years, I can attest to the excitement of being the first person to see a bloom that never existed before.

Like tubers and cuttings, dahlia seedlings grow to full height and produce blooms in their first growing season. They also produce tubers that can be dug, divided, and stored for future planting. If you like the blooms from a seedling, you can save the tubers and grow a clone of that same variety the following season.

Dahlia hybridizers refer to some plants as "second-year seedlings." These are plants grown from a tuber that came from a first-year seedling; they are new, typically unnamed varieties grown for a second year. Often breeders will grow new varieties for 3–7 years, observing all of their characteristics and traits before giving the variety a name and introducing it to the market.

"Lulu Island Mom' and 'Steve Meggos'.

Heather Henson with a dried flower bouquet.
Photo by Megan Timm of Brighter by Megan photography.

Heather Henson, Alberta, Canada

Heather Henson of Boreal Blooms grows annual and perennial cut flowers in the boreal forest of Alberta, Canada. She sells her blooms through a CSA, the farmer's market, custom bouquets, and full-service and DIY weddings. Through trial and error, Heather has developed strategies for growing dahlias in an unforgiving climate with a short but intense growing season. Her dahlias are planted in June, yet they receive 19 hours of daylight at the summer solstice (June 21st), compensating for the late planting date. Heather is assisted by her two daughters, her son, and two part-time employees. They have been growing flowers together for over 10 years.

Heather's mother grew fruits and vegetables that were harvested and canned for the long winter. There were flowers in her yard when she was growing up, but they were for outdoor color, not cut flowers. When Heather's children were young, she and her husband lived for several years in Belgium. Their home was in an urban apartment building, leaving Heather no garden to tend. Across the road was a flower market. Heather watched as people bought flowers each week. She came to appreciate the European tradition of having a vase of fresh flowers on the table. She soon became a regular customer at the market and fell in love with indoor cut flowers.

When her family moved to Cold Lake, Alberta, Heather tore out her lawn and planted fruits, veggies, and flowers on every spare inch of her small lot. Then, by fate, Heather read a blog post about Erin Benzakein of Floret Farm growing and selling cut sweet peas. That got her thinking about selling cut flowers from her small garden. It worked, and eventually, she rented a half-acre farm plot ten minutes away from her home. She grows tulips, peonies, ranunculus, zinnias, and 400 to 500 dahlias in high hoop tunnels. Because her growing season ends in October, she dries flowers, including dahlias, for use in bouquets and arrangements for winter weddings and events.

When she is not tending her garden, bringing flowers to the farmer's market, or designing arrangements for a wedding, Heather is the co-host of the Sustainable Flowers Podcast. Since 2017 Heather and her friend Clara Qualizza of Meadow and Thicket have been interviewing growers and sharing their passion for sustainable cut flowers.

Heather's Website: borealblooms.com
Heather's Instagram: @borealblooms

'KA's Papa John' grown from a cutting. Photo by Iris Wallace.

3. CUTTINGS

MAKING CUTTINGS

CUTTINGS CAN BE MADE FROM A single dahlia tuber, a tuber clump, or a pot root. Pot roots are intentionally made the season before by planting a small tuber or cutting in a four-inch (10 cm) pot. The plant is then grown all season in the small pot, restricting tuber growth and producing a miniature tuber clump. Making cuttings from a single tuber can yield 5 to 10 plants; cuttings from a pot root can yield 50 to 100 plants; Cuttings taken from a tuber, a tuber clump, or a pot root all result in plants that are clones.

Starting a cutting bed requires some advance planning. It takes about two to six weeks to "wake up" tubers from winter storage and another two to three weeks to grow a cutting for planting. So, as a rule of thumb, start a cutting bed eight to ten weeks before your last frost date. You can use this website (almanac.com/gardening/frostdates) to enter your ZIP code and find your last frost date. If you don't get frost wait until eight to ten weeks before your nighttime low temperatures reach 50° F (10° C).

Like all things relating to dahlias, the speed at which a tuber will wake up differs based on the variety and the specifics of your particular cutting bed. My 'Cafe au Lait' tubers sometimes wake up in about two weeks. Likewise, I have some varieties that can take almost nine weeks to wake up. So, ten weeks before your last frost date is a good time to start if it's your first time taking cuttings. As the years go by, you will learn to adjust your start date depending on the varieties you grow. Keeping records every year is always a good idea.

A cutting bed can be simple or elaborate. It is basically a plastic container filled with high-quality potting soil held at a warm temperature with grow lights above it.

Your grow lights don't have to be the professional type. Many growers use inexpensive shop lights from home improvement stores. Whatever tub or pot you use must have small holes at the bottom and a pan below it to catch excess water. If you want to make a large cutting bed, you can find large tubs with catch basins at stores that sell hydroponic supplies.

Next, fill your tub with six inches (15.2 cm) or more of high-quality potting soil. If you set up your cutting bed indoors, the ambient room temperature may provide enough warmth for your tubers to sprout. I keep the potting soil in my cutting bed between 65 and 70°F (18.3 to 21.1° C). I monitor the temperature with a soil thermometer buried three inches (7.6 cm) into the potting soil. If the indoor temperature is low, you may want to use a heat mat under your container to keep the potting soil at the right temperature. If you use a heat mat I suggest also using a probe controller that will keep the soil at 70° F (21° C). If the soil reaches 80° F (26° C) the tubers could rot.

You will also need a grow light 10 inches (30 cm) above your cutting bed. Once the tubers sprout, they need 14 hours of light each day to "trick" them into thinking it's spring. Grow lights can add significant heat to a room. To keep my room from getting too warm, I run my lights at night when

CUTTINGS vs. TUBERS

Dr. Keith Hammett, a plant pathologist and leading dahlia expert with 60 years of experience growing and hybridizing dahlias, believes that cuttings produce better plants than tubers. He reasons that tubers are made up of old plant material. When a tuber is planted, it is one-year-old plant tissue. Older plant material has had more opportunities through cell division to accumulate mutations. Dr. Hammett explains that this is why the body of a 70-year-old does not look the same as it did when that person was 20 years old and why we are not as vigorous in old age as we were when we were young. In contrast, a cutting is 100% new plant material. When planted in the garden, it is only a few weeks old and is less likely to have damaging mutations that can occur with age.

Another reason Dr. Hammett cites the benefits of cuttings over tubers is that there is a more direct connection between the roots of a cutting and the above-ground part of the plant. When we plant a tuber, the roots grow underground from the base of the tuber. For nutrients to reach the above-ground part of the plant, they must travel through the tuber. If it is rotting, or is in poor health, it could restrict the flow of nutrients. However, a cutting has an entirely new root system that connects directly to the plant stalk. With no tuber in the way, there is no restriction of water or nutrients between the roots and the plant above.

the ambient temperatures are lower and electricity is less expensive.

Once my cutting bed is ready, I pull the tubers I will use out of cold storage. Tubers with thin necks are at high risk of drying out and withering under grow lights; I save them for planting in the garden and use thicker-necked tubers for the cutting bed. I make a plant tag with the date for each tuber as it goes into the cutting bed; I will follow up with the date each tuber produces a sprout. This way, the next time I make a cutting bed, I can better predict how long each variety will take to sprout.

With individual tubers, I bury each tuber into the potting soil up to the crowns with the tubers at a 45° angle. The tuber body and neck will be under the potting soil and just the crown will be protruding. I place my plant tag just behind each crown to identify each tuber. Tubers can be placed close together, leaving a one-inch (2.5 cm) space between them.

Giving advice on watering is difficult because each grower will use a different-size container and a different potting mix. Some potting soils have added wetting agents that keep the soil moist. Also, some rooms are warmer or have higher humidity than others. After the initial planting, I give the tubers a good watering in. This settles the potting soil around the tubers. When I initially water my tubers some water will come out of the bottom of my container. After this first heavy dose, I water to keep the soil moist, but not too wet. You must continue to give the tubers a small amount of water, or they will not sprout. Sprinkle water on the surface just enough to moisten the potting soil.

Once the tubers sprout, every day I use my finger to judge whether or not the potting soil is moist. In my cutting bed, once the tubers have sprouted, on average I water them every other day. That being said, my cutting bed is inside of my home where it is warm. In a cooler setting, a cutting bed may require less water.

To complete my bed, I install several yellow sticky insect traps at soil level to catch fungus gnats that sometimes hatch from the potting soil. I buy 5 by 7 inch (12

Dahlia cuttings in rooting cubes.

x 17 cm) yellow sticky trap sheets online from Arbico Organics. I cut these into strips, mount them on small sticks (shish kabob skewers work well), and set them perpendicular to the soil, right at the soil level. Gnats tend to walk rather than fly so placing the traps at soil level catches them as they walk around. You can see a video of me setting up my cutting bed on the Kristine Albrecht YouTube channel. Look for videos 172, 173, 174, and 175.

The warm temperature, the slight moisture, and the prolonged exposure to light trick the tubers into thinking it is spring, and green shoots start to grow from the eyes on the tubers. They will grow straight up towards the light. In about three weeks, some of the tubers will have produced enough green growth for the first cuttings. When a shoot has developed two or three leaf pairs, it is ready to be harvested. Many growers use scalpels to slice cuttings from the tuber, however, that method requires sterilizing the scalpel in a 10% bleach solution between each cut to avoid spreading a disease or virus. Alternatively, I often keep a separately labeled scalpel on hand for each individual tuber.

Another method I use, I call a "pull." I take hold of the shoot below the lowest set of leaves and wiggle it in a small circular pattern like I'm removing a loose tooth. It will separate right where the shoot meets the tuber crown. I hold the shoot above the point where it separates so my fingers do not spread disease or virus between tubers. As a result, I don't need to sterilize any tools or my fingers between pulls. After taking a pull from a tuber, new growth is stimulated just outside the pull location, and more shoots begin growing.

Once the cutting or pull is taken, I strip off the two side leaves and transfer it to a medium where it can develop roots. The cutting needs four things at this stage: water, air, humidity, and heat. Growers use many media, including sand, potting soil,

1. Filling the cutting bed w/ potting soil (sand below).

2. Pulling out soil to make a trench.

3. Nestling tubers into the trench.

4. Tubers in potting soil with crowns left unburied.

and vermiculite. Some choose to make soil cubes with the help of a compaction tool. I use Root Riot cubes made by Hydrodynamics International of Lansing, MI. There are other similar products available from other suppliers. I like the Root Riot cubes because they have lots of little crevices that work well to supply air to the developing roots. These cubes come with a pre-made hole for the pull, and each cube fits snuggly into a 50-cell tray. First, I make sure that the cube is moist before placing my pull into it. Next, I set my 50-cell tray onto a solid bottom tray placed on a heat mat with a soil probe thermostatic switch, keeping the cubes at 72° F (22.2° C). You can see a short video of me taking a pull on the Kristine Albrecht YouTube channel. Look for video 129.

I then make a plant tag with the name or number of the pull and place it in the space between the rooting cube and the tray. I add about 1/4 inch (.63 cm) of water to the bottom tray. Because these pulls have no roots, keeping them hydrated until they develop a root system is critical. Using a Mondi 2-liter Mist and Spray pump sprayer, I mist the pulls with water once a day and cover the 50-cell tray with a clear plastic dome. Clear domes designed to fit over the trays are available at stores that sell garden or hydroponic supplies. I hang a grow light at about 16 inch (40 cm) above the top of the dome. The lights are on for 14 hours each day.

After 10 to 14 days, cuttings typically have small roots. You can check this by gently taking the rooting cube out of the tray. If you see roots around the cube's outside edges, your cutting is ready to be transplanted. If no roots are showing, give your young plant more time. If roots are visible, gently remove the rooting cube from the tray, roll it in a mycorrhizal inoculant, and repot it into a four-inch (10 cm) pot filled with potting soil.

Green shoots growing from a tuber clump in a cutting bed.

Taking a cutting.

Taking a pull.

Mycorrhizal inoculants provide a biological connection between roots and nutrients present in the soil. Be sure to transfer plant tags with each plant. If the pull is starting its life in early spring and it's cold outside, keep the four-inch (10 cm) pots on the heat mats (no domes at this stage) without grow lights for 24 hours. They have been in a sheltered environment under humidity domes and need time to acclimatize in drier air before exposure to bright lights. After that, they can go under the grow lights and on a heat mat until the weather warms up. You can see a short video of me moving cuttings into small pots on the Kristine Albrecht YouTube channel. Look for videos 130 and 162.

HARDENING OFF

When it comes time to plant young plants outside, you can't expose them to full sun all at once. They have a fragile new root system and new tender leaves. They must go through a transition period that gardeners call hardening off. To harden off, I put young plants outside in full shade for about four days. This should be done when the temperatures during that day are above freezing. If the nights are mild, I will leave the plants out at night too. If the forecast is for freezing temperatures overnight, I bring the plants in at night and put them back outside during the day. Once they have been out in the shade for four days, I will give them a half-day of full sun for two or more days. After that, the little plants are ready to be planted and receive full sun all day.

I like to grow small plants until they are two to four inches (5 to 10 cm) tall before putting them in my hoop house. I do this because the larger a plant is the better its survival chances. After they are acclimated I put them in a simple hoop house that provides the plants some shade, warmer temperatures, and some protection from wind, rain, and insect pests. You can see instructions on building an inexpensive temporary hoop house on page 48.

Once the threat of overnight frost has passed, cuttings can be transplanted from their four-inch (10 cm) pots into the garden beds. When I plant my cuttings in the soil, I make holes larger than the pot. I then tip the cutting out of its plastic pot and gently set it into the hole, pushing the native soil up around it, ensuring that the soil and the potting mix make good contact. Finally, I will start them off with a bit of fertilizer, especially if the soil is still a bit cold. I use AgroThrive, a liquid concentrate with an N-P-K value of 3-3-2.

I have described the process of making cuttings or pulls with tubers. That is an excellent place to start if you have never made cuttings, however, more experienced growers often take cuttings from a pot root or tuber clump. Pot roots are made when a plant is grown to full size inside a 4-inch (10 cm) pot for an entire growing season. At the end of the season, what results is a "pot-bound" miniature tuber clump. These small tubers do not get divided. Instead, they are left intact as a tight miniature clump. Making a cutting or taking a pull from a pot root is exactly the same as from an individual tuber. What distinguishes a pot root is its ability to produce a few dozen to 50 or more cuttings (or pulls) from one clump, many more than one can make from a single tuber.

You may be wondering what to do with an individual tuber after taking cuttings from it. I don't plant tubers in the ground after I have used them to make five to ten cuttings as the process depletes the tuber. So after a tuber has given me cuttings, I dispose of it. The only exception to this rule is when I take only one or two cuttings from a tuber. In that case, it still has plenty of reserve energy to send up additional vigorous sprouts in the spring, so I will plant it.

David Hall, England

David Hall of Halls of Heddon Northumberland, England produces approximately 100,000 cuttings each year.

Stripping off the lower leaves.

Pushing a cutting down into a rooting cube.

Adding a small amount of water to the bottom tray below cuttings.

The scale of his operation required him to develop methods for mass production. Yet several of his techniques might interest the home gardener or farmer-florist looking to simplify or scale up their cutting beds.

David's cutting beds are filled with full-size tuber clumps and pot tubers. These clumps take up too much room for a single cutting bed container. Instead, David uses rectangular plastic mushroom or tomato crates approximately 15 by 12 by 4 inches (38 x 30 x 10 cm) filled with potting soil and perlite for his cutting beds. He can add or subtract crates as needed. Each crate holds about six to eight tuber clumps or up to 20 pot roots. The sides of the crates have many holes; but because the crates are pressed tightly against each other, the soil stays in place. Heat mats under the crates are set to 64° F (18° C).

Once the cuttings are taken, David places them into 20-cell trays filled with potting soil inside a greenhouse. The natural daylight is enough for most varieties to root and grow. David adds a few extra hours of light from grow lights for varieties that are in high demand or are particularly slow growers. At this stage of development, cuttings need consistent moisture. Instead of a humidity dome, David covers a full bench of cuttings with a single layer of fleece row cover (Agribon). He mists the row cover as needed to keep the cuttings underneath hydrated. As the young plants grow, they collectively push up on the row cover, so he keeps a close eye on them at this stage. The young plants can get damaged if the cover is left on even just a day or two too long. In his climate, David finds his early season cuttings take 20 to 28 days to root and make a "mini plant" (rooted cutting) of a size suitable to send out to customers. After the spring equinox, with more light, the rooting time to salable plant size decreases to 14 to 20 days.

CARING FOR CUTTINGS THAT ARRIVE BY MAIL

When ordering cuttings from a supplier, it is best to have them arrive after your last frost date. That way, you can plant them in the soil after a few days of hardening off (see page 42).

Rolling the rooting cube in mycorrhizal inoculant.

Making a hole in the potting soil for the rooting cube.

Settling the cutting into potting soil.

Watering in the cutting.

When a cutting arrives at our doorstep by mail it needs immediate care. Cuttings are small plants with leaves and roots; they need light, water, and the right temperature to survive. Open the box the day your cuttings arrive. They have been traveling for several days in the dark and they need light.

If your young plants arrive and there is still a risk of overnight frost you will want to pot them up, keep them at room temperature, and let them grow a bit before planting them outside. Open up the clamshells that they were shipped in and gently pull out the foam wedge the plant is rooted in. Don't attempt to break apart the foam plug—doing so will damage the fragile young roots. Remove any blackened leaves that may have died on the journey. Fill a four-inch (10 cm) pot with high-quality potting soil. Make a depression in the center of the potting soil and sink your plant with its rooting cube deep into it, right up to the first set of leaves. Transfer the plant tag to the small pot so you can keep track of the variety. Once the potting soil is pressed around the root plug give your new plant a drink of water and diluted water-soluble fertilizer. I like diluted AgroThrive for my young cuttings. I use one and a half times the water recommended on the bottle. You can see a short video on potting up rooted cuttings at the Kristine Albrecht YouTube channel. Look for video 130.

Once hydrated, wait a day or two before putting your plants under the lights. After the plants have acclimated from their greenhouse environment to grow lights, I recommend having the lights on 14 hours

Typical clamshell packaging for a cutting arriving by mail.

a day. Hang the lights six inches (15.2 cm) above the tops of the plants. If the temperature outside is not below freezing during the day, you can put your plants in the shade outside in the daytime and bring them inside under grow lights at night. Be sure to acclimate the plants before they go out into direct sunlight. This is done by placing plants outside in the shade for four to five days before putting them in direct sunlight. Once acclimated your young plant will do fine in full sun. Remember, dahlias cannot tolerate frost, so if the forecast outside calls for freezing temperatures, bring your plants inside. You can see a short video on acclimating plants on the Kristine Albrecht YouTube channel. Look for video 100.

Hoop house frame (2x4s & 60d nails).

Five gallon pots as a base for plywood.

Plywood shelf with cut out for access.

10' PVC pipes slip over the 60d nails.

Agribon row cover installed over pipes.

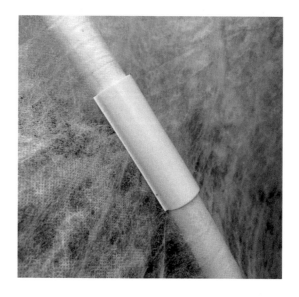

*Snap clips (from Johnny's Select Seeds) secures
the Agribon to the pipes.*

48

Continue watering your young plants. The top of the potting soil should be dark and damp to the touch. If the potting soil is light-colored and dry, give the plants a little more water. When the risk of frost has passed you are ready to plant your cutting outside in the soil or in a container. Be sure the plants are acclimated for several days in the shade before replanting. Plant them so the first set of leaves is at ground level.

If your plants arrive in the mail and you are past your last frost date you can prepare to plant them directly into the soil. Remove the clear plastic clamshell they arrived in and remove any blackened leaves that might have withered in transit. Leaving your plants in the media they came with, set your cuttings outside in the shade for two to three days. While they are in their tiny sleeves, water them twice a day. It is advisable to bring them in at night. This process of acclimating them is critical before they receive direct sunlight.

Once acclimated, pull the rooting cubes out of their sleeves. Do not break apart or tear the rooting cubes. They hold the plant's fragile root system. Plant each cube directly into soft moist soil burying it to the first set of leaves. Transfer the plant tag to the soil so you know which plant is which. Water them right away and give them a dose of diluted water-soluble fertilizer such as AgroThrive.

Young plants require more daily attention than mature plants. They must be watered every day for a week or two to help get them established. I also recommend sprinkling some Sluggo Plus on the leaves and around the plants to protect them from slugs, snails, and earwigs. If you are experiencing very hot weather it is a good idea to shade these young cuttings until the weather cools off. Fabric on wooden stakes works well, as does a propped-up umbrella.

Checking on young plants in the hoop house with my sister-in-law Janet.

Lorelie Merton in her dahlia patch. Photo by Hannah of Florelie Seasonal Flowers.

Lorelie Merton, Australia

Lorelie Merton of Bungaree, Victoria grows dahlias under the name Florelie Seasonal Flowers. Bungaree is a small hill town a little more than an hour west of Melbourne in the southern Australian state of Victoria. Lorelie is a cut flower farmer selling dahlias, bearded irises, ranunculus, zinnias, and peonies to nearby florists and designers. She also sells dahlia tubers. Lorelie grows just under 8,000 dahlias each year, including her own 'Florelie' varieties.

She cultivates a one-acre plot on a 20-acre parcel of land. Her dahlia patch is on flat ground surrounded by pasture. There are no nearby trees to block the sun and no hedgerows to harbor snails and slugs. Aside from an occasional strong wind storm, Lorelie's location and climate are excellent for growing dahlias. She even avoids roaming bands of kangaroos due to her position between two main roads. Dahlia growers in less-fortunate locations have to erect tall fencing to keep kangaroos away from their dahlias. Lorelie, her husband, and their three children also raise sheep, who are fed damaged tubers that cannot be stored or sold.

Because of strict import regulations, Australian dahlia growers have a limited selection of dahlia varieties. Even within the country, dahlia tubers cannot be shipped to three out of eight Australian states and territories. As a result, Australian breeders are in high demand for their ability to increase the diversity of dahlia stock. Lorelie's breeding program has resulted in 40 introductions to the Australian market.

The size of Lorelie's farm requires her full-time effort and help from Hannah, her one permanent employee. They are assisted by Lorelie's husband, Ethan, who works as an agronomist for a vegetable seed company. Ethan is Lorelie's "farm consultant" and has developed tractor-based systems for growing dahlias each year. Lorelie was not always a flower farmer. She started growing dahlias while working as a speech pathologist before switching to full-time farming in 2021.

Lorelie's Website: florelie.com.au
Instagram: @florelieseasonalflowers

'KA's Apricot Jam'.

4. PLANTING DAHLIAS

PLANTING BED LAYOUT

IF YOU ARE PLANTING DAHLIAS AS ornamentals or accent plants in a garden, give them a space about 20 to 30 inches (50 to 76 cm) wide to spread out. If you are planting multiple plants in a dedicated planting bed, the individual plants can be closer together.

My planting beds are 30 inches (76 cm) wide. Each bed has two rows of dahlias planted diagonally across from each other. If you were to hop back and forth down my rows from one side of the bed to the other, the plants would be in a zig-zag pattern (see graphic below). For average-sized dahlias, my plants in each row are 16 inches (45 cm) apart. The A and AA-sized dahlias (dinner plate size), I plant 24 inches (60 cm) apart. Two rows of plants ensure that I can comfortably reach in and cut blooms from either side. One year, I planted my beds with three rows of seedling dahlias. I found that the plants in the middle row were crowded and it was a challenge to harvest blooms and care for

the plants in that middle row. My friend Iris made me a chart that tells me how many plants I can get in each bed based on bed length and plant spacing. When I am planning out my garden each winter I use Iris' chart along with plot maps of my planting areas.

My planting beds are raised about three to ten inches (7.6 to 25 cm) above the native soil. I don't recommend that for everyone. My farm is located on land that has a gentle slope. Before raising my beds, I found that the lower ends of my beds were collecting more irrigation water. This made it difficult to judge exactly how much water the plants in each row needed. By raising the beds above the native soil level, and leveling the rows, my plants received more consistent watering. There are no wooden or metal forms on the edge of my raised beds. I mound up the soil with no extra support structure.

The paths between my rows are three feet (91 cm) wide. That might seem excessive. However, it is necessary because as the plants grow up, they also grow out. Mature

53

	Maximum number of plants in each row PLANT SPACING in Inches (2 Rows-Zigzagged)												
Row Length	4"	5"	6"	8"	9"	10"	12"	16"	18"	21"	22"	24"	inches apart
20 feet	120	96	80	60	53	48	40	30	27	23	22	20	
25 feet	150	120	100	75	67	60	50	38	33	29	27	25	
30 feet	180	144	120	90	80	72	60	45	40	34	33	30	
35 feet	210	168	140	105	93	84	70	53	47	40	38	35	
40 feet	240	192	160	120	107	96	80	60	53	46	44	40	
50 feet	300	240	200	150	133	120	100	75	67	57	55	50	
60 feet	360	288	240	180	160	144	120	90	80	69	65	60	
70 feet	420	336	280	210	187	168	140	105	93	80	76	70	
80 feet	480	384	320	240	213	192	160	120	107	91	87	80	
90 feet	540	432	360	270	240	216	180	135	120	103	98	90	
100 feet	600	480	400	300	267	240	200	150	133	114	109	100	

The plant spacing chart made by my friend Iris.

plants will branch out and crowd that three-foot-wide path quickly. If you plan on pulling a wagon full of flower tubs through your paths at peak season, I encourage you to make them four or five feet (1.2 to 1.5 m) wide.

If you don't have room for a full-sized bed of plants, you can still enjoy growing dahlias. For example, I have a 10-inch (25 cm) wide bed wedged between my house and a concrete walkway on the south side of my house. Every year I grow a single row of dahlias in this strip of soil, and those plants grow to full size and produce beautiful blooms.

Galena Berkompas, Washington

Galena Berkompas of Micro Flower Farm in Vancouver, Washington has a small growing area and a lot of dahlias. She maximizes her cut flower yield by spacing her plants nine inches (22 cm) apart. That may seem too close for comfort; however, dahlias grow quite well when crowded together. Her plants grow to full size and produce blooms like plants spaced further

apart. Because more stems and leaves are tangled together, Galena always removes the lower mature leaves on her plants to increase airflow. An added benefit of the tight spacing is that once the plants are corralled with stakes and twine on the bed perimeter, the mass of plants holds itself up in the wind. One downside to planting so close together is that Galena has noticed a smaller tuber yield compared to plants she grew 12 inches (30 cm) apart.

Heather Henson, Canada

Heather Henson of Boreal Blooms in Cold Lake, Alberta plants her dahlias 12 inches (30 cm) apart. With this tight spacing, she has observed no reduction in bloom production. The close spacing allows more plants inside her 14 by 80-foot (4.2 x 24 m) hoop tunnels. It also encourages the growth of longer stems. Because Heather's farm is so far north (54.4° N), her plants don't grow as tall as they do in lower latitudes. Her average dahlia plant will grow to about three feet (91 cm). By planting her dahlias close together, they compete for light and grow taller than they would if spaced farther apart. Because Heather uses no tractors or tillers on her no-till farm, the paths between her beds are only 12 inches (30 cm) wide. These narrow paths work because she diligently holds the spreading stems using the corral method with rebar stakes and baling twine. I discuss staking methods on page 101.

WHEN TO PLANT DAHLIAS

Dahlias are typically planted in the spring after all threat of frost has passed and when the soil temperatures start to warm up to 50 to 60° F (10 to 15.5° C) or warmer. Your planting date will depend on your location. Dahlias can't tolerate freezing temperatures, so your planting date should be after your last frost date. If you don't get frost, wait until your nighttime low temperatures will reach 50° F (10° C). You can find your local frost date here: almanac.com/gardening/frostdates.

After the last frost date, most dahlia growers plant tubers directly in the ground. It may take two to six weeks for a shoot to emerge above the soil (depending on variety and soil temperature) and another two and a half to three months before the first bloom. Some open-center varieties will produce blooms as quickly as 40 days. In Santa Cruz, if all my tubers are planted by April 15th, I can expect my first blooms by mid-July. Planting after the last historic frost date is, of course, not an exact science. You could experience a rare late frost after planting. However, since it typically takes a couple of weeks for a sprout from a tuber to break the soil's surface, you do have a time buffer in the event of an unseasonal frost.

Heather Henson, Canada

Heather Henson of Boreal Blooms in Cold Lake, Alberta plants her dahlias between mid-May and the beginning of June in a 14 by 80 foot (4.2 x 24 m) hoop tunnel. She pre-sprouts her tubers indoors, giving them a four to six-week jump start on tubers taken right out of cold storage. Pre-sprouting tubers is necessary for Heather with her short growing season. Without a covered tunnel, she would only have dahlia blooms for two weeks before frost killed her plants. By putting greenhouse plastic over the tunnel hoops at the end of August, Heather's dahlias will bloom for six to eight weeks.

WHERE TO PLANT DAHLIAS

Dahlias need at least 6–8 hours of full sun each day throughout the entire growing season. Even better, if you have a choice, plant them where they will receive sun all day long. As a rule of thumb, dahlias grow

Transplanting a cutting from a 4 inch pot into native soil.

Planting beds in early season.

best where you would plant a tomato plant. If planted in a shady spot, dahlias will grow tall and leggy. The exception to this advice is for growers in hot climates. Planting dahlias where they will receive afternoon shade could benefit plants if your temperatures are consistently high. While dahlias like the sun, they do not grow well when they get too hot.

Dahlias like well-drained soil and want their feet consistently moist, but not soaking wet. They do not grow well in boggy soil but don't like the soil to dry out between watering as this can damage the root tips. Finally, it is important not to plant dahlias directly under or near mature trees with shallow roots. The tree's established root system will rob your plants

of water and nutrients and lead to smaller plants and fewer blooms.

Ideally, your dahlia garden is close and accessible to your house or farm. Dahlias benefit from close observation and daily care. Quality care is more likely if plants are close at hand.

PREPARING BACKUP PLANTS

Not all dahlias that are planted survive. Some get taken down by gophers. Others will rot underground or have extreme pest pressure when young and fail to thrive. When I lose a plant or pull out a plant, the result is a blank spot in my planting bed. I could plant a new tuber or germinate a seed to fill that spot; however, nurturing a

ROOT COMPETITION

My farm has a row of tall pines on the north side of my planting beds. Fortunately, trees on the north side do not block the sunlight. I like the trees because they provide a shady work area on hot days. However, it took me several years to realize that the plants closest to the trees were consistently smaller and less vigorous than the surrounding plants. Likewise, when I dug up my tubers, those nearest the trees were not as plump as the others and were entwined with roots. The nearby tree roots were attracted by the water I gave my dahlias.

The ideal solution would have been to move the beds away from the trees. However, I didn't have that option because my farm is small. Instead, I dug a 30-inch (76 cm) deep trench between my planting beds and the trees. Once the 60-foot (18m) long trench was dug and the tree roots were cut, I inserted a root barrier into the channel before putting the removed soil back. Root barriers are made of 60 mil polypropylene and are commonly used to keep bamboo shoots from running. They are suitable for over 50 years of service underground. The severed roots that remain under my dahlia beds slowly decomposed. The roots on the tree side of the barrier will stop or turn and grow in a different direction. It was a big job to dig such a deep trench and cut several dozen roots; however, I now have plants that grow beautifully right up to the edge of my beds.

plant that is not the same size as the surrounding plants is not ideal. For instance, if I plant a tuber in the blank hole, that tuber could rot because I am now watering the plants in that bed, and green plants need more water than tubers do. Likewise, if the plants in my bed are 12 inches (30 cm) tall and I fill a blank space with a tuber or a small cutting, the more mature plants will shade it from the sun and it will not reach its full potential.

I have found that the best solution for bare spots in my beds is to fill in with plants of similar size. Every year when I am making my cuttings, germinating my seeds, or planting my tubers, I pot up 10 to 20 percent extra in 4-inch (10 cm) or 1-gallon (3.7 L) pots ready to transplant should the need arrive. If I get lucky and only a few of my plants are lost, my backup plants make fantastic gifts that I can give to friends and neighbors. Who wouldn't want to receive a healthy young dahlia ready to be planted?

STRATEGIES FOR EARLIER AND LATER BLOOMS

Depending on daily temperatures and dahlia variety, tubers planted in early May, for example, will typically produce their first blooms in late July. I am often interested in extending my growing season to get blooms earlier. I am anxious to see my new dahlias grown from seed. Early blooms are also a gift to my florists and designers who enjoy the luxury of dahlias by Mother's Day. Sometimes a grower will want to jump-start their season to have blooms ready for an early wedding or event. In some climates, with extra effort, this can be done.

For me in Santa Cruz, this effort starts each year right around the end of December. I set up a cutting bed to start making cuttings and start germinating my seeds. I discuss these two germination methods elsewhere in this book. Six weeks after I start this process my seedlings and cuttings are large enough to be planted. After an acclimation period, my plants go directly into a prepared bed in the ground in early February. Because the ground is

Low metal hoops with Agribon row covers for early-season blooms. The metal hoops I buy from Johnny's Select Seeds. They are 54" Wire Support Hoops.

still a bit cold and plants have difficulty taking up nitrogen in cold soil, I add some organic nitrogen fertilizer.

My beds are then covered with low metal hoops and Agribon row cover. During the day, the plants in the bed have one layer of row cover to keep them warm and allow in as much sun as possible. At night I typically add one or two more layers of row cover depending on the expected low temperatures. At night, the triple layers of row cover give the young plants a six to eight-degree F (3.3 to 4.4 C) boost in temperature.

There is another reason for extending my growing season. As a hybridizer, show grower, and cut flower farmer, I wear a lot of hats during the year, and there never seems to be enough time to get everything done. In particular, hand-pollinating blooms for my breeding program takes time. So if I can get plants blooming

sooner, I can start making hand crosses and collecting seeds before the rush of the cut flower season. In addition, getting some plants in the ground early relieves me from having to plant out everything at the same time.

Although having blooms in May is exciting, there are a few downsides. Although my young plants are protected, there is always the fear that a cold snap could kill some plants. Also, the pressure from aphids in early spring can require early spraying with horticultural oil or the release of ladybugs inside the Agribon tunnels (See the section on managing pests on page 155). You can see a short video of me spraying young plants for aphids on the Kristine Albrecht YouTube channel. Look for video 178.

One other simple strategy for early-season blooms is to leave a portion of your tubers in the ground over the winter if your climate allows for it. That way when the temperatures are just right, the tubers will sprout and your season will be off and running. If you employ this strategy, I recommend digging up these tubers every other year as tuber clumps grow larger each season. These large clumps can produce too many sprouts at once which will cause crowding that can lead to smaller blooms and increased powdery mildew. Two other considerations, if you plan to leave tubers in the ground, are potential damage from gophers or rot. If your plot is prone to gopher activity you may not want to leave tubers in the ground all year long. If you have a high water table, an unusually wet year, or soggy soil you could experience rotted tubers.

If you are looking to harvest blooms as late in the season as possible, you can delay your planting. A couple of years ago, my daughter announced she was getting married in mid-October and wanted lots of dahlias for her wedding. Even though I am in California, mid-October is a bit late to harvest blooms in their prime. By October, plants are switching over to making seeds. As a result, the blooms are smaller, have a lower petal count, and often pop open their centers. In addition, the weather gets cool, slowing plant growth and bloom production.

That being said, I saved one long bed on my farm for the wedding and planted it six weeks later than usual, at the end of May. As the season progressed, the wedding bed was behind the other plants on my farm. Just before the wedding, those blooms were more full and beautiful than the

One year I added strings of lights inside my low hoops to raise the air temperature at night. The lights didn't add much warmth but my neighbors loved the nighttime garden art installation.

Late-season dahlia blooms from my farm on my daughter's wedding arch.

surrounding blooms from plants that were started six weeks earlier. I was able to plant late and harvest late because, in my climate, there is typically no frost until December. In colder climates harvesting blooms in mid-October may not be possible.

PLANTING IN 4-INCH (10 cm) SINK POTS

While most dahlias are planted directly in the soil or grown in above-ground containers, they also grow well in plastic pots sunk into the ground called "sink pots." I use this technique with all of my seedlings and those cuttings that I want pot roots from. There are several benefits to this planting method.

First, if I planted all my new seedlings or cuttings 16 inches (40 cm) apart, the

At left: my daughter's wedding
with late October dahlia blooms.
Photo: Woodmancy Photography

required space would exceed the land I have. If you are a dahlia breeder, however, and plan to pull out a majority of first-year seedlings mid-season, plants in native soil four inches (10 cm) apart will have entwined roots. Pulling out selected plants could damage the roots of their neighbors. For this reason, I plant all my first-year seedlings 4 to 8 inches apart (10 to 20 cm) in 4-inch (10 cm) sink pots.

Second, the mini tuber clump (a pot root) that results from growing plants in sink pots is easier to store when dug up in the fall. Pot roots are ideal for use in a cutting bed the following season.

Once my seedlings are growing in four inch (10 cm) plastic pots and are hardened off, I dig two four-inch (10 cm) deep trenches on either side of my dahlia beds and nestle the potted seedlings into the trenches. I ensure the pot top is level with the top of the soil. I plant these sink pots right up against each other down the row resulting in the plants growing four inches (10 cm) apart. I then push the soil around the pots, set my drip tape over them, and mulch the soil.

My beds have three rows of drip tape irrigation. The two outside rows of drip tape lay over the sink pots and deliver water directly to them. The third drip line in the middle of the bed provides moisture to the soil. These plants will send roots through the holes in the pot to seek additional water and nutrients. I don't want those spreading roots to encounter dry soil. Using sink pots I can grow 300 seedlings in a 50-foot (15 m) bed, saving space in my garden.

Although it seems counterintuitive, these plants will grow almost to full size, and, most important for breeding purposes, they will bloom. This allows me to evaluate each seedling and decide if it will be kept for another year. Ninety-five percent of these new seedlings will not meet my breeding goals and will be discarded. Pulling out unwanted seedlings is where this method really shines. Because the plant roots are mostly confined to the sink pots, they pull out of the ground easily without disturbing the roots of neighboring plants.

Growing dahlias in small sink pots does change tuber production. They make a tight clump of pot roots by the season's end. Although small, these clumps will have viable eyes and produce plants the following year.

The plants I grow in sink pots are cuttings or seedlings. Neither of these has a tuber to start with, so they fit comfortably into the small pots. If your tuber fits in a four-inch pot, great. If it doesn't you can use a larger pot.

Pay extra attention to supporting plants grown in sink pots. Because their root system is not woven wide into the soil, sink pot plants are top-heavy and more likely to fall over. I use the corral method to support my plants grown in sink pots. See the section in this book on staking dahlias on page 101.

PLANTING IN LARGER SINK POTS

If you live where water is precious or have a problem with gophers, consider growing your dahlias in two or three-gallon (7.5 or 11 L) sink pots. Advantages of this method include:

1. Gopher protection. I have planted over 300 plants in two-gallon (7.5 L) sink pots in an area with gophers. Only two of the 300 plants were lost to these underground pests.

2. Ease. Dropping a tuber or plant into a sink pot and pulling out that pot at the end of the season is a breeze. Much easier than digging tubers out of the native soil.

3. Water savings. Plants in sink pots require less water. Instead of watering a large patch of native soil, water can be concentrated and preserved inside the pot.

4. Cool feet. Dahlias like their roots to be cool. A container above ground receives sunlight and heats up. A sink pot is underground and keeps dahlia roots cool, even on the warmest day.

To plant in a larger sink pot, dig a large hole in your soil to accept the pot. Sink the pot into the ground with just about one inch (2.5 cm) sticking above soil level. Next, fill the pot with high-quality potting soil and plant your seedling, tuber, or cutting as you would in native soil. Not all garden pots are the same. Source the thickest plastic pots (with a bottom hole) you can find. Then, backfill the hole, so the pot is firmly packed in the soil. Your plant will grow just fine inside the confines of the plastic pot because dahlias are shallow-rooted and don't have a long taproot. Most importantly, your plants will be protected from gophers, moles.

Photo at right: four inch sink pots planted with three lines of drip tape.

Dahlias growing in 1 gallon (3.8 L) sink pots.

GROWING DAHLIAS IN ABOVE-GROUND CONTAINERS

Growing dahlias in containers provide a great deal of flexibility. It is a good option for those who don't have land available for a planting bed. It is also a good option if your land is in the shade but you have a sunny spot on a deck, patio, or driveway. We need not plant only dwarf dahlia varieties in containers. Dahlias that grow to four or five feet can thrive in a container.

Containers for planting dahlias can be as small as 2 gallons (7.5 L), but many growers use 5-gallon (19 L) pots. If working with oversize tubers, a larger pot might be required. Regardless of size, it is critical to start with a clean container. If your container has soil and roots from a previous planting, it could hold disease or insect eggs. Empty your containers and spray them out with a strong stream of water, followed by a ten-minute soaking with a 10% bleach solution, followed by rinsing and drying the container. New containers do not require cleaning before use. Potting soil should only be used for a single growing season. In addition to possibly harboring diseases, the soil nutrients will be spent from the previous year.

Another benefit of a sink pot is soil quality. I recommend filling your sink pot with high-quality potting soil. Good potting soil is balanced for optimal plant growth. If the prospect of amending an entire plot of land is too much for you to tackle, you can provide your plants with high-quality soil inside sink pots instead.

When I plant in large sink pots, I feed my plants with liquid plant food such as diluted fish emulsion a few times in a season. In smaller 4-inch (10 cm) sink pots, roots will escape through the holes in the pot and pull in nutrients from the native ground. However, a 2-gallon (7.5 L) sink pot is large and deep enough that the roots will mostly stay within the container, necessitating additional feeding. For a video on planting sink pots, see the Kristine Albrecht YouTube channel and watch videos 145 or 182.

Fill your container part-way with pre-moistened, high-quality potting soil. Potting soil can take hours to days to thoroughly moisten, depending on how dry it was when packaged. You want to avoid planting a tuber into bone-dry soil. If the holes at the bottom of your container are large, you can use a pot shard, rock, or a paper coffee filter over the hole to hold the soil in. You want to fill the pot so that the soil level is six inches (15 cm) from the top.

Next, place your tuber into the soil with the crown (or eye) of the tuber in the center. This is often only possible if the tuber is small. With a large tuber, place the crown as close to the center as possible. The tuber should be lying flat, as if it's being put to bed. If the tuber has a sprout or you pre-sprouted your tubers, make sure the sprout is facing up. If your tuber has no sprout, laying it on any side will do. New sprouts that emerge will detect gravity and grow toward the sky. Before you cover the tuber, push a stake into the potting mix two to four inches (5 to 10 cm) from the crown of the tuber. Top off your container with potting soil, stopping two inches (5 cm) from the top. Make a plant tag, attach it to the stake, or sink it into the soil. Finally, top off the last two inches (5 cm) with your favorite mulch or aged compost.

If you plant your tuber earlier than your last frost date, you must keep it inside a greenhouse or a room protected from the elements, or you can start your tubers indoors under grow lights while your nights are still below freezing and put them outside when the frost abates. While indoors, hang a grow light six inches (15 cm) from the top of your shoot. Keep the grow light on for 14 hours each day. When it is time to set your container outside, put it in the shade during the day and back in at night for a week or so as it adjusts to full sun. Setting a new plant out into the direct sun can shock it. After one week of hardening off in the shade (see page 42), the new plant can move into full sun.

Watering plants in containers is the trickiest part of the process. The soil in containers dries out faster than native soil. In addition, plant roots in containers can't branch out and search for moisture. They only have access to the limited amount of soil inside the container. Therefore, your watering regimen with containers will have to be more frequent. Depending on your climate and the local temperatures, you may have to water your plants daily. Push your finger down into the soil and feel for moisture. If the soil is moist one inch (2.5 cm) down, don't water it and check again the following day. If it's dry give it some water. If your container is in a spot where the sun hits it for much of the day, this added heat will dry out your soil quickly. Providing fabric, wood, or metal panels to block the sun from striking the pot directly will help keep your container cool.

POTTING SOIL

Even though it is called potting soil, these mixes contain no soil. Instead, they are typically a blend of moss, fine bark, perlite, vermiculite, and compost. The organic matter (compost and moss) feeds your plants, while the other ingredients hold your plant roots and keep the mix from compacting.

Once your plant has two or three sets of leaves, I recommend pinching out the growth tip to make your plant branch and produce more blooms (see Pinching Out Dahlias on page 109). As your plant grows, tie it every 12 inches (30 cm) to the stake in your container to ensure it doesn't fall over or get blown over in the wind. Potting soil does not have the same structure as topsoil and does not support the roots as firmly.

Because potting soil is made with sterilized material, it does not have the flourishing biology of natural soil. The missing bacteria, fungi, and worms leave potting soil less able to supply nutrients to your plant over an entire growing season. For this reason, you will want to fertilize your plants, typically once a week.

Finally, plants grown in containers are more prone to frost and freezing damage than plants in native soil. This is because containers are exposed above ground where cold air can chill the soil inside the container. Plants in native soil have a vast storehouse of heat in the soil as ground temperatures are slower to react to cold air temperatures. As the season progresses in the fall, keep an eye on the overnight low temperatures and move containers inside if freezing temperatures are in the forecast. You can see a short video about planting in containers on the Kristine Albrecht YouTube channel. Look for video 84.

EARLY SEASON DAHLIA CARE

Suppose you left a tuber clump in the ground over the winter. In that case, in spring you may see several sprouts emerging from the soil at once. If they are all left to grow, the resulting plant could be crowded with shoots and promote the growth of powdery mildew. I recommend poking your fingers underground to the tuber clump and snapping off all but the two best-looking sprouts. These two survivors will grow happier and healthier than if all the sprouts were allowed to grow.

Sometimes a young plant grown from a tuber will wilt in the sun. Unlike healthy plants, these struggling plants may have leaves and stems that are flagging or drooping. Instead of giving up on a struggling plant, I like to intervene and give it a second chance, especially if it is a rare or highly anticipated new variety.

The first step in determining the problem is to give the plant some extra water. If this doesn't improve the situation within 24 hours, it's time to dig out the tuber for inspection. A flagging young plant can result from a tuber that is softening or rotting. Carefully dig up the tuber and squeeze it. Next, rub your fingers over the surface of the tuber. If you feel a soft spot or the tuber skin is shiny and slimy, you have a rot problem. The best remedy is to use a knife or sheers to cut off the rotted part of the tuber and replant it. If the plant is over 12 inches (30 cm) tall, it will need to be cut back to 8 inches (20 cm) and replanted.

If the young plant has developed new roots, you can remove the entire rotted tuber and replant with just its new roots. However, a plant uprooted and replanted may not be able to heal in intense direct sun. Instead, give the plant water and provide shade for a week or two. These interventions succeed about half the time. For a video on aiding a plant with a rotted tuber, go to the Kristine Albrecht YouTube channel and watch video 150.

When your tubers send new green growth above the soil or you plant new seedlings or cuttings, they will attract slugs, snails, and earwigs. If left unprotected, your new dahlia sprouts will likely be eaten. To give them the best chance to grow into full-size plants, I recommend sprinkling Sluggo Plus on your soil around the new shoots as soon as sprouts appear. Regular Sluggo only protects against slugs and snails. Sluggo Plus also protects against earwigs, sow bugs, and cutworms. If the Sluggo Plus you sprinkled on the soil gets consumed or washed away, reapply it. For more information, see the section in this book on Slugs, Snails, and Earwigs on page 155.

At right: "KA's Apricot Jam' growing at the farm.

Galena Berkompas of Micro Flower Farm. Photo by Dani Winters.

Galena Berkompas, Washington

Galena Berkompas started Micro Flower Farm on an urban half-acre (2023 sq m) in Vancouver, Washington she shares with her husband and four children. She didn't grow up farming or growing flowers. Like much of Washington state, the home she grew up in was populated with abundant trees. Under a canopy of shade, gardening wasn't a top priority.

Galena's love of gardening started following a life-changing trip with her husband and children to England. The British are excellent gardeners. Their cool and mild climate is almost perfect for growing plants. Galena was struck by how people turned even the smallest plot into gorgeous gardens. City-dwellers with no land of their own tended verdant plots in common allotments. In England, Galena saw how gardening could transform the land and encourage a slower way of life with time to appreciate natural beauty and the passage of the seasons.

On her return home, she set herself the goal of cultivating her own land, no matter how small. Today she grows over 1,500 dahlias in a climate with a six to seven month dry growing season. The rest of the year, it rains. In addition to dahlias, she grows spring flowers like roses, tulips, and ranunculus that she sells at her driveway farm stand. Galena is a no-till organic gardener who prioritizes healthy soil and healthy plants through companion planting.

She is curious, friendly, and effusive. When she gets interested in something, she is relentless in her pursuit of knowledge. In a very short time, she has developed skills and techniques that keep her dahlia plants happy. Not content to keep her knowledge to herself, she teaches live online workshops for budding flower farmers and maintains an active and educational Instagram account.

Galena's Website: microflowerfarm.com
Galena's Instagram: @microflowerfarm

5. GROWING DAHLIAS FROM TUBERS

PURCHASING TUBERS

DAHLIA TUBERS ARE AVAILABLE FROM several sources. Some growers buy tubers from a local garden center or big box home renovation store. The tubers purchased at these outlets are typically not "named" varieties. They will probably not be highly sought-after varieties or the latest introductions from dahlia breeders. The first dahlias I grew were gifts from a friend who purchased tubers at a big box store. They were not named but they were beautiful and I fell in love with growing dahlias. There is nothing wrong with growing generic varieties purchased from a large retailer. In fact, for new growers who are just learning how to grow dahlias in their particular climate, buying inexpensive tubers is an excellent idea. Nothing is more disappointing than paying top dollar for a fancy new introduction and then losing it.

Dahlia tubers come in different configurations based on their country of origin. In the United States, tuber suppliers typically divide their clumps. When you purchase tubers in the U.S., you will likely receive one large individual tuber that has been separated from a larger clump. Most suppliers guarantee that each tuber has a viable eye. Tuber eyes look similar to the eyes on a potato. The eye on the tuber crown will sprout and produce a plant. Outside the U.S., tubers sell in clumps or half-clumps with three to five small-size individual tubers connected to the tuber crown. When these reach their destination, some tubers are often broken or damaged. A clump with broken tubers should perform just fine as long as one tuber is well-connected to the crown with an intact neck. Cut off the broken tubers that don't have a solid connection to the crown.

Photo at left: unnamed 'KA's' seedling.

If you are a more experienced grower and are looking to purchase a specific variety by name, you would likely order online for arrival at your doorstep in the spring. Most tuber suppliers open online catalogs between October and January for shipping in the spring, typically in April and May. Some suppliers with popular varieties that sell out quickly open sales in September. The most popular varieties at these early sales will often sell out in minutes. I advise getting on the mailing list of any supplier you are interested in purchasing from so you don't miss the opening rush of their online sales.

The best site for finding suppliers of a specific variety is dahliaaddict.com. This site is the work of Amanda Sargent and her husband. The Dahlia Addict homepage lists varieties alphabetically. Once you find the variety you want, the site lists all the suppliers who sell it. It also lists the price, sold-out status, catalog opening date, and

Viscot surgical markers.

Artline garden markers.

satisfaction rating from customer reviews. The registration fee is under $10 and is worth every penny. The site has a trivia page listing the most offered and searched-for varieties. Those who register with Dahlia Addict have access to a news page that lists when each supplier opens their sales, restocks popular varieties, or makes changes to their sale dates. The dahlia community is fortunate to have Amanda and her husband doing this vital work.

If you have a dahlia society in your area, check to see if they have an annual tuber sale. My local society has a tuber sale in April each year. Society members donate their extra tubers, which are sold to fund their work such as hosting dahlia shows. These sales can be a great way to pick up

varieties you have been looking for at a reasonable price with no shipping costs. Because growers in your area donate all the tubers, you will likely get varieties that grow well in your climate. Finally, a society tuber sale is an opportunity to talk with dahlia experts, ask questions, and support a community nonprofit organization.

HANDLING TUBERS THAT ARRIVE BY MAIL

Although you may purchase tubers online in the fall or winter, suppliers typically don't ship them until spring, closer to planting time. When your tubers arrive on your doorstep, it is critical to open the box, remove them from the material they are wrapped in, and inspect them. Tubers are alive and must be cared for so they stay that way. Some suppliers ship tubers in sealed plastic bags. That is fine for the journey through the mail, but they need to breathe, so opening up the bags is a good idea. If the tubers are not individually labeled, it is a good idea to do so. I like to use Viscot surgical-grade skin markers, Sharpies, or garden markers.

Check your new tubers for rot. If any tuber part is soft and yields to the touch, it is rotting. A rotten tuber will not produce a healthy plant. If you find rot, contact the company you purchased the tuber from immediately. If your tubers are healthy and you are going to plant the tuber within a week of arrival, you can keep it stored in a dark place at room temperature. If you are waiting longer, however, you will need to store them as you would over the winter. In my climate, that is in a cool dark place in peat moss at around 43° F (6.1° C). For information about storage mediums and moisture control see page 201.

WAKING UP TUBERS IN THE SPRING

The downside of putting tubers into the ground straight from cold storage involves unpredictable weather and the chance that unseasonal rain could rot them while your tubers are waiting for warmer temperatures. Tubers typically don't have roots. Therefore they cannot take up water, making them susceptible to rotting underground if the soil is very wet. By putting them in the ground cold and waiting for them to wake up, you give up a level of control.

I prefer to wake my tubers up in a controlled environment, on my schedule. This method gives me the advantage of knowing which tubers are viable and which are not. If a tuber, for whatever reason, does not sprout, I will not waste my time, energy, and garden space planting it.

My method for waking up tubers is simple. About two to three weeks before planting, I pull my boxes of tubers out of cold storage and bring them inside my house, where the temperature is between 65 and 68° F (18.3 to 20° C). The time it takes to wake up tubers varies by type. For instance, my 'Cafe au Lait' tubers will wake up two weeks after coming out of cold storage. I know a tuber has woken up when a small green, white, or purple sprout emerges from the tuber crown. Other cultivars can take up to two months. The average of all the dahlias I've grown is about 18 days. I suggest keeping good records of how quickly your tubers wake up so that in future years you will get to know when each of the varieties you grow should come out of storage.

Moisture is also a trigger for waking up tubers. I live in a dry climate. If a tuber comes out of cold storage feeling dry, I will add a couple of tablespoons of water to the storage medium (for a shoebox-sized container) and put the lid back on the box. The warmth and a small amount of moisture will cause tubers to sprout. Warming up tubers inside my home allows me to plant only those viable and ready to grow. You can see a couple of short videos about pulling tubers out of winter storage and waking up stored tubers on the Kristine

Albrecht YouTube channel. Look for videos 131 and 133.

MANAGING LONG WHITE TUBER SPROUTS

Sometimes when we open up our boxes of tubers after their winter storage, we find that a few have developed white sprouts. If a sprout is three inches (7.6 cm) or less, you can leave it intact when you plant the tuber. However, these sprouts can be up to 12 inches (30 cm) long; planting a tuber with such a lengthy sprout would encourage the growth of a leggy plant.

There are two options for handling long tuber sprouts. First, they can be cut off 1/4 of an inch (0.63 cm) from where they originate on the tuber and discarded. The tuber will develop more sprouts when it is planted. The second option is to multiply your dahlia stock by rooting the sprout, treating it much the same as a cutting or a pull. You would cut off the sprout 1/4 of an inch (0.63 cm) from the tuber, saving only the two to three inches (5 to 7.5 cm)

Rooting the tip of a long tuber sprout.

73

furthest away from the tuber. See page 37 to learn how to root a sprout. You can see a short video about rooting a long white tuber sprout on the Kristine Albrecht YouTube channel. Look for video 116.

EXPERT TIP: PRE-SPROUTING TUBERS

If you live where the growing season is short and you'd like to get blooms earlier in the year, you can do more than warm up your tubers; you can pre-sprout them. This method allows you to plant a tuber with roots and leaves, putting your plants weeks ahead. Planting a tuber with a root system can also be a significant advantage if you live in a climate with late spring and early summer rain. The risk of rot declines once a tuber develops roots for taking up water.

Pre-sprouting tubers will result in leaf growth. Leaves provide the plant with energy from the sun. The more leaves you have at planting time, the stronger your young plant will be, and the sooner you will get blooms. Regardless of your storage strategy or storage medium, I suggest starting to pre-sprout your tubers six weeks before your planting date.

You will need to gather five things for pre-sprouting: A grow light, some plastic tubs

Pre-sprouted tubers develop roots and leaves, making them more resilient for planting.

or deep trays (with a few holes in the bottom for drainage), a bottom tray to catch excess water, plant tags, and moist high-quality potting soil. In addition, if you are pre-sprouting in a cold garage or greenhouse, you will need a heat mat set at 55° F (12.7 C) under your tray. Start by writing out plant tags for each tuber you will be pre-sprouting. Lay down a 4-inch (10 cm) layer of potting soil in your tub or tray and dig out a trench in the potting soil with your hand. Without allowing them to touch each other, nestle your tubers into the soil trench, making a row across the long end of the container. The tubers should be angled up at 45°, keeping the crowns above the soil. Finally, place the plant tags behind each tuber crown.

After the first row of tubers is in the soil and the plant tags are in place, repeat the process of digging out a trench, and piling up the soil to cover the first set of tubers. Make sure not to cover the tuber crowns. They should be exposed to the air. Set in the second row of tubers behind the first row. Again, place their plant tags and cover the tuber bodies with potting soil leaving the crowns exposed to the air. Repeat this process until your tray is full. Finally, water lightly to settle the soil around each tuber.

Place the tray full of tubers eight to twelve inches (20 to 30 cm) below a grow light for 14 hours per day, tricking the tubers into thinking it is spring. If your tray is in a warm room, you should be set. If your tray is in a cold garage or an unheated shed, place a seed starting heat mat underneath your tray set at 55° F (12.7° C). Keep an eye on the moisture level in the tray, especially if you are using a heat mat; you want to keep the soil slightly moist but not dripping wet. In time the viable tubers will make roots and send up shoots from their crowns, and because of the 14 hours of light from the grow lights, they will develop leaves.

After your last frost date, you can bury your sprouted tubers with their new leaves above ground. If your sprouted tuber has sent up multiple shoots, break off all but two of them when you plant it. If your shoot is short and has no leaves, place the tuber in the soil just as if it was not pre-sprouted. If your shoot is tall and has developed leaves, place your tuber in the soil a bit deeper than you usually would. Deeper planting will support the larger shoot at its base. Using this method, your dahlia plants will typically be one month ahead of where you would have been had you planted an unsprouted tuber. Even though I live in a warm climate with a long growing season, I use this method to make my season even longer. You can see a short video about pre-sprouting tubers on the Kristine Albrecht YouTube channel. Look for video 96.

PLANTING TUBERS

After their last frost date, most growers plant their dahlia tubers directly into the ground in spring. You can use this website (almanac.com/gardening/frostdates) to enter your ZIP code and find out your last frost date. If you don't get frost, wait until your low nighttime temperatures will reach 50° F (10° C).

A good rule of thumb is to base your planting distance on bloom diameter: plants with ten inch (25 cm) or larger blooms are planted 24 inches apart (61 cm) while smaller blooming varieties can be placed 16 to 18 inches apart (40 to 45 cm). I plant two rows of dahlias per bed, and I offset each row. Hence, the plants are diagonal to one another, allowing me to get the proper distance between plants in a narrower bed

Dahlia tubers come in all shapes and sizes. Some are long and thin. Some are short and fat. Some are as round as a billiard ball. Tuber size and shape do not matter much. Some of the largest dahlia varieties produce undersized tubers, yet tubers of any shape or size can produce a healthy, vigorous plant.

It's not uncommon to find sprouts of all lengths coming from your tubers when you remove them from winter storage. If a sprout is shorter than two inches (5 cm), you can plant your tubers with the sprout. If the sprout is longer than three inches (7.5 cm), I recommend cutting it off 1/4 of an inch (0.63 cm) from the crown.

Before I plant my tubers, I make up plant tags for all the varieties that will be going in the ground. I like writing out all my tags while sitting at a table rather than writing up tags in the field. My tubers are stored by variety in boxes. I drop the tags in each box, and I am ready to start planting. Next, I dig a hole about 6 inches wide (15 cm) and 4 to 6 inches deep (10 to 15 cm). If the tuber I am planting has roots, I will sprinkle them with Mykos mycorrhizal inoculum, which contains beneficial fungus. This extends the reach of the plant's roots and increases the uptake of water and nutrients. I then lay the tuber horizontally at the bottom of the hole like I was putting it to bed. If a tuber does not have protruding roots, I will not use the inoculum as it is only viable in the soil for a couple of weeks (Mykos only benefits a tuber if it has existing roots, which can take up to four weeks to establish).

If I can identify an eye on the crown of the tuber, I face it toward the sky. Although every tuber must have an eye to make a plant, if I can't see one at planting time, I don't worry about it. All my tubers that are stored over winter had an eye when I divided them. Eyes can go flat during winter storage. If a tuber has sprouted, that is also fine. I face the shoot upward and bury it along with the tuber. It will find its way to the soil surface. It is okay if the shoot breaks off while handling the tuber. It will sprout again. Before filling the hole with soil, I push a 12-inch (30 cm) bamboo stick into the ground right next to the crown on the tuber. These small sticks serve three functions. First, as time passes, I watch for new growth to break out of the soil near each stick. Second, these sticks allow me to see where I have placed tubers

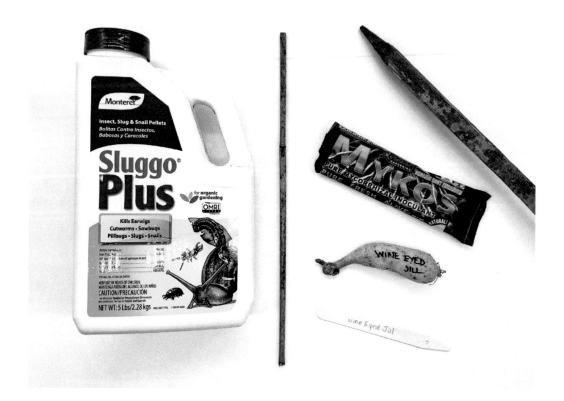

The items I gather when I am planting tubers. Sluggo Plus is needed if your tuber is pre-sprouted and has leaves. Small bamboo sticks mark the location of your tubers if you plan to stake your plants as a group. A tall garden stake is used if you stake plants individually. A plant tag identifying your tuber variety is needed. Finally, if your tuber is pre-sprouted and has roots, I sprinkle a little Mykos mycorrhizal inoculum in the hole to extend the root system.

once my mulch is applied. Because my plant tags are small, I would never see them without the sticks, as they might be buried in the mulch. Third, if most tubers have sprouted but some are lagging behind, the sticks show me where to dig to investigate. These sticks are just markers, not support stakes. I will set up support stakes later using the corral method described on page 102.

Suppose you have just a few plants and decide to support each one individually. In that case, I recommend sinking a five or six-foot (1.5 or 1.8 m) stake in the ground after digging your hole and just before planting your tubers rather than the small stick. I recommend driving your stakes into the ground when you are planting. If you wait to put a stake in the ground after filling the hole, you might accidentally

skewer the tuber and damage it. With a stake next to a buried tuber, you will know exactly where to look for the emergence of the first shoots. Once the stake is in place, refill the hole with soil so the tuber is buried 4 or 5 inches (10 or 12 cm) underground.

It is important to label each tuber at the time you plant it. Once it is covered with soil, it will be impossible to know the variety in each hole. I put my half-inch by six-inch (1.2 by 15 cm) white plastic plant tag into the soil right up against the stake. This gives it support and reduces the chance it will get bent or broken.

If your soil is dry, it is best to moisten it a few days before planting. Bone-dry soil will dry out your tuber. Likewise, drenching your soil at planting time could lead to tuber rot. Tubers contain moisture, and the warmth of the soil promotes growth. Typically, if your soil stays moist, you won't need to water your planted tuber until the first shoot appears above the ground. If you live in a dry climate however, and your soil dries out while waiting for a shoot to appear, sprinkle the soil once a week or so with a bit more water, so your tuber doesn't shrivel. You can check the soil moisture by sticking your fingers three inches (7.5 cm) underground. The two exceptions where watering a freshly-planted tuber is different is if you are planting it in a container or it already has an existing root system. See the section on planting in containers on page 64.

1. Making a 4 or 5 inch hole.

2. Setting a stake at the tuber crown.

3. Covering the tuber and securing the plant tag.

4. Water your sprout once it emerges from the soil.

David Hall of Halls of Heddon in his display garden.

David Hall, England

David Hall's grandad served in WW1 as a volunteer stretcher bearer and, returning home as a wounded veteran, he was advised to find an outdoor job. As a keen allotment gardener, he and his wife Barbara decided to move with their young family and start a plant nursery near the village of Heddon on the Wall. David still operates the nursery today as Halls of Heddon. The wall in the village name is Hadrian's Wall, a 73-mile stone fortification built in 122 AD by the Roman Emperor Hadrian. It marked the boundary of what, at the time, was Roman Britannia and the unconquered land to the north called Caledonia.

For 103 years, David's family has been raising nursery plants for gardeners all over England. Originally they grew delphiniums, pansies, and chrysanthemums. Then, in the mid-1920s, they expanded into dahlias. Their mail-order business of cuttings and pot tubers started just before WWII. During the war, when food production was a high priority, dahlias were grown in beds between vegetable plants. In the 1950s, David's father was a national champion dahlia exhibitor.

The first mail-order catalog was produced in 1931 and featured chrysanthemums, dahlias, delphiniums, pansies, and violas, among other plants. Today David oversees the propagation and sale of 100,000 dahlia cuttings and 10,000 pot tubers every year from two nursery locations. In addition, he plants a show garden of 7,000 dahlias on 1.25 acres (5,050 sq m) that is ablaze with color in September, allowing customers to see how new and favorite varieties grow and bloom. For many dahlia growers in England, a trip to the show garden is an annual ritual.

In recent years David's team has been collecting seeds and developing a line of in-house varieties. The introductions are primarily open-center varieties that bloom profusely, one of which, 'Hadrian's Sunlight', was awarded the Royal Horticultural Society's Award of Garden Merit soon after introduction. All of his variety names start with Hadrian's, in honor of the stone wall in his village. His most popular in-house variety is 'Hadrian's Midnight'. You can see all of his varieties on his website. Use the search box and type in Hadrian's.

David's Website: hallsofheddon.com
David's Instagram: @hallsofheddon

Three woman dahlia breeders at the Triple Wren Dahlia Festival.
Me on the left, Noni Morrison in the middle, and Sandy Boley at right.
Noni is the hybridizer of 'Salish Twilight Girl'. Sandy is a hybridizer with
her husband Steve. Their varieties start with 'Sandia, "Irish', and 'SB's'.

6. Growing Dahlias From Seed

HOW DAHLIAS MAKE SEED

WHEN I FIRST STARTED GROWING dahlias I had no idea they could be grown from seed. I was focused on purchasing tubers from my local nursery or from my dahlia society. For me, tubers were the way dahlias were propagated. Unlike tubers, seeds produce dahlia plants that are not clones of the parent plant. Instead, they are unique and unrepeatable. Like a litter of puppies, each seed in a dahlia seed head is different from its "seed-mates." What I eventually learned is that every dahlia variety we grow started out as a single seed.

I think breeding new dahlia varieties is the most exciting part of growing dahlias. If you want to learn how to breed unique dahlia varieties look for my book *Dahlia Breeding for the Farmer-Florist and the Home Gardener*. It's a step-by-step guide to breeding new dahlia varieties from seed. It covers breeding strategies like hand pollination, open pollination with culling, and seven other strategies for generating new dahlia varieties.

Dahlia blooms start their life as a bud. Interestingly, after they bloom and get pollinated, they end their life as a seed head that looks similar to the original bud. If you collect dahlia seeds or do some deadheading, it is important to know the difference between a seed head and a new bud. Dahlia buds tend to be round. Often they look a bit like a ball that has been paddled flat at both ends. The immature petals inside are covered by green bracts that protect the developing bloom. Even with these green protectors, it is often possible to see the color of the petals showing through the green. Seed heads, however, show no petal color underneath. Instead, they are grassy green and shaped more like an acorn than a flattened ball. As they age, the tip of the head typically turns dark brown or black.

COLLECTING SEEDS

Once a dahlia bloom is pollinated by bees or humans and is left on the plant for at least six weeks, the seeds inside the seed head will mature. The best clue that the seed head is ready to harvest is at the tip. It will typically turn brown or black. When this occurs, it is time to peek inside. Peel back a few of the bracts and look at a seed. It's like peeling back a corn husk to see the kernels. If the seeds are light green or white, they still need time to mature. Push back the bracts and give the seed head a week or two before checking again. Seeds are most likely mature if they are elongated, stiff, and brown or black. The six-week maturation period is not universal. Seeds from open-center varieties tend to mature sooner. Seeds from giant dahlias tend to mature later.

Seed heads on a plant mature best in dry conditions. If rain is in the forecast, I recommend covering them to keep them dry. An umbrella works well. I don't recommend covering the seed heads with plastic bags. In my experience, the condensation inside a plastic bag can rot a developing seed head. When a big storm is in the forecast, and I want to protect many developing seed heads, I use paper corn tassel bags. These are long, narrow waterproof paper bags designed for hand-pollinating corn plants. They are available

The life cycle of a "KA's Mocha Katie' bloom from bud (on the left) to seed head (on the right).

from a company called Midco at midcoglobal.com. Once on their website, type "Tassel Bags" into the search window. I use the medium size bags. Any of the bag colors will do. These bags come in quantities of one thousand, so finding a friend to split the order might be helpful.

I am often asked if immature seed heads can be cut from the plant, brought indoors, and set into a jar of water to finish maturing. I don't recommend this. If developing seeds required only hydration, this technique might work, but it takes more than water to make seeds. Making

A mature dahlia seed head.

seeds is a dahlia plant's most energy-intensive task in its lifetime. The plant supplies the developing seeds with sugars, amino acids, hormones, and starches. When we cut a seed head from the stem, those nutrients and energy sources are severed. A far better strategy, if wet weather is coming, is to cover the seed heads and allow the plant to continue to bring the seeds to maturity.

Once your seed head is mature, cut it off the stem. The plant that produced the seed head is called the seed parent. If you keep track of your seed parents, write the name on a paper bag and drop the seed head in. Then, take it indoors to a clean table. Break open your seed heads and separate the black seed from the papery chaff. The thin chaff in a seed head is the dried-out paleal bracts that support each petal from behind when in bloom. Some seeds may be smaller or lighter than others, and some will be more square. Seeds that are light green were not pollinated and will not be viable. The larger dark seeds should be dried and saved. Lay them out on a paper towel with their tag, so you know the seed parent (if you are keeping track). I lay them out to dry for 24 hours at room temperature. You can see a short video of me taking apart a seed head on the Kristine Albrecht YouTube channel. Look for video 158.

After the seeds have dried I put each batch in 3½ inches by 2¼ inches (8.2 x 5.7 cm) paper coin envelopes. I write an X (for "cross") and the name of the seed parent. I also jot down the year on the envelope to know when the seeds were collected and any notes I think are relevant to these seeds. Although you can germinate seeds collected years earlier, fresher seeds tend to be more viable. Once secure in their envelopes, store your seeds in a cool, dry place indoors. Don't store them in a barn or a hot or moist environment, or where rodents can get to them. I keep all my envelopes of seeds in a sturdy cardboard shoebox on a bookshelf in my office. The seeds I collect in the fall will sit inside their envelopes for four to five months before spring germination.

Not all seeds from a seed head will be viable. Some may never have been pollinated. Others may have needed more time to fully mature. The more you work with dahlia seeds, the better you will get at telling which seeds are viable. In general, mature, viable seeds are dark and have a bit of a "belly" on them. Very flat seeds typically will not germinate. One surefire way to tell if a seed is viable is to cut one open. If you have a group of seeds from a single seed head and want to know if any are viable, cut one of them in half with a sharp knife. Non-viable seeds will be empty. All you will see is the seed coat with nothing inside. If you see something inside the seed, squeeze it out. Viable seeds will have a white paste that will ooze out when

you squeeze it. That is the endosperm, the food that supplies the energy the embryo will need to germinate in the spring. You can see a short video of me looking inside seeds on the Kristine Albrecht YouTube channel. Look for video 170.

In years when I have more seeds than I can

A corn tassel bag over a bloom.

plant, I can freeze them to preserve their viability. I place my coin envelopes in a sealed plastic freezer bag and store them in the coldest part of my kitchen freezer. If you plan to freeze seeds, ensure that they are thoroughly dry. Freezing wet or moist seeds could generate ice crystals and damage the future viability of the seed.

Dick Parchell, a dahlia breeder I know, has successfully germinated seeds that were stored for 30 years in a freezer.

GERMINATING SEEDS

Watching a dahlia open its first bloom is the reward many growers anticipate most. For me germinating dahlia seeds is one of my favorite parts of dahlia growing. Although they look inert, the seeds are alive. Most of the mass in a seed is the endosperm, the food needed to sustain the embryo inside once it starts to sprout.

Dahlia seeds are programmed to germinate when the moisture and temperature levels are right in the spring. In the right place, under the right conditions, seeds come to life with a tiny shoot breaking free of the hard outer coat. Every dahlia we grow in our gardens was once a seed that waited for its moment. I never tire of watching seeds come to life.

Six weeks before I want to plant my seedlings in the ground, I start germinating my seeds. Many dahlia seeds are not viable and will never sprout. Instead of a non-viable seed taking up space under the grow lights, I pre-sprout them and only nurture those that will produce a plant.

Seeds need three things to germinate: optimum temperature, moisture, and air. Seeds have very little water, which helps them survive dormancy. To start the process of germination, we need to rehydrate them. Once absorbed, water will give rise to enzymes that "wakes up" the embryo inside the seed. Water also swells the seed and causes the seed coat to split open, however, too much water chokes out needed air and can lead to rot.

Seedlings in four inch pots.

84

Me with a "bouquet" of dahlia seed heads.

I germinate my seeds between moist paper towels to give them an ideal balance of water and air. I start with 20 half sheets of paper towels stacked on top of each other like a lasagna. I then fold the entire stack of 20 in half. I run the stack of paper towels under a cold water faucet to get it completely wet. I then squeeze the stack gently to wring out the excess water. Next, the entire moist towel stack is laid flat on a dinner plate. Finally, I peel back almost all the pieces of paper towel like opening a book, leaving three to five sheets at the bottom, flat against the plate.

Next, I pour about 30 seeds out and spread them out on the open paper towel. I write with a pencil on a plastic plant tag the information from the coin envelope (X plus the seed parent name). Once the seeds are spread out, I lay the plant tag on the paper towel with an inch or so sticking out (like a bookmark in a book). I then lay down three to five more sheets of moist paper towel on top of those seeds and repeat the process. Next, another tag is written and placed with an inch or so sticking out for each successive layer. If I offset each plant tag from the one below it (like the tabs of a file folder), I can quickly flip through the layers of seeds. When I'm

SEED BANKING

Seeds hold the promise of the survival of the species. Nature has optimized a seed's chance for survival with seed banking. If every seed in a seed head sprouted simultaneously, survival could be at risk under the wrong environmental conditions. For instance, what if all the seeds from a seed head sprout at the same time as a hatch of hungry grasshoppers? Or what if a spell of hot, dry weather sets in just after every seed has sprouted? In these circumstances, all the seeds in a seed head could be lost.

Nature protects against this risk with seed banking. In a seed head full of seeds, one inherited trait is the number of days it takes for a seed to germinate. My experience with dahlia seeds is that some will sprout in two days. Most will sprout in four to ten days. A few will sprout in 12 days. A tiny number will sprout in 20 to 22 days. In this way, the species' future has a better chance of survival. If the first set of seeds sprouts early and the grasshoppers eat all the young plants, the seeds that wait 20 days will rise from the soil after the grasshoppers are gone. Seed banking is critical to remember when you are sprouting your seeds. Not all seeds are viable; however, those that are will sprout in their own time, according to nature's way.

done, I have a stack of layered seeds, as if they are nestled in the pages of a book.

After I have layered all the seeds in a paper towel stack, I wrap the entire stack, including the plate, with plastic wrap. I am trying to keep the paper towels from drying out. Next, I write the date on the plastic wrap using a permanent marker. Finally, I place the plate where it will stay between 72 to 75° F (22 to 23° C). Warmth is a necessary condition for the germination of seeds. If they are cold, they will not germinate. My kitchen has an old Wedgwood stove with pilot lights; the shelf above the stovetop keeps my seeds at just the right temperature. I use an infrared non-contact thermometer to monitor the temperature of my seeds. Dahlia seeds do not need light to germinate. You can see a short video of how I germinate dahlia seeds on the Kristine Albrecht YouTube channel. Look for video 95.

Dahlia seeds typically germinate in two to ten days, with some germinating later, up to 22 days. I open the plastic wrap and check my dahlia seeds once or twice daily. The first sign of germination is a thin white root that will appear out of the pointed end of the seed. If the paper towel is drying out, I use a spray bottle of water to moisten it, being careful not to get it dripping wet. I like to check seeds often because their root tips can grow into the fibers of the paper towel. If the root tip becomes too embedded in the paper fibers, it can get damaged when I remove it. If I can't free up an embedded root tip, I cut the paper around it with scissors. The small piece of paper attached to the root tip won't interfere with the growth of the seedling.

Once the seeds germinate, I remove them from the paper towel and transfer them into a wet seed starting mix. Any ungerminated seeds are transferred to a fresh paper towel stack on the fourth or fifth day. I do this because warm moist paper towels can get contaminated with bacteria and affect seed germination. Every so often, the black outer seed casing will fall off of the shoot. That's okay. It did its job and is no longer needed.

After day ten, I will more closely inspect the remaining un-sprouted seeds. Some of these may just be late spouters; however, experience has taught me that many un-sprouted seeds at day ten are probably not viable. To determine the viability of these remaining seeds, I will use my fingers to gently roll them on the paper towel. The black shell will usually come apart if they were never pollinated or have a defect. It will be evident that there is no viable seed inside.

If a seed does not fall apart when I roll it, and it is firm with a slight "belly," I will keep it and hope it will eventually sprout. Seeds that are flat and lightweight generally don't sprout as well. My average germination rate is 20-50% depending on the seed and pollen parents. Germination rates vary depending on the varieties being crossed and the pollination method used.

If your paper towel develops mold, there are three possible remedies. First, it could be that your paper towel is too wet. Try again and, this time, wring out more of the water. Another solution might be to change the paper towel every few days. Finally, you can mix up a 5% bleach solution in a spray bottle and give your seeds and the towel a spray every few days.

Once my seeds have sprouted, I immediately root them using a high-quality seed starting mix in a plastic 72-cell seedling tray. These trays can be found at garden centers, hydroponic supply stores, or online. Seed starting mix is different from potting soil. It has a finer texture and is sterilized for young shoots. Each cell in the tray has drain holes in the bottom. I use a bottom tray without holes to water my seedlings from the bottom up. Watering seeds from the top can dislodge them or disturb their growth in the soil. I recommend getting your 72-cell tray ready for seeds on the same day (or a day before)

LABELING SEEDLINGS

I am sometimes asked why I make an X in front of the seed parent name on my plant labels. Why don't I just put the name of the seed parent, like, 'Jomanda'?

I use the X because it differentiates my plants grown from cuttings and tubers from those grown from seed. Plants from tubers and cuttings are clones of the mother plants. Seeds, on the other hand, are unique and don't produce blooms identical to the mother plant. By putting an X in front of the name, I know that while the plant was an offspring from 'Jomanda', it is not an exact clone of 'Jomanda'. Instead, it is a unique seedling with its own set of traits.

you set your seeds onto the moist paper towel. I do this because some seeds sprout very quickly. Fill the cells in your tray with seedling mix and fill the bottom tray ¾ full of water. Set the top tray into the bottom tray for about half a day until the seedling mix has soaked up some water and it glistens slightly on the surface. This process can happen more quickly as every seedling mix is different. After soaking, pull out the bottom tray and dump all but one-quarter of an inch (0.6 cm) of the water.

I use the 72-cell trays because four-inch (10 cm) pots would take up too much room with the number of seeds I start. If you have a manageable number of seeds and want to root them in four-inch (10 cm) pots, that will work fine. If you use a four-inch (10 cm) pot, I recommend filling most of the pot with potting soil with some seedling mix in the center where you will place your seed.

In addition to having trays ready to receive sprouted seeds, you will need a source of light and a source of warmth. If you

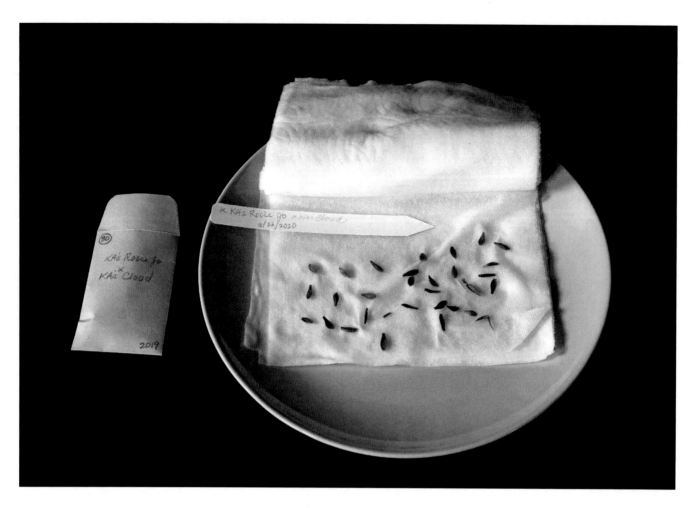

Seeds placed on to moist paper towel.

already have a seed-starting facility, use that. I don't have a greenhouse, so I use seed-starting heat mats and grow lights. My heat mats are 2 by 4 feet (60 x 120 cm), and I set my 72-cell trays on them. When plugged in, they give off warmth and keep the soil at the right temperature. I use a digital thermostatic switch with a soil probe, so the mat cycles on and off automatically, keeping the soil at 72° F (22° C). The grow lights I use are also 2 by 4 feet (60 x 120 cm) and will illuminate four of the 72-cell trays at a time. I hang them, so the lights are three to five inches (7.6 to 12.7 cm) above the soil's surface. That might sound too close, but when the seeds are young, they need intense light to grow and to avoid getting leggy. My grow lights are on a timer to give the sprouted seeds 14 hours of light each day. Where I live, electricity is less expensive at night.

Therefore, I have my grow light on overnight. As the plants grow I move the lights up to maintain the three to five-inch (7.6 to 12.7 cm) spacing above the plant leaves.

Now that we have our 72-cell trays and heat and light systems ready, let's return to germinating seeds. Once I have a sprouted seed, I make a plant tag that identifies the seed parent and germination date. Next (using a pencil), I make a small hole in the seed-starting mix deep enough to hold the small white root and half of the seed. I place the seed into the hole with the root facing down and gently squeeze the soil around the sprouted seed. Half of the seed (the un-sprouted end) is now sticking up out of the soil. Next, I place the appropriate plant tag in the cell with the seed. Finally, from above, I gently moisten the seed with a light spray of tap water from a spray bottle (I use a Mondi two-liter "Mist and Spray" pump sprayer). I do this to settle the soil around the newly-planted seed. I repeat this process for each sprouted seed until the 72-cell tray is full. Next, I place the tray on the heat mat and under the grow lights, even if it is not yet full. Filling a 72-cell tray can take days, and the first seedlings need heat and light.

I keep my eye on the soil moisture, touching the top of it periodically to test its dampness. When the 72-cell tray needs more water, I fill the bottom tray about three-quarters of the way full and place the top tray into the water, where it can soak up the moisture from below. I leave the top tray in the bottom tray for a few minutes until I see the top of the soil getting glossy. That tells me the water has wicked from below to the top of the soil. I then lift off the top tray and pour off most of the excess water leaving one-quarter of an inch (0.6 cm) in the bottom tray.

When seedling roots start breaking through the holes in the bottom of the 72-

Seeds in moist paper towels covered in plastic wrap.

Germinated seeds.

Planting the root tip into seedling mix.

The first leaves (cotyledons).

Seedling with true leaves.

Seedling potted up in a four inch pot.

A seedling ready for planting.

EIGHT REASONS SEEDS DON'T SPROUT

There are several reasons why a seed may not be viable and will never sprout. Here is a partial list.

- A seed may have been taken from its seed head too early and is not fully mature. Most seed heads must stay on a plant for about six weeks after fertilization to be viable.

- A seed may have rotted in the seed head due to too much moisture during gestation.

- A seed could have come from a poor seed parent. Not all dahlia cultivars are good at making seeds. Some dahlias have beautiful blooms, healthy plants, and robust tubers but are poor at making seeds. Likewise, some seeds may have been pollinated with pollen that is not viable because the pollen parent is sterile or the pollen was wet.

- A seed could have an unusually thick seed coat. Although the seed is viable, the thick shell will not yield to the shoot inside. In this case, you can sand the edge of the seed coat with an emery board to allow water to enter and germination to start. Sand only the edges of the seed coat. Avoid sanding the pointed tip, as that could damage the sprout inside.

- A seed could be too cold to sprout. Therefore, when germinating seeds on a moist paper towel, they must be kept at 72 to 75° F (22 to 23° C).

- The seed may not sprout if the paper towel is too dry. Likewise, a seed may rot and fail to germinate if the paper towel is too wet.

- A seed may fail to sprout if it is not fertilized. Not all seeds in a seed head get pollinated. Although they may look viable, some are empty shells with no possibility of sprouting.

- A seed might not be viable if the seed head received too much rain, heavy dew, or a deep freeze after it was pollinated. Generally speaking, it is best to keep seed heads dry after pollination.

cell tray, they are ready to be repotted. I fill up four-inch (10 cm) pots with premium potting soil. Again, I will fill up a bottom tray with water and let the four-inch (10 cm) pots soak up moisture from below for at least 15 minutes and as long as two days. Some potting soils contain a wetting agent and soak up water quickly. Others can take a day or two to hydrate fully. I will also water the potting soil from above before transplanting the seedlings if needed.

To transplant the seedlings, I make a hole in the soil of the four-inch (10 cm) pot large enough and deep enough to accept the plant and its soil from the 72-cell tray. Then, using two butter knives, I gently pry out seedlings from each cell (taking the soil with it) and nestle them into the larger pots, gently pressing the soil in around them. I then transfer the plant tag to the new pot. It is essential throughout a seedling's life that the plant tag follow it wherever it goes. If the seedling starts its life in early spring and it's still cold outside, I keep the four-inch (10 cm) pots on the heat mats and under grow lights until the weather warms up. If the weather is warm when I start seeds, I put the small plants directly outside in the shade. When these small plants are newly repotted into four-inch (10 cm) pots, they must be gradually introduced to full sun. I typically keep them in the shade for three to five days before planting in native soil.

In nature, small plants get buffeted by the wind. This movement stimulates them to develop stronger stems. However, there is no wind indoors, and the tiny plants indoors can develop weak stems. This is solved by placing a fan in the room where your seedlings are growing. An oscillating desk fan six to eight feet (1.8 to 2.4 m) away from your plants is ideal and creates more random wind patterns than a fixed fan. Jostling your tiny plants with a fan indoors will help them grow strong.

I grow these repotted plants until they are three to four inches tall before putting them into the garden. A bigger plant with a better root system is better equipped to

resist pests and cool temperatures. Over the years I have planted seedlings in multiple ways. When I was first starting out I planted them with the spacing I used for my plants grown from tubers: 18 to 24 inches (45 to 60 cm) apart. Eventually, I realized that since seedlings are a surprise package, many were not varieties I was interested in regrowing in future years. Now I grow my seedlings four to eight inches apart (10 to 20 cm) because 95% of them will be removed and discarded after they produce their first few blooms. In addition to closer spacing, I now grow all my first-year seedlings in sink pots. This

Pulling seedlings out of a 72 cell tray with two butter knives.

allows me to remove individual plants without disturbing the roots of the neighboring plants. Closely-spaced sink pots are also a great idea if you have limited garden space and want to grow as many seedlings as possible. If you are interested in planting in sink pots, you can read more about them on page 61.

When it comes time to plant your seedlings outside, you cannot transition them all at once. As with cuttings, young seedlings need to be hardened off. You can find information on hardening off young plants on page 42.

When I plant seedlings into my garden beds, I sprinkle them with Sluggo Plus. These organic and pet-safe pellets protect young plants from slugs, snails, earwigs, sow bugs, and cutworms—critters that would love to chew plants down to their stems. It's important to sprinkle the product in the plant canopy and on the ground around the plant. Regular Sluggo will only protect against slugs and snails. Sluggo Plus adds protection against earwigs, sow bugs, and cutworms.

Gently placing a seedling into a four inch pot filled with potting soil.

SEEDLING TERMINOLOGY

A dahlia plant grown from a tuber or a rooted cutting is a clone. It will grow, produce blooms, and perform identically to the parent plant. A plant grown from a dahlia seed is the first generation of a new cultivar that is unique and unrepeatable. Plants grown from seed are called seedlings.

"First-year seedling" refers to a unique plant grown directly from seed. A first-year seedling is a unique plant with no identical siblings or offspring. If you grow a dahlia plant from a seed, you witness something no one else has ever seen. It is lost forever if a grower loses a first-year seedling through disease, pests, or drought. If a first-year seedling survives and produces viable tubers, there is a path to growing and multiplying it in future years.

A second-year seedling is a plant grown from a tuber or a rooted cutting from a first-year seedling. Hybridizers grow new varieties for several years to observe their traits, growing habits, productivity, disease, and pest resistance and ensure that their genes are stable. Because most breeders only name a new cultivar once it has been under observation for several years, second-year seedlings typically have a number, not a name. Every subsequent year a seedling is grown for observation, another year is added on. That is why we sometimes hear about third-year or fourth-year seedlings. Eventually, if a seedling is worthy of introduction, it will get a permanent name.

BUYING SEED

Growing from seed is different from growing cuttings or tubers. When we buy cuttings or tubers, we purchase a clone. We know how the resulting blooms will look. Buying seeds is the opposite. It allows us to grow something that has never existed before. Each seed that germinates will produce a new dahlia cultivar.

I recently searched online for dahlia seeds and found many sites offering them. Some advertise their seeds as a mix of open-centered varieties. I would expect these cultivars to produce mostly open-centered blooms. My search did turn up an ad for 'Maki' seeds on a popular online site. 'Maki' is a large pink and purple informal decorative dahlia introduced in 1980. What we must remember is that every dahlia seed is unique and there is no guarantee that seeds taken from a 'Maki' seed parent will look like a 'Maki'. Those seeds will likely produce mostly open-center blooms and look nothing like 'Maki'. Seeds from a 'Maki' bloom could be any color. They can also be small or large and in any variety of forms. Such is the reality when buying dahlia seeds.

The six colorful seedlings above are seed-mates from the same seed head from the white pompon seed parent next to the snips.

COTYLEDONS

Early on, a tiny seedling depends entirely on its internal food supply (the endosperm) to grow. As it develops, however, it switches to energy from light. Inside the seed are the cotyledons, often called seed leaves or cot leaves; these are the first temporary ready-made leaves that expand and break out of the seed casing. Their job is to turn light into sugar and fuel the new plant while it constructs its first real leaves. Notice that the cotyledons don't look like dahlia leaves. When the first set of real dahlia leaves appear, the cotyledons will wither and die.

Meanwhile, the tiny root is burrowing into the soil. Although roots are not glamorous, they have three essential jobs. First, they provide the plant with an underground structural foundation to keep it from blowing over in the wind. Second, they take in water, nutrients, and minerals. Finally, they store excess energy in tiny underground tubers.

The tiny embryonic root is what scientists call "positively geotropic." This means the root knows which way is down and will push down into the soil. On the other hand, the cot leaves and their embryonic shoots are "negatively geotropic," meaning they push up, against the forces of gravity, toward the sun.

You have probably heard the terms monocot and dicot. About one-third of all flowering plants are monocots, like wheat, corn, and grasses. Dahlias, and 200,000 other species, are dicots. Monocot and dicot refer to the number of cotyledons a germinated seed produces. Monocots burst forth with a single cot leaf. Dicots, like dahlias, germinate with two.

Melissa Smith of Fraylick Farm. Photo by Emily Barbee.

Melissa Smith, South Carolina

Ten years ago, Melissa Smith founded Fraylick Farm in Traveler's Rest, South Carolina. Set in the foothills of the Blue Ridge Mountains near the border with North Carolina, she had visions of gorgeous dahlias, sweet peas, and cosmos blooming in abundance in her field. Unfortunately, that dream collided with the stubborn reality of her hot, humid climate. According to Melissa, "My climate has everything dahlias hate."

Melissa farms one acre (4046 sq m) of cut flowers. Because her average summertime temperatures hover around 90° F (32° C), she has developed creative strategies to keep her plants thriving. In addition to being a cut flower farmer and tuber supplier, Melissa is a skilled communicator and maintains a lively blog sharing what she has learned from a decade of flower farming in the heat.

Melissa's plants benefit from a setting within a grove of tall trees. While her plants receive full sun in the middle of the day, they are shaded in the heat of the afternoon. In a hot climate, nearby trees can serve as a much-needed source of shade.

You can sign up for a free "Dahlia Lovers" newsletter on her website. Her focus in these frequent messages is sharing growing advice, successes, failures, and results from her new variety test garden.

Melissa's Website: fraylickfarm.com
Melissa's Instagram: @flwrtherapy

7. DAHLIA FIELD CARE

GROWING THE RIGHT VARIETIES

WE LIVE IN A TIME WHEN DAHLIA growers can easily share pictures with people worldwide. Therefore, it is natural to want to grow everything beautiful that we see online. However, not all dahlia cultivars grow well everywhere. Therefore, finding out what grows well in your garden is essential.

Our dahlia plots are unique. They exist in specific places with varying soils and climates. Our soil may not be like soil 1,000 miles away. Our garden's pests and diseases may differ from those in a warmer or colder climate. The length of our growing season and the hours of sunlight each day depend on our latitude. More importantly, every dahlia cultivar is different. They have different preferences for heat and cold and are tolerant of various pests and diseases. I have struggled to grow some dahlias that I have seen others grow easily. Likewise, there are varieties I can grow beautifully that friends elsewhere tell me they struggle with.

One of the most important things we can do in our gardens is to observe our plants closely and keep records of their performance. Over time we will learn what varieties work well in our gardens and grow those with confidence. While it is tempting to try to grow every beauty we see, ultimately, our joy comes from plants that thrive. I encourage you to try growing new varieties. You will never know until you try. However, if a particular cultivar does not do well for you after a few years of trying, let it go and grow the dahlias that thrive in *your* garden.

At left: 'KA's Snow Jo' & KA's Mocha Jake'.

Heather Henson, Canada

Heather Henson of Boreal Blooms in Cold Lake, Alberta has a very short and intense growing season. Therefore, she must grow cultivars that mature quickly and give her blooms before a hard frost arrives. Heather does not grow any large or dinner plate dahlias. She also does not grow 'Cafe au Lait'. They take too long to bloom in her short summer. Likewise, because her plants grow shorter than in most climates, she avoids short, stocky varieties like 'Silver Years'. Over time, Heather has found that ball dahlias, mini balls, and decorative dahlias work best in her climate. A few of her best performers are 'Jomanda', 'Mary's Jomanda', 'Linda's Baby', 'Peaches-N-Cream', and 'Cornel Bronze'.

WATERING DAHLIAS

Watering is the trickiest part of dahlia care. Water requirements are determined by the makeup of your soil, your climate, the amount of mulch you use, and how much wind or fog your site receives.

Dahlias originated in the well-drained volcanic soil of Mexican and Central American hillsides. Although they require a lot of water, they like their roots constantly moist, but not water-logged. Dahlias are shallow feeders. They take up water in the first 12 inches (30 cm) of soil. They don't send a tap root deep into the ground.

I check my soil regularly. Using my hand, I dig down a few inches and ensure that my soil is moist but not dripping wet. I don't dig down too far, only about four to eight inches (10 to 20 cm). I also keep a sharp eye on my plants for signs of flagging or wilting. This might be an indication that more water is needed. When my plants are young, I typically water them once each week. In summer, when the plants are larger and the temperatures are higher, I typically water every other day.

During the summer, Santa Cruz will experience a few heat waves that last for days and, in rare cases, weeks. On the hottest days, I shower my plants with a gentle rain head on my hose to cool the plants. Like us, they love to be cooled down with a shower when it gets too hot. I am often asked if overhead watering dahlia plants in the day's heat will burn the leaves. The answer is no. High heat can burn leaves with or without water, but wetting down your plants in the heat of the day will not cause them to burn. Giving your plants an overhead shower on hot days is the best thing you can do for them.

If I am expecting high heat for an extended period I will switch to pulse watering. This involves giving your plants water multiple times over a day rather than one deep watering. For example, instead of watering once for 30 minutes, I will water my plants three times during the day for 10 minutes. Those three watering times will be spaced out in the morning, mid-day, and evening.

Pulse watering puts water shallowly in the soil where the plants can use it. It encourages the water to spread out wider, not deeper. It also makes water more available to plants all day long, when they need it. Although I currently pulse water only when temperatures rise, I am experimenting more and more with using this method year-round on a few of my rows to see how the plants perform. Some growers in hot climates use pulse watering with five-minute soakings up to six times per day. John Menzel in Australia experienced temperatures up to 120° F (49° C). You can read about how he used shade cloth and pulse watering to keep his plants hydrated on page 129.

Galena Berkompas, Washington

Galena Berkompas of Micro Flower Farm in Vancouver, Washington doesn't start watering her plants until her dry season starts in June or July. She then overhead waters her dahlias every other day. Galena uses Melnor oscillating sprinklers, the kind we used to run through as children. Melnor makes about a dozen oscillating sprinklers covering 2,400 to 4,500 square feet (222 to 418 sq m) of garden space. She puts her sprinkler up on a platform so the water stream will not get blocked by the plants. She has also used Wobbler sprinklers from Neversink Farm on a pole with a stake at the bottom to hold the sprinkler firmly in the ground with the sprinkler head high above the plants.

While some dahlia growers worry that overhead watering harms plants, Galena credits her lack of powdery mildew to her watering regimen. She believes the regular "rain" from her sprinklers washes away powdery mildew spores before they can take hold on her dahlia leaves. Galena has her sprinklers on timers that run between 3:00 am and 4:00 am to reduce evaporation. During rare heat waves, she waters every day instead of every other day.

Lorelie Merton, Australia

Lorelie Merton, of Florelie Seasonal Flowers in Bungaree, Australia irrigates her dahlias using soil-level drip emitters on her high clay soil. She waters deeply but not as often as others in her climate. She will water two or three times per week for an hour, depending on the temperature. She believes that this regime of deep irrigating with periods of rest in between builds resiliency in her plants and her tubers.

STAKING DAHLIAS

Fully grown dahlia plants can't support themselves in a stiff wind or when weighed down with rain. Unless you grow shorter varieties (typically used in gardens as border plants), you will need to provide your plants with some support. The need for plant support is universal regardless of how your plants are propagated. Plants from tubers, cuttings, and seeds all need to be supported. The two ways to support your plants are individually or collectively. It's best to install your plant supports when you plant your tubers, seedlings, or cuttings.

POUNDING IN STAKES

We have all struggled with pounding stakes into the ground in our gardens. If the stake is made of soft wood, like redwood or cedar, using a hammer will split and splinter the top end of the stake. Using a hammer can also cause hand injuries from the stake itself or the hammer.

When I was first learning how to grow dahlias, a member of my local dahlia society took me under his wing and taught me several garden tricks. His name was Dean, and he was 91 years old. One tool Dean showed me is still in use at my farm, the stake pounder. Dean took a 12-inch (30 cm) long piece of 2-inch (5 cm) wide galvanized pipe and screwed a galvanized cap on one end.

Slipping the pipe's open end over the stake, he could quickly pound it into the ground without splitting or injury. The rounded pipe cap does not split or splinter the ends of the stakes, which means they last for years and years. Unfortunately, Dean is no longer with us, but I think of him every time I pound in my stakes. You can see me using Dean's stake pounder on the Kristine Albrecht YouTube channel. Look for video 101.

When staking individual plants, I suggest any garden stake except bamboo. The hollow stems on bamboo can harbor earwigs, sow bugs, slugs, and snails. Cedar, T-stakes, or rebar stakes will all work well. I use redwood stakes that are 1-inch square (2.5 cm) and about five or six feet (1.5 to 1.8 m) tall.

For individual staking, I recommend sinking your stake before you plant your tuber. I plant my tubers with the tuber crown about two inches (5 cm) from the stake. Pounding a stake in after the tuber is planted could result in tuber damage. In addition, having a stake right next to your tuber helps you know where your tubers are planted. This is important when looking for new growth and preemptively placing slug and snail protection. Place your plant tag up against your stake for protection and easy identification. Once your plant starts growing, you can use twine or specialized garden ties to wrap around the body of the plant.

I recommend the "corral method" if you are staking an entire bed or row of dahlias. This method supports many plants at once and is less work than using individual stakes. It involves setting up a perimeter of stakes and wrapping twine to hold all the grouped dahlias. I put my stakes in and string my twine when I plant my dahlias.

I start by placing redwood stakes at all four corners of the bed. I then pound in stakes every four feet down the long sides of the bed. Again, T-posts, rebar, or wood stakes will work fine. The first layer of twine sits 10 inches (25 cm) above the soil around the outside perimeter of the bed. Starting at one post, I stretch the twine tight and loop it around the next post and repeat until I am back to where I started. Then, at the same level and starting in one corner, I zig zag my twine diagonally from a stake on one side of the bed to the other. When I reach the end, I reverse direction and tie the twine in a zig-zag pattern crossing over the twine I just strung. This process makes a series of Xs running down the inside of the bed. Once the first level of twine is complete, I run twine in the same pattern 10 inches (25 cm) above the first level. I will then make one more twine level 10 inches (25 cm) above the second level.

When I am done, I have three levels of twine wrapping around the bed perimeter and zig-zagging into the bed's interior. I use a braided black polypropylene twine that is 1/8 of an inch (.3 cm) thick. I like this twine because it does not stretch or sag when it gets wet, like natural fiber twine does. It is also very durable; I roll it up and reuse it every year. My local garden center sells only cotton twine. I found the

polypropylene twine at a nearby wholesale agricultural supply store. I prefer black twine over white because it lasts longer and blends well with dark green foliage. If you cannot find this locally, you could buy baling twine online. This is inexpensive and sold in large rolls for securing hay and straw bales. The only downside of baling twine is that it comes in bright colors like yellow, orange, or blue. Therefore, I find it distracting when I photograph my plants. However, if you don't mind the bright colors, baling twine is a great value.

Polypropylene twine is reusable and rolls up after use for easy storage until the following season.

Two levels of twine installed over young plants
that are protected from frost by row cover.

There are several reasons why I prefer the corral method over the Hortnova netting (a white netting that looks like a tennis court net). First, the twine goes up quickly and comes down quickly at the end of the season. Unlike netting, I can remove the twine from the tangled mass of plants by pulling it through them and rolling it up on a small piece of wood for future use. The Hortnova netting is almost impossible to remove from the mass of plants at the season's end. Second, I find a small roll of twine much easier to store all winter than a mass of netting. Finally, I like to photograph my varieties during the growing season. The black twine blends well with the dark green foliage for photography. I find photographing plants with the white netting running through the leaves distracting. You can see a short video of how I stake my plants on the Kristine Albrecht YouTube channel. Look for video 152.

David Hall, England

For David Hall of Halls of Heddon in Northumberland, England staking dahlias is part of a streamlined system that

103

accomplishes three things simultaneously. First, just before planting, David lays down his rows of drip tape irrigation. He then rolls out a lightweight metal crop support mesh (similar in size and structure to plastic Hortnova netting, except made of metal) on top of his drip tape, across the entire bed. The squares in the mesh are 8 by 8 inches (20 x 20 cm) and serve as guides for his plants' 16-inch (40 cm) spacing. Using this method, he doesn't have to lay down a wood or cardboard spacing guide. Finally, he raises the mesh off the ground once his dahlias are planted.

The mesh is held up by tension from strong wooden posts on all sides of the planting bed. A pair of posts are pounded into the ground on one end of the bed. The tops of the posts lean away from the bed. Another pair of posts on the opposite end of the bed is pounded partway into the ground with a slight lean into the bed. The posts are pulled back and away from the bed ends and pounded the rest of the way. This outward lean keeps the mesh under tension. This same process is repeated on the perimeter of the beds on both of the long sides, using lighter stakes 1.25 inches (3.8 cm) square. David raises the mesh as the young plants get taller, always keeping it just above the new

growth. As the dahlias are growing quickly at this stage, it only takes a few days before the net provides positive support. He stops raising it when the first buds appear. The plants grow through the mesh and are ultimately held firm at about 2/3 of their final height.

When the growing season is over, the plants are cut down and released from the mesh. After clearing the soil of plant debris, the mesh is lowered back to the ground, where it serves its third function. David secures the drip irrigation to the mesh panel using paper-coated wire ties (like those used on plastic bread bags). He then rolls up the metal mesh for storage (along with the attached drip tape) until the following season. In the spring, David unrolls the metal mesh on top of the soil and removes the small wire ties. His drip irrigation lines are all in place, and he is ready to plant dahlias again, using the mesh as a plant spacing guide.

Gabriela Salazar, Mexico

Gabriela Salazar of la Musa de las Flores in the mountains west of Mexico City uses a simple and beautiful method to stake the dahlias in her 3 by 65 foot (1 x 20 meter) beds. First, Gabriela installs 1-inch (2.5 cm) square wooden stakes on all sides of her dahlia beds, each about 3 feet (1 m) high.

Gabriela Salazar's natural twine plant supports. Photo by Laura May Grogan.

Then, using natural fiber twine, she builds a gridded layer of twine 12 inches (30 cm) above the soil. Because her stakes are close together, the twine grid looks like a solid net (like a Hortnova net). Her natural fiber grid is far more beautiful than premade netting. Finally, Gabriela completes the process with a second grid of twine 12 inches (30 cm) above the first layer. The result, with natural wood and twine, gives her garden a soft and organic feel.

In my garden, I have tried using natural fiber twine; however, it sagged when wet

At left: crop support mesh at Halls of Heddon. Photo by David Hall.

with dew. Gabriela's garden is completely covered by a protective translucent plastic canopy, keeping her twine dry and taut. The close 12-inch (30 cm) spacing of her stakes also helps to keep the twine from sagging.

Emily Avenson, Belgium

Emily Avenson of Fleuropean in Belgium does not stake her dahlias. In her clay soil, dahlia plants don't grow tall. She plants them very close together, as close as six inches (15 cm) apart. The branching stems of the plants entwine and hold each other up in the wind. Having said that, blooms that get wet with rain are heavy and more prone to wind damage. For this reason, if rain and wind are forecast, Emily deadheads her mature blooms. Occasionally a plant will slump over from the wind. Emily leaves those plants on their own. The bent-over stems eventually turn and start growing toward the light. Emily loves the resulting blooms with curvy stems. They add movement and drama to her naturalistic floral designs.

Lorelie Merton, Australia

Lorelie Merton of Florelie Seasonal Flowers in Bungaree, Victoria does not stake her dahlia plants. She plants most of her varieties 16 inches (40 cm) apart. Her pompon varieties are planted 8 inches (20 cm) apart. Lorelie relies on her full-grown plants to hold each other up should there be wind. Plants that fall over, she culls from her field and won't grow again. Over time, she only grows varieties with strong stems that can fend for themselves. With about 8,000 dahlia plants to care for, this "survival of the fittest" approach saves Lorelie the time, effort, and expense of pounding hundreds of stakes into the ground and installing and removing twine or netting.

MULCHING DAHLIAS

Once my plants are 6 inches (15 cm) high, I apply a 5 to 8-inch (12 to 20 cm) layer of mulch on top of my planting beds. I'm not afraid to pile it on. Mulch is one of the greatest gifts we can give our young plants. My preferred mulch is rice straw. California is a large rice producer, so rice straw is plentiful and inexpensive where I live. What you might use for mulch will largely depend on what is abundant and affordable in your area. That could be wheat straw, barley straw, or oat straw. All of these will work well. It's important to use straw, not hay. Straw is the left-over stalks of grains. These stalks typically have no seeds. Hay is full of seeds, and if you spread it on your beds, you will be spreading unwanted seeds. If you see seeds in the bale, don't use it.

I use straw successfully because no rain falls on my farm between May and October. In wet climates, straw can absorb water and become a heavy, sticky mess or provide habitat for slugs and snails. If you receive summer rain, check with dahlia growers in your area and see what they use for mulch. I know dahlia growers in the U.K. who successfully use sheep wool as mulch!

On the paths between my planting beds I use black landscape fabric (weed cloth) that stays in place permanently. I use a thinner layer of rice straw to cover this fabric because uncovered landscape fabric gets hot in my climate. Covering it with straw keeps me and the ground cooler.

If you live near deciduous trees, you have a free source of mulch in the fall in the form of leaves. Leaves can make excellent mulch as they are abundant, usually free, and full of nutrients that fungi love. Fungi in the soil break down the leaves, making nutrients available to our plants. The downside of using leaves is the labor they take to gather and prepare. Laying down several inches of full-sized leaves creates a "mat" of material that hinders air and

Rice straw mulch in my dahlia patch.

water movement. When using leaves as mulch, you will want to break them down into smaller pieces. Use a leaf chipper or spread them on the ground and run over them with a power mower. For many years I spent hours collecting leaves, chopping them up with a mower, and adding them to the top of my soil. My local newspaper featured a picture of me on the front page one day, calling me "the leaf-collecting lady." As my farm grew and the demands on my time increased, my leaf-collecting days were numbered.

Finally, I don't recommend wood chips alone in planting beds for dahlias, as decomposing cellulose leaches nitrogen from the soil. A friend of mine decided one year to put wood chips on her dahlia beds. For four years she had below-average plant growth. She ultimately tried to remove all the chips from her beds, but much of it had migrated down into the soil where it took years to break down as it robbed her soil of nitrogen.

'KA's Mocha Blush'.

David Hall, England

David Hall of Halls of Heddon in Northumberland, England uses organic municipal compost from grass clippings and tree and shrub prunings, which is thoroughly composted to recognized standards, ensuring it is free from pathogens, weed seed, etc. After shallow tilling of his beds, he applies a two-inch (5 cm) layer of the municipal compost as a mulch. Since he started using green waste mulch, his worm population has increased by 300%. The worms in his garden beds improve soil drainage and reduce erosion during the rainy season. In addition to better soil health, David credits the mulching for a reduction in weed growth, saving hours of labor through the growing season.

One surprise benefit David has observed since he started using organic mulch is a dramatic reduction of dahlia smut. This soil-borne fungus causes irregular spotting on lower dahlia leaves when humidity levels are high. David believes that the fungal spores spread in dry months when the soil is dustier. Now that he mulches his soil, it stays moist, and the fungal spores don't spread. In addition, David sees reductions in fungal spores since switching to permanent grass paths between his dahlia beds. When they were bare soil, some spores would be spread to the beds from rain splash on the dirt paths.

Emily Avenson, Belgium

Emily Avenson of Fleuropean in eastern Belgium doesn't cover her dahlia beds with mulch. The year-round rain that falls in her climate doesn't require her to maximize soil moisture. As a result, she does get weed growth. However, she doesn't see significant regrowth after an intense weeding in June. She plants her dahlias six inches (15 cm) apart. At that distance, they grow into one another and shade the soil below, retarding weed growth. Emily plants her dahlias close together for two additional reasons. First, she has limited bed space and wants to maximize her harvest. Second, she relies on close planting to provide support in the wind without staking.

Philippa Stewart, England

Philippa Stewart of Justdahlias in Cheshire, England mulches her dahlia beds with aged cow manure blended with wood chips. Her neighbor raises cows and gives her the farm's year-old manure pre-mixed with wood chips. Philippa reports that it is a bit stiff and takes work to spread evenly, but it is a low-cost source of soil-fortifying mulch.

PINCHING OUT DAHLIAS

Once your young plants from seed or cuttings start producing leaf pairs, I recommend pinching out the main growth tip. This technique is sometimes called "stopping" or "pinching off." Pinching out is one the most important tasks you can do in your garden if you desire a lot of blooms. If you don't pinch out your plants, you will give up the potential for dozens of extra blooms in a season.

You will want to pinch out varieties that produce large or giant blooms after three leaf pairs. Varieties with small or medium blooms get pinched out after four to five leaf pairs. The center growth tip (called the apical meristem) produces hormones that suppress the branching of the axillary buds below it. Removing the upper growth tip reduces those hormones and triggers branching in the lower canopy, and, ultimately, the production of more blooms. Dahlia plants that are not pinched out will grow tall and produce a single bloom sooner but produce fewer blooms over a season.

I am often asked if I pinch out both my seedlings and named varieties. I do because I sell my seedlings as cut flowers in addition to breeding new varieties. For strictly breeding purposes pinching out is not necessary. A breeder need not see dozens of blooms to determine whether to

1

Pinching out a young plant.

2

110

3

4

The black rings in this photo show where the plant will push new lateral branches.

Cut above a leaf axil for a hollow stem.

keep or reject a new variety. By pinching out my seedlings, I generate many more blooms that I can sell to florists and designers. They may not be varieties I will keep for another year, but often they produce beautiful cut flowers.

Some growers wait until their plants are 18 to 36 inches (45 to 91 cm) high before pinching out. Because the plant is already quite mature, this method often results in a hollow stalk open to the sky that can collect rain and potentially rot your tubers. A hollow main stalk also provides a habitat

Cut across the leaf axil for a solid stem.

for earwigs and other dahlia pests. In addition, pinching out when the stalks are thick and hollow requires a cutting tool that could spread disease or virus from plant to plant.

I pinch out my plants when they are young, before the main stem is hollow. The smaller solid stem will scar over in a few days, and I don't have to worry about it collecting water or making a habitat for pests. In addition, at this stage of growth, no snips are required. Instead, I bend over and snap the tender center growth tip with my fingers. Because my fingers never come in contact with the resulting stem wound (the location where a virus or disease can enter a plant), I don't need to disinfect between plants. I recommend snapping off the growth tip in the morning when your plants are cool and well-hydrated.

Pinching out young plants is an act of faith. You are removing a healthy, growing stem apex today for more lateral branches and blooms tomorrow. As a result, you will be rewarded with a bushier, more robust plant and many more blooms.

Suppose you are late pinching out your plants and are concerned about a hollow stem. In that case, there is a clever trick I learned from Warren Vigor, a friend and dahlia grower in Victoria, Australia. Warren taught me to cut across the stem at the leaf axil, the location on the stems where the leaves attach. If you cut, you will leave a solid stem, not a hollow one. Thanks for the tip, Warren!

You can see short videos of me pinching out young plants on the Kristine Albrecht YouTube channel. Look for videos 85, 163, 176, 180, and 181.

Heather Henson, Canada

While I recommend pinching out your dahlia plants, there are exceptions to every rule. For example, Heather Henson of Boreal Blooms in Cold Lake, Alberta is so far north that her growing season is very

'KA's Snow Jo'.

short. With her dahlias under protective plastic high hoop tunnels, they will bloom for six to eight weeks. Pinching out would delay her first blooms by two weeks, reducing her dahlia harvest by 30%. For this reason, Heather does not pinch out her plants. Instead, she lets the main growth bud produce its first bloom naturally. Then, she harvests that bloom by cutting deep down the stem, below the third leaf axil. That deep cut will encourage branching and result in more blooms without the lengthy delay caused by pinching out a younger plant.

DISBUDDING FOR BETTER BLOOMS AND TUBERS

When plants develop new buds, they typically appear along with two smaller side buds. Looking down the stem from the main bloom, find the first set of leaves. You will usually find two (sometimes three to five) smaller buds at that leaf axil. If the side buds are left to mature, they will compete with the main bud for energy and decrease the size and beauty of your blooms. In addition, the main bud is more mature than the side buds and opens first. If left on the stem, the side buds grow tall, remain closed, and stand higher than the main bloom. When we cut the main bloom, we disconnect the two side buds from the plant and they will never open or mature into a bloom.

Disbudding is the removal of two or more side buds, which improves the quality and size of your blooms. To disbud, keep your eye on your emerging buds and remove the side buds as they appear. This requires no tools. Just grab hold of the side buds and bend them over. They will usually snap right off. You don't want to pinch them off with your fingernail or a tool. Rather, you want to bend them over and have the stems snap off cleanly at the leaf axil.

I remove my side buds when they are small, about the size of a pea. They are easy to "roll" off with my finger at this size. It is never too late, however, to disbud. If you don't see the two smaller buds on first inspection, gently open the leaves closest to the main bud, and you will likely see them hiding in the leaf axil. Even if the side buds have three-inch (8 cm) stems, they can still be removed to help the main bloom. Disbudding is best done in the morning when the plants are cold and crisp. The wound where the bud stem grew will heal over. Don't remove the leaves near the buds, only the buds themselves. The leaves closest to the main bloom provide the nutrients and energy required for the bloom to fully develop.

There are varietal differences in the size, shape, and exact location of side buds. In general, they are round and stand on small green stems, however, they can appear in a variety of sizes and shapes.

Sometimes one of the side buds is large, and its companion is small. Some are narrow and tall, almost teardrop shape. You might also observe side buds in unexpected places. There can be multiple buds originating from the leaf axil where one would expect only two. In some rare instances, the main bud is not the dominant bud; the main bud might have been damaged or deformed, and one of the side buds took its place. When I encounter this situation, I remove the weak main bud and the smaller side bud, promoting the larger side bud as the new main bloom. After disbudding for a couple of hours, you will get a better feel for how to find and recognize the variety of side buds.

Because I disbud, there are no secondary buds to contend with when I harvest my blooms. I cut my stems just above the second leaf axil from the bloom. So, traveling down the stem from the bloom, I go past the first set of leaves (where earlier I removed the side buds) and cut just above the second set of leaves. The plant will produce two new branches with main and side buds at that axil. Using this method, my blooms typically have 12–18 inch (30–45 cm) stems. If I prefer an even

114

The side buds outgrow the main bud when not disbudded.

longer stem, I will move down to the third leaf axil and cut right above it. Of course, as with all things related to dahlias, there are varietal differences. Some dahlia varieties, like 'Cafe au Lait', have naturally short stems and a short distance between leaf axils. To have a workable stem for this variety I have to cut my blooms down three or more leaf axils.

One benefit of disbudding your plants is the opportunity to observe and groom them regularly. Disbudding requires up-close observation, and while doing so, you will inevitably find issues that need attention or intervention. You will likely find deformed buds to be removed, the first signs of powdery mildew, and insects that can be picked off your plants and squashed. Disbudding once or twice a week in peak season provides me with the

Main bud with three side buds before disbudding.

opportunity to look closely at my plants. You can see videos of me disbudding plants on the Kristine Albrecht YouTube channel. Look for videos 86, 87, 102, 104, or 155.

FERTILIZING DAHLIAS

Every garden plot is different, and a soil test will give you a window into what your soil might be missing. The best thing you can do for your plants is to give your soil only those things it needs based on a soil report and nothing more. I don't recommend adding fertilizers to your soil without having a "road map."

There are two basic types of fertilizers: organic and synthetic. These two work in different ways. Adding fertility to your soil with organic matter like leaves, compost, worm castings, blood meal, fish emulsion, or manure has long-term benefits. The large molecules in organic matter break down slowly, often over years, into smaller molecules that plants can eventually use. Synthetic chemical fertilizers are different. They are in a form that plants will use almost immediately. Synthetic chemicals lend themselves to immediate compensation for soil lacking in one or another critical nutrient. In addition, synthetic fertilizers do not add organic matter to the soil for long-term fertility.

The general-purpose fertilizer we find at our local garden center has three numbers on the label. These indicate the relative levels of nitrogen (N), phosphorus (P),

116

Main bud after three side buds are disbudded.

and potassium (K). The N-P-K levels that plants prefer differ by species. Dahlias like about twice as much phosphorus and potassium as nitrogen. A good N-P-K fertilizer for dahlias would be a 5-10-10 or a 10-20-20 mix. We would add too much nitrogen in proportion to phosphorus and potassium if we used a 10-10-10 fertilizer. Manure is a popular soil amendment. It has an NPK profile of 1-1-1. Adding too much manure could build up nitrogen levels in our soil.

Nitrogen is an essential plant nutrient and is present in most garden fertilizers. It occurs naturally in the soil as a breakdown product of organic matter. Nitrogen-fixing bacteria in soil work in tandem with some root nodules to absorb nitrogen directly from the air. The difference between nitrogen levels in a no-till planting bed and a tilled bed is significant. Due to high organic matter reserves, no-till soil can have five times more available nitrogen than tilled soil. Therefore, fertilizer use will be greatly reduced if you practice no-till methods in your garden.

Based on my soil test, I use a small amount of blood meal when I plant my dahlias in the spring (six pounds or 2.7 kilograms per quarter acre). My soil report has shown me that my potassium and phosphorus levels are high. Blood meal is 12-0-0. It allows me to give my plants nitrogen without adding more potassium or phosphorus.

Unnamed 'KA's' seedling. Photo: Jan Palia

Fertilizing without the benefit of a soil test can be risky because you could inadvertently add compounds that you already have too much of. Any fertilizer you add to your soil should serve only to supply nutrients deficient in your soil. If our soil has sufficient organic matter and is alive with microbes and worms, your plants probably have most of what they need to grow well.

Phosphorus and potassium levels in most soil are ample for the growth of our plants. Adding too much phosphorus can harm soil organisms. Unless a soil test reveals a shortage of these two nutrients, you most likely do not need to add more. The one exception to this is very sandy soil. If you have a high sand content, do a soil test and closely examine your potassium levels.

There is one time during the year when I add some diluted liquid organic fertilizer to my soil: when I plant young seedlings or cuttings very early in the spring and the soil and the air temperatures are still a bit cold. When small plants are set into cold soil, their ability to take up soil nutrients is diminished. For this reason, I give young starts a single application of diluted organic liquid fertilizer when I plant them. The product I have had good results with is AgroThrive. They have two different organic liquid fertilizers, a general-purpose blend and one formulated for fruiting and flowering plants. The product for fruits and flowers has a higher level of potassium. Because my soil is already quite high in potassium, I use the general-purpose blend. You can decide which product to use based on your soil test results.

REMOVING LOWER LEAVES ON MATURE PLANTS

As our plant grows taller, the upper canopy shades the lowest leaves on the plant. As a result, the lower leaves become less effective at photosynthesizing. In response, the leaves at the bottom of the plant grow larger, hoping to compensate for the shade by increasing their size. The next time you look at your full-sized dahlia plants, notice that the largest leaves are at the bottom of the plant and the smallest leaves are at the top.

'Elma Elizabeth', 'Sandia Panama', 'Kenora Lisa'.
Photo: Jan Palia

119

Upper, middle, and lower leaves all from the same plant.

Even with their larger size, the lower leaves eventually cannot gather enough light to add much energy to the plant. At that point, the plant will start transferring the water and nutrients from the lower leaves to the ones higher in the canopy. This is why, over time, the lowest leaves start to yellow and dry out. Eventually, these leaves will wither and fall off the plant. As a new grower, I can remember thinking I was doing something wrong as the lower leaves died. Now I know it is a natural process.

Removing the lower leaves provides a couple of benefits. First, it increases the airflow in the lower canopy, slowing powdery mildew's growth—it is in the older lower leaves where powdery mildew typically shows up first. Second, dahlia blooms get more energy from the leaves that they are closest to. Removing lower leaves allows the plant to shift precious energy higher in the canopy, where the upper leaves can support the development of better blooms. You can see a video of plants with lower leaves stripped on the Kristine Albrecht YouTube channel. Look for video 163.

The lower leaves stripped from a mature plant.

DEADHEADING SPENT BLOOMS

Deadheading is the term flower farmers use to describe removing blooms once they have passed their prime. Deadheading keeps a plant looking fresh and encourages the plant to produce more blooms. If a bloom is left to mature on a plant it will get pollinated and start to develop a seed head. This process signals the plant to slow down flower production. The exception to deadheading all of your spent blooms is if want to leave some for seed collection.

I cut my dahlias for florists and designers once or twice a week. While I am cutting blooms I take the opportunity to deadhead any old blooms at the same time. I have a system to do this. I am right-handed, and I hold my clippers in my right hand. I use my left hand to reach for the bloom stems and can hold several blooms at once. I stagger the height of the blooms in my left hand, so the petals are not rubbing against each other. If I see a bloom that needs deadheading, I will cut it and tuck it under my left armpit until I reach a bin to toss out the spent blooms. Deadheaded blooms don't need to be carried carefully like fresh blooms, which is why I tuck them under my arm. You can see a video of me deadheading one of my plants on the Kristine Albrecht YouTube channel. Look for video 166.

121

Me with a 'Maki' bloom at the Monterey Bay Dahlia Society show.

PLANTS ARE MODULAR

Dahlia plants are built from repeatable modular sections. Unlike animals, young plants don't have a predetermined adult shape they will grow into. Instead, depending on environmental stimuli, they will grow more in one direction or less in another direction as needed. Each modular section holds a leaf, a node (where the leaf attaches), an axillary bud (wedged between the leaf and stem), and the internode (the length of stem between each leaf node). By reproducing these modular sections over and over, a plant can grow tall, wide, recover from an injury, or change its shape to capture more light. Look closely at a dahlia plant, and you will see these modular sections repeated from the tuber crown to the bloom.

Plants need this modularity to survive in an uncertain world while rooted in one place. For example, if a tall tree shades one side of a plant, it can grow bigger on the sunny side to capture more light.

Animals don't require this flexibility. Their mobility allows them to seek sun and shade as needed. Also, animals must grow into a predetermined symmetrical shape to move about. Imagine the difficulty of walking if one of our legs grew to be twice the size of the other. Yet, that is what plants do with their stems and branches.

Lorelie Merton, Australia

In Bungaree, Australia, Lorelie Merton of Florelie Seasonal Flowers, deadheads her plant by simply pulling mature blooms off their stems. She then feeds those blooms to her sheep. For two reasons, Lorelie prefers this method over cutting the stems of old blooms. First, with 8,000 plants, she needs to be efficient with her time. Popping blooms off with her hands is much faster than holding snips and finding the proper stem to cut. Second, using her hands to remove a bloom from its stem does not create a cut and, therefore, does not require her to sterilize tools between plants.

You may ask what Lorelie does with the lone stems that are now conspicuously sticking up on her plants without blooms. She cuts them off the next time she returns to that plant to cut blooms for her florists and designers. At that time, she has her snips and sterilizes them between plants. That is the perfect time to remove the lone stems. However, instead of having to sterilize tools twice (once for deadheading and once for harvesting blooms), she only has to do it once, saving a lot of time and trouble.

Lorelie uses Metho, an Australian-made methyl alcohol, to sterilize her tools instead of bleach. She has developed a quick way to move through her dahlia patch and sterilize tools between plants. Using a small bucket filled with alcohol, she carries two sets of identical snips. After cutting from one plant, Lorelie drops the snips into the alcohol and moves to the next plant. She then pulls the second pair of snips out of the bucket and starts cutting. The first pair of snips is soaking in the tub as she works. By rotating the snips after each plant, Lorelie doesn't have to dip and wait. She always has a pair of snips in her hands and a second pair being sterilized.

HOW BLOOMS CHANGE IN LATE SEASON

We grow our favorite dahlia varieties for the traits we love. Those could be for color, strong stems, tight bloom centers, a large number of blooms, long vase life, or bloom size. Unfortunately, the plant's priorities change as the growing season winds down. Making seeds for the next generation becomes the top priority. This results in an accelerated maturation process, where blooms are smaller and

DAHLIAS ARE AN INFLORESCENCE

Dahlias belong to the Asteraceae family. This is one of the largest flowering plant families and includes daisies, marigolds, sunflowers, cosmos, zinnias, lettuce, and chrysanthemums. This family used to be known as Compositae – a name that aptly describes the structure of a dahlia bloom. Technically speaking, a dahlia bloom is an inflorescence; a composite of individual flowers: ray florets and disc florets. The ray florets are the showy petals, while the disc florets are the reproductive parts found in the center. Typically, disc florets are yellow, but varieties have been selectively bred to be red or brown. Both disc and ray florets are easily seen in open-center dahlia varieties. In fully double varieties, the disc florets are hidden behind the mass of ray florets until the bloom matures fully and the bloom "pops its center." In the accompanying photo, a single dahlia bloom has been dissected into its individual florets, with the ray florets notably larger than the disc florets. The green structures at the base of the bloom are bracts, which protect the bud while it is still developing.

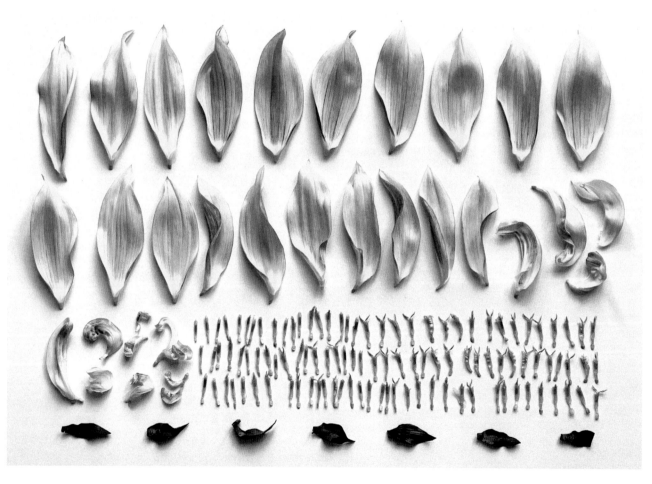

A dahlia bloom reduced to individual parts. The large parts are ray florets. The small tubular parts are disc florets.
Each one of these 138 parts are individual flowers. The green parts are bracts that hold the immature bud.

their centers pop open sooner for easier fertilization. The prioritization of seed production robs energy from the stems, making them smaller and weaker.

In addition to the plant's internal priorities, the world outside changes. As fall approaches, fewer hours of sunlight leave the plant with less opportunity to photosynthesize. In addition, the nights grow colder, affecting the plant's metabolism. As a result, blooms are smaller, and their color may change.

Fortunately, none of these changes carry over with the plant's genes to the next generation. They are just temporary, due to the time of year. Tubers from a weaker plant with diminished blooms at the season's end will produce a healthy plant with all the traits we love the following year.

HOW VARIETIES CHANGE OVER THE YEARS

As octoploids, dahlias have complex sets of genes. This results in a diversity of form, size, and color. However, it means that most cultivars have a finite life span. Dahlia Addict (dahliaaddict.com) is currently the best database of available dahlia varieties in the United States. Although they list 3,100 varieties available, tens of thousands of varieties have been introduced over the last 150 years. Where have they all gone? Some fell out of fashion, and growers stopped growing them. Some were lost when the last tuber finally rotted or was not dug up. Some likely had little virus tolerance and stopped being grown. Some of these varieties were lost because their valued traits degraded or changed over time.

Every time cells are replicated (as they are in the production of a new tuber or cutting), the replication is not always 100% perfect. Over the years, these imperfect replications accumulate and can eventually make the variety less desirable to growers. For example, dahlias with tight centers can start producing blooms that show their disc center. Plants that once had strong stems can start making weaker stems. Bloom colors can change or fade. Varieties that once produced copious blooms no longer do so. Pest resistance or virus tolerance can be lost, or tuber production can taper off.

While we would love our favorite varieties to live on forever, the odds are against them. There are, however, some varieties that have stood the test of time; they've been growing continuously for decades, still desired for the traits that made them popular when they were first introduced. 'Union Jack' is still being grown. It was introduced in 1882. Likewise, 'Thomas A. Edison' is still growing. It was introduced in 1929. I grow 'Little Bee's Wings', which was introduced in 1909. Why have these varieties survived when most of the introductions of their day are gone? We don't know, but these varieties could have virus tolerance. It could be that their genes are more stable than most dahlia varieties, or they produce plentiful tubers that store well over winter.

As growers, we can help our favorite varieties to stay strong and beautiful as long as possible. If we notice a plant that does not look healthy and is not performing well, we can dig up the tubers and dispose of them. When we divide and share tubers from an unhealthy plant, we pass on the degraded stock, further weakening that variety. Every tuber we keep or share should be from a plant that grew well and produced blooms that are worthy and true to that variety. Finally, we must fully appreciate the varieties that make us happy in our gardens because they may not be around forever.

GROWING DAHLIAS IN HOT CLIMATES

Melissa Smith, South Carolina

Melissa Smith of Fraylick Farm in South Carolina has spent years experimenting with growing dahlias as cut flowers in a hot climate. Her summer temperatures push dahlias outside of their comfort zone. Through trial and error, however, she has figured out how to grow happy plants in the heat. Her most interesting adaptation is when she chooses to plant her dahlias.

In a warm climate, a grower can start plants early in the season. By pre-sprouting tubers or making winter cuttings, growers in a warm climate can plant early and have dahlia blooms by mid-May. However, Melissa takes a contrary approach. Although her last frost date is April 15th, she holds off planting her tubers until late May or early June. Green shoots don't peek above the soil until mid or late June. She is trying to avoid caring for full-grown plants in July, the hottest month on her farm and the time of high pest pressure.

Melissa irrigates her dahlias using four rows of pressure-compensating drip tape, one for each row of dahlias in her beds. She waters her plants every day during the growing season. On the hottest days in summer, her plants will get water twice a day. She gives her irrigation system the day off when she has a day of rain. For weed control and moisture retention, Melissa lays woven black weed cloth on her beds with holes 12 inches (30 cm) apart for her plants.

When dahlia plants are full-size, they require a lot of water to stay hydrated. The large number of stems, leaves, buds, and blooms put great demands on a plant's metabolism. When daytime temperatures get too hot, plants shut down. As a result, most blooms don't mature, and those that do are small and poorly formed. Melissa can't sell these inferior mid-summer blooms.

By starting late, her plants will be immature and without buds or blooms during the mid-summer heat. She aims for her plants to reach full height and bloom in mid-August. By that time the daytime temperatures have decreased, and her plants give her beautiful blooms in late August, September, and the first half of October, when weddings and events are in full swing.

In spite of planting late with a goal for blooms at the end of summer, some plants will sprout, grow quickly, and be at full height during the July heat. Melissa uses "tough love" with those plants to get them back onto her blooming schedule. She cuts these full-size plants halfway down to the ground. If a plant originated from a tuber clump over-wintered in the ground, Melissa would cut it back more, leaving six-inch (15 cm) stalks. Dahlias are survivors; their secret weapon is the energy stored in tubers. The tuber will send up new green shoots. The re-sprouted plant will grow and bloom six to eight weeks later in time for cut flower season. By cutting down mature plants during the hottest time of year, Melissa gives them a second chance in more favorable conditions to finish the season in full bloom. A side benefit of these regrown plants is that their tender new shoots and first leaves emerge when pest pressure is lower in August than it is in early and mid-summer.

In the hottest months, Melissa helps her plants beat the heat by applying kaolin clay. Kaolin is a natural powdered mineral that can be purchased at a low cost and mixed with water. The brand of clay she uses is "Surround." It is available in 25 pound (11.3 kg) bags from Arbico Organics. It can be sprayed onto plant leaves and stems with a backpack sprayer. Melissa sprays kaolin on her dahlias once every ten days during the heat of summer. The clay turns the plants (and the weed cloth) a grey-white color. This reflects light, cooling the plants and giving them sunburn protection. During times of summer rain, Melissa may have to apply the clay more often.

Because the clay blocks only the infrared part of sunlight, it does not interfere with photosynthesis. Infrared light is not used by plants for energy production; it is, however, the spectrum of sunlight that generates heat. Another benefit of clay application is the potential to protect plants from insects and powdery mildew. The fine clay dust irritates and confuses some insect pests and hinders their ability to feed and lay eggs. The insects affected by clay applications are leafhoppers, Japanese beetles, coddling moths, and cucumber beetles. Finally, kaolin clay interferes with the ability of powdery mildew spores to penetrate the leaves of dahlias.

When her plants start opening their first blooms, Melissa stops spraying the clay. No florist wants blooms or stems covered in white clay dust. She then sets up water sprinklers in her field and gives her plants mid-day showers. The overhead water cools her plants, washes off the remaining clay residue, and, in her climate, holds off the growth of powdery mildew. Powdery mildew develops on leaves if the moisture level is just right. The mildew can't take hold with too little or too much moisture. Drenching her leaves daily in South Carolina's high humidity helps her keep powdery mildew in check.

Kaolin clay on Melissa's plants in the heat of summer. Photo by Melissa Smith.

Melissa's dahlia plot is surrounded by trees that provide partial shade. Photo by Melissa Smith.

Melissa's dahlia field is nestled in a hollow and bordered on three sides by tall trees. This gives her plot full sun mid-day with some morning and afternoon shade. In hotter climates, having a source of shade for the hotter parts of the day can make the difference between robust plants and those that struggle.

Melissa's dahlia beds have permanent low-tunnel hoops over them. The hoops are made from bent metal electrical conduit, held in place with three-foot (1 m) pieces of iron rebar pounded into the ground. The open ends of the conduit slip easily over the exposed rebar and are held fast by friction and gravity. When Melissa plants dahlias in May or June, she covers the metal hoops with a 30% sun-blocking shade cloth. Built-in ropes hang down from the shade cloth and clip into ground-level eye hooks on the side of the wooden raised bed. The shade cloth will protect her plants as they are getting established and will be removed when they outgrow the height of the shade shelter.

Melissa also has two permanent walk-in 14 by 90 foot (4 x 27 m) plastic-covered hoop houses where she plants 800 shorter-stemmed varieties. In the mid-summer heat, these hoop houses are covered with a 30% sun-blocking shade cloth. In addition, she has permanently mounted electric fans to increase air circulation in the summer. The hoop house's extra warmth and wind protection encourage these shorter varieties to grow taller and produce longer stems for cut flowers. She has found that the plants grown all season in the covered hoop houses change color slightly in response to less light.

128

Gabriela Salazar, Mexico

Gabriela Salazar of la Musa de las Flores in the mountains near Mexico City has a fairly mild climate. Her town of Valle de Bravo sits at 6,000 feet (1,828 m) above sea level and avoids the extreme heat in the Mexican lowlands. The traditional time of year for planting dahlias (February and March) are the two driest and hottest months. Therefore, Gabriela waits to plant her dahlia tubers until the end of March or early April, with hopes for the first blooms in June.

The next challenge she faces is protecting her plants from the heavy rain that falls between June and September. The mountain storms are so strong that dahlia plants left unprotected would be destroyed when hail storms move through. Gabriela protects her dahlias with a translucent plastic canopy over her beds. She does not use a hoop house or a greenhouse. In her humid climate, those would trap too much moisture. Instead, her canopies sit high on wooden posts over her dahlia beds like a giant umbrella. They keep the plants below safe from rain and hail while allowing for the free flow of air. In addition to heavy rains, Gabriela's mountain location receives strong summer winds. She protects her garden beds with six-foot (2 m) high walls on all sides.

John Menzel, Australia

In Victoria, South Australia, John Menzel pioneered dahlia growing methods in an unforgiving hot and dry climate. John was an active dahlia breeder, show grower, dahlia judge, and author for years. His dahlia cultivars all start with "Winkie." He wrote a book widely read in Australia titled, *Dahlias in Australia, The Winkie Way.*
John tested different shade cloth fabrics to protect his plants from the extreme heat that reaches 120° F (48.8° C). Shade cloth lets in most of the light but reduces the field heat. He found the best material to be 50% knitted white or beige shade cloth. He found that black and green cloths encouraged the growth of foliage at the expense of blooms.

After forty years of experimenting with various watering regimes, John found pulse watering to be the most effective in his climate. Pulse watering involves applying small amounts of water several times during the day. He found that traditional prolonged watering created a teardrop-shaped water pattern in the soil that delivered water below the dahlia's root zone. Pulse watering delivers a more horizontal-shaped water pattern in the soil, delivering water within the root zone. With pulse watering, John estimated he reduced his water usage by 80 percent.

WHY DO DAHLIAS SHUT DOWN IN THE HEAT?

The underside of dahlia leaves have tiny pores called stomata. These allow the passage of carbon dioxide and oxygen during photosynthesis. Water vapor also passes through the stomata, cooling the plant on a warm day. Stomata are flanked by two guard cells. The plant can open or close the stomata by increasing or decreasing the water pressure inside the guard cells. For instance, to retain moisture they close every night when photosynthesis stops.

When outside temperatures rise dramatically a plant will close its stomata to retain as much water as possible in order to survive. However, energy production stops because photosynthesis cannot occur with the stomata closed. This is why our plants shut down in very hot weather. Without the ability to make energy from the sun, they enter a dormant state until the weather cools down and the stomata can reopen.

Gabriela Salazar's translucent canopies protecting her dahlia beds. Photo by Laura May Grogan.

He also found that pulse watering allowed his plants to recover from extreme heat events quicker than when they were watered traditionally. John's pulse watering regime gave his plants five minutes of drip irrigation every day at 8:00 am, 10:00 am, 12 noon, 3:00 pm, 5:00 pm, and 7:00 pm. John calculated that each plant received 2.5 cups (600 ml) of water when pulse-watered six times a day. John used wheat straw or pea straw as mulch to keep moisture in the soil and retard weeds. John is no longer alive, however, his wife Ann continues his work. You can find more information about "The Winkie Way" at winkiedahlias.com.

PREPARING FOR THE END OF THE GROWING SEASON

As the dahlia season winds down and I am about 30 days from digging up my tubers, there are three primary tasks I focus on. First, if I haven't removed the lower leaves of my plants earlier in the season, I do it now. Many of these leaves will be brown. In the late season, these leaves can restrict air circulation in my plot and encourage the growth of powdery mildew. I strip all the lower leaves up to about 16 inches (40 cm) from the ground.

Second, I focus on my plant tags. With the lower leaves removed, I cross-check each tag with the blooms on the plants. I want to make sure that all the variety labels are correct. This must be done while I still have blooms. Once dahlia plants are cut down, they all look the same, and it will be impossible to double-check that the tags are correct. Finally, using marking tape (plastic tape with no adhesive), I indicate which plants I want to grow the following year.

At right: stripping lower leaves at summer's end. The organza bags exclude bees for dahlia breeding.

Third, I slowly wean my plants off of extra water. If I have been watering daily, I cut back to watering every other day. After a week or ten days, I will cut back to watering every third day. After another week, I will stop watering altogether. The only exception is if I am waiting for some seed heads to fully mature. They require six weeks on the plant after pollination to reach maturity and need water every three days that entire time.

If you have applied fertilizer regularly to your plants, you should stop 30 days before you dig up your tubers, because you want the plant to focus its energy on tuber production, not growing more leaves and blooms. You can see a short video of me checking my tags and stripping lower leaves on the Kristine Albrecht YouTube channel. Look for videos 118 and 163.

FAVORITE TOOLS AND SUPPLIES

GARDEN SNIPS

I have worked with many types of clippers or snips over the years. As a cut-flower farmer, I always reach for snips to cut blooms or divide tubers. My favorite is the

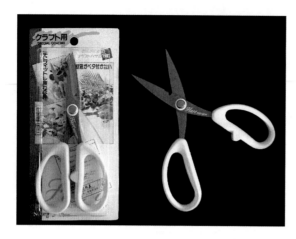

My favorite garden snips.

Silky Teflon Floral Scissors manufactured in Japan. They have smooth high-carbon steel, non-stick cutting surfaces with a serrated section near the base. They even have a notch for cutting floral wire. The blades are 2 inches (5 cm) long. They are wonderfully ergonomic. One big benefit of these snips is the Teflon-coated blades. They won't rust when repeatedly dipped in bleach solutions for sterilization. I have found two places that sell these snips in the U.S. The first is Hida Tool in Berkeley, California (hidatool.com). They have a website, and they do ship them. On their site, search for "Silky Teflon Floral Scissors." Another outlet is Bernal Cutlery in San Francisco (bernalcutlery.com). They have a website, and they also ship. On their site, search for "Flart Floral Snip."

FINGER-CUT GLOVES

There are tasks around the garden that require dexterity and a feel for your plants. Disbudding is just such a job. You need to feel the small buds and roll them off with your fingers, not with a gloved hand. Since I am in the sun most days I try to stay covered up to protect my skin. I wear big-brimmed hats for my face and long sleeves for my arms, however, the backs of my hands are vulnerable to sun exposure. To solve this problem I cut the fingertips off of my garden gloves. This allows me the dexterity and feeling that I need while protecting the back of my hands from the sun. Believe me, this little trick is a game-

changer. I learned it from my sister-in-law Peggy who is a dermatologist.

GARDEN PRUNERS

For heavier stems and light woody pruning, I find the ARS 140LDX Pruners to be the best. The blades are made with high-carbon steel and a chrome coating for longevity and rust resistance. They are eight inches (20 cm) long and have a three-inch (7.5 cm) blade. I love the soft PVC handles. These are available online. There are two options for these tools: the 140DX and the 140LDX. The model with the "L" has a longer blade. Those are the ones I prefer.

PLANT TAGS

I plant over 1,800 plants each year, so my plant tags need to be affordable. I use simple white plastic rectangular garden tags six inches (15 cm) tall and 0.8 inches (2 cm) wide. I buy them online for about $3.00 per hundred tags. I write on these tags with a pencil. Pencil marks will survive in the sun and still be readable. I made the mistake years ago of using a black Sharpie to mark my plant tags. Although Sharpies are fine for marking tubers, their ink will fade in the sun.

MITSUBISHI PENCILS

As stated above, I use pencils to mark variety names on my plant tags, however, not all pencils are created equally. My absolute favorite pencil is the Mitsubishi 9850 HB. I love these old-school wooden pencils. They sharpen easily, write smoothly, and, best of all, have a quality white rubber eraser. I buy these by the box full online, and they make me so happy.

OSCILLATING MULTI-TOOL

When I dig and divide my tubers, one of the most challenging tasks is cutting apart large tuber clumps, particularly the tough stalk sections of the crown. For years I struggled with big loppers to break the stalks apart. Finally, I tried using my husband's multi-tool a few years ago and I have never looked back. This tool has changed how I divide tubers. The oscillating blade cuts through the most rigid stalks with ease. The model I use is a 20-volt cordless Oscillating Multi-Tool made by DeWalt. There are plenty of other cordless multi-tools out there from different manufacturers. If you already have some cordless construction tools, you would likely want to buy the same brand, so your batteries are interchangeable between devices. If you divide a lot of tubers, this tool is a must. One important detail is to purchase the right blade for the job. There are a multitude of blades available for these tools. The 2.5-inch (6.3 cm) wide coarse tooth blade that works best for dividing tubers is made for cutting wood. The blades designed for cutting metal have teeth that are too small to work well with tubers. You can see a short video of me using my multi-tool on the Kristine Albrecht YouTube channel. Look for video 89.

ORGANZA BAGS

These fine mesh bags are made primarily to hold party favors for brides and event hosts. You can find them at craft and fabric stores and online. These colorful bags come in many sizes. I use larger bags that are 12 by 16 inches (30 x 40 cm) for giant blooms. I use the 6 by 9 inch (15 x 22 cm) size for smaller blooms. Dahlia breeders use these bags to cover a closed bud and exclude pollinators in preparation for hand pollination. The mesh is small enough to exclude all sizes of bees and flies.

The second reason dahlia growers use organza bags is for pest control. There are times during the year when keeping chewing insects off the blooms may not be

Disbudding with finger-cut gloves.

possible. As they bloom, covering a bud with an organza bag is a surefire way of keeping chewing insects off the petals. If you are experiencing chewed petals and your pest controls are not doing the job, bagging your buds is an excellent solution. One downside is that it is a lot of work taking the bags on and off the blooms. Also, the bags are flat and can result in rubbed and bruised petals. This is particularly true with larger-sized blooms. Even with the largest bags, damage can still occur.

My Instagram friend @practical_girl came up with a simple alteration that changes the shape of these bags allowing blooms to open up with less damage. This sewing trick changes the shape of the top of the bag from flat to a box shape, like the bottom of a paper shopping bag. To make this alteration, fold one corner of the top of the bag and sew a seam that runs perpendicular to the top seam on the original bag. Next, do the same on the other side. Once the new seams are sewn, cut off the spare triangular section of the bag above the new seams. The result will be a bag with a square top that provides ample room for your flowers to bloom. You can see a short video of me modifying organza bags on the Kristine Albrecht YouTube channel. Look for video 159.

WATERING NOZZLE

I have tried dozens of watering nozzles over the years. By far the best for watering plants gently is the Dram 1,000 hole 11 GPM Water Breaker. It's made from durable plastic and has a stainless steel nozzle head with 1,000 tiny holes. This nozzle allows me to give my plants a high flow of water without the high pressure that can result from other nozzles. No matter how high I turn up the water, the flow coming from this nozzle is gentle and will not damage plants or erode the soil. I also like that this nozzle has a soft rubber rim around the edge so that when I drop it on the ground it does not dent. This nozzle is particularly well suited for drenching young plants without damaging them. I combine this nozzle with a shut-off valve so that I don't have to run back to the hose bib when I want to stop watering.

'KA's Mocha Jake'.

Emily Avenson of Fleuropean. Photo by Anna Doshina.

Emily Avenson, Belgium

Emily Avenson is the creative spirit behind Fleuropean, located in eastern Belgium. She hails from Oakland, California but fell in love with Europe and eventually married and settled there. In her new home, she discovered the joy of growing fruits and vegetables in a lush, green environment, unlike the dry hills of her hometown. For her wedding, she was determined to grow her own flower arrangements from seed, starting with cosmos, nigellas, and sweet peas. This led to a newfound love for growing flowers and a passion for floral color, texture, and form.

Emily has been growing dahlias in her home garden since 2010, using seasonal plants and unique elements like fruit tree branches in her floral designs. She photographs her arrangements, often using a black background and soft foreground light, recalling the mood of a Rembrandt still life.

Emily's floral designs caught the attention of a wedding planner, leading to her growing and designing flowers for weddings. However, her wedding work was short-lived. Weddings require planting hundreds of identical plants in a limited color palette. Emily prefers to work with a diverse range of flowers, including those with "confused colors," varieties that produce blooms across a spectrum of colors that blend well with others.

Emily responded to requests from followers on social media to visit her garden and learn floral design. This ultimately led her to find her true calling as a teacher. She moved her garden to a historic property near her home, which includes larger beds for growing flowers, a studio for instruction, and living quarters for visiting students. Today Emily leads small groups of international students, sharing her passion for flowers and naturalistic design. As an anthropology major, she values the personal connections and exchange of ideas with her students as much as she does the art of floral design. It's a collaborative learning experience for both her and her students.

In 2012, Emily started leaving small bouquets on park benches, bus stops, or doorsteps for someone to find. Each bouquet had a tag instructing the finder to report its final destination on a website. She called these acts of kindness "Lonely Bouquets." The idea quickly caught on in Belgium, then in England and California. The idea eventually went worldwide. The last Sunday in June is now recognized globally as "Lonely Bouquet Day."

Emily's Website: fleuropean.com
Emily's Instagram: @fleuropean

A dahlia plant with powdery mildew in late season.

8. DAHLIA DISEASES

BACTERIA, FUNGI, AND VIRUSES RELY ON our plants as hosts. However, the healthier your soil and the more vigorous your plants are, the better they will resist diseases. Like almost everything relating to dahlias, the effects of disease are often related to variety. Some varieties seem better able to resist or coexist with diseases better than others do. By growing different varieties over many years, you will become familiar with which varieties are more disease-tolerant in your region.

POWDERY MILDEW

Powdery mildew is a common name for several fungal species spread through airborne spores. As the name suggests, leaves and stems on infected plants look as though they are dusted with a grey-white powder. Humid days and cool nights create an ideal environment for mildew. Unfortunately, powdery mildew is not something we can eliminate in many climates. It is more something that we have to learn to keep in check. It will not usually kill a plant, but it does reduce its ability to photosynthesize, resulting in smaller blooms, weaker stems, and fewer tubers.

The key to keeping mildew in check is starting a spray regimen before the white powder appears. Immature mildew spores are on the leaves before the powder shows up. The white powder is evidence of mature mildew spores. I spray my rooted cuttings and seedlings when they reach a foot (30 cm) tall. I spray plants from tubers a week or two after the first leaves emerge. I use Monterey Bay Horticultural Oil, which is OMRI approved for organic gardening. This product is sold as a concentrate and must be diluted before use. It is essential to spray both the upper and lower side of the leaves. I spray with a battery-powered backpack sprayer every ten days throughout the growing season. I spray in the late afternoon when the sun is low in the sky. Spraying plants when the sun is up is not recommended as it can burn the leaves. Even though horticultural oil is OMRI-approved, I wear a mask and clothes covering any exposed skin. An added benefit of regular spraying is that horticultural oil helps control aphids and thrips.

If you want to reduce powdery mildew without spraying, consider spacing your plants 3 feet (1 m) apart. Extra space between plants increases airflow and reduces mildew. In addition to spraying, I remove the older lower leaves of my plants once the plant gets to full height. This also helps to improve airflow through the plants. In addition, the older lower leaves tend to be infected with mildew first.

CROWN GALL and LEAFY GALL

Crown gall is a disease caused by a soil bacterium called *Agrobacterium tumefaciens* that enters dahlia tubers through a wound. The bacterium produces auxins, the same substance used in rooting hormones. The auxins promote excessive and disorganized knobby growth, mostly at the tuber crown. It is easy to spot because it looks similar to cauliflower. A tuber with crown gall will not produce healthy shoots. Therefore, it is effectively useless in the production of a healthy plant.

Crown gall.

Occasionally we see a disorganized mass of green shoots and leaves from a tuber crown. These will not produce a healthy plant. Growers often refer to this condition as leafy gall. Leafy gall in other plant species results from an infection from a bacterium called *Rhodococcus fascians*. Although symptoms in dahlias may look similar to those found in other species, the cause is unknown. At this time the necessary scientific work to confirm leafy gall in dahlias has not been done.

There is no treatment or cure for either of these conditions. It is best to dispose of infected tubers and the soil immediately surrounding them. It is essential to clean any tools or gloves with a bleach and water solution if they have touched an infected tuber or plant.

I often receive questions from growers asking if their tubers have leafy gall. What I see most often is a tuber that is a bit over-enthusiastic at producing new shoots. For example, suppose a tuber is in a cutting bed, and a cutting is taken. In that case, the tuber is stimulated to push new shoots around the location of the cutting. Typically the tuber will produce three to five secondary shoots. However, some tubers go a little crazy and produce more.

A similar situation can occur after taking tubers out of winter storage. If a long shoot that sprouted from a tuber while in storage is broken off, a similar cluster of shoots will emerge around the scar from the original shoot. That is perfectly normal.

PHYTOPHTHORA (Crown Rot) and PYTHIUM

Phytophthora and Pythium are soil-borne pathogens that can affect dahlia tubers, roots, and crowns. While these are two separate species, I group them together because they are both classes of water molds and the remedies are the same. They are often called fungi because they produce hyphae-like underground strands the way fungi do.

With sufficient soil moisture, Phytophthora and Pythium spores survive for many years. They are activated when the soil is consistently soggy or waterlogged. The symptoms of infection are tuber crowns or tuber necks that are dark brown, with a broken, crumbly surface. Infections can cause cankers or rot on the surface of the tuber crowns or tuber bodies. Infected tubers must be discarded. Interestingly,

A condition on dahlia tubers many growers refer to as leafy gall.

141

Phytophthora was the cause of the devastating 1845 Irish Potato Famine.

The most important factor in managing these diseases is moisture control. Growing your dahlias in well-drained soil is key. The appearance of Phytophthora or Pythium could be a sign of overwatering or excess standing water in the soil. If you tend to have wet or soggy soil most of the year, it is advisable to mound up your rows or build raised beds. My dahlias can experience infections when we have an unseasonal deluge of rain in the fall just before digging the tubers.

Phytophthora is often called crown rot because it infects plants at the root crown right where the tuber connects to the stem. From there, it can spread up into the stem and into the tubers. If Phytophthora or Pythium is a problem, it is best not to hand or overhead water your plants. Instead, use drip tape that waters the plant roots while keeping the crown dry. When setting up drip tape for young plants, it is necessary to locate it close to the plant crown. However, backing the drip tape away from the crowns as the plant grows is the best practice for helping to prevent infection. Plant crowns kept consistently wet will invite water molds that could eventually rot underground tubers.

Finally, if Phytophthora or Pythium is a serious problem in the garden, one can transition to growing dahlia in containers. Plastic pots, sink pots, or fabric grow bags filled with potting soil will defeat the water molds. Fresh potting soil is free of the spores that cause the disease. Indeed, many large-scale commercial growers have started growing entire crops in containers to avoid soil-borne pathogens and diseases.

A tuber clump with Pythium.

Three dahlia seed heads with varying degrees of Botrytis infection.

BOTRYTIS CINERIA (Flower Blight)

Botrytis is a fungus that infests dahlia plants under warm and moist climatic conditions. It is most commonly found in dahlia blooms. As the fungus takes hold, the bloom petals fade, wilt, and ultimately rot. Botrytis prefers temperatures between 65 and 75 degrees F (18 to 24 C) and high humidity. It is most commonly associated with grape, strawberry, and blackberry infestations.

On my farm, I see Botrytis on my maturing seed heads in the late season. As fall weather turns more humid, the seed heads retain moisture, and the fungus gains a foothold inside them. This is especially true of the giant dahlia varieties; their seed heads are so large and dense that they stay wet deep inside. As a result, seed heads with this fungus are easy to spot. Instead of being smooth and grassy green on the outside, they are brown and look like they are falling apart. Deep inside, the seeds and the chaff are rotted and slimy.

I don't use any treatments to fight Botrytis. On my farm, it only affects the seed heads in the late season. While I regret the loss of some seeds, the injury to my breeding program is minor, so I have a live-and-let-live attitude to this particular fungus.

However, Arbico Organics does sell a competing fungus that can be applied to dahlia plants. This harmless fungus takes up residence on the plants and out-competes the Botrytis fungus. Several chemical fungicides are also available to fight off Botrytis.

VIRUSES

Although it may feel like a recent phenomenon, virus infections in dahlias is not new. Viruses and dahlias evolved together. Wild species dahlias developed a tolerance for viruses that allowed both plants and viruses to co-exist, however, once humans started selectively breeding dahlias, the traits favored by breeders had more to do with size, color, and form than with virus tolerance. Our modern cultivated dahlias are showier than their ancient ancestors; however, only some are prepared to thrive side by side with viruses.

Dahlia growers have been observing and discussing virus infection for over a hundred years. In 1925 author W.H. Waite wrote about mosaic viruses in the *Little Book of Modern Dahlia Culture*. In 1946 the Portland Dahlia Society published *Practical Dahlia Culture*, which mentions Mosaic, Ring spot, and Spotted wilt virus. Finally, over forty years ago, Dr. Keith Hammett wrote about the Cucumber mosaic virus (CMV) and Tomato spotted wilt virus (TSWV) in his 1980 book, *The World of Dahlias*. Dr. Hammett's book even uses the motto we often hear today: "If in doubt, throw it out."

In the 1930s, the American Dahlia Society (ADS) began requiring all exhibited blooms to include leaves so that judges could detect virus infection; if the leaves of any entry showed symptoms of a virus, it was disqualified. Today, the ADS still requires leaves on all entries, and leaf health and appearance is still a part of the overall score.

I am often asked how prevalent viruses are in the dahlia community. Fortunately, in the U.S. we have some excellent data on this. The ADS has spent more than $1 million over 25 years studying viruses. They support an annual testing program for local dahlia societies and vendors, reporting results for six virus strains. In 2022 the ADS undertook a wide range of tests for vendors and dahlia societies. The 2022 average virus infection rate from all club and vendor samples was 57%. This infection rate is in keeping with the ADS multi-year average of 40 to 60% viral infection in tested samples, however, it turned out that those results were not the full story.

In the last few months of 2022, researchers at Washington State University (WSU) completed genome sequencing of the Dahlia mosaic virus (DMV). They were curious why their tests had not detected any DMV infection for six years, and were worried that the DMV tests were no longer effective. They went on to discover that DMV had mutated, thus their tests could no longer detect it. In January 2023, the WSU lab developed a new test for the mutated DMV. They began the process of retesting frozen leaf samples from the 2022 season. The results from dahlia societies and vendors returned DMV infection between 60 and 100 percent. When the new results from the DMV tests

were merged with those for all the other virus strains, 13 percent of the samples were free of viral infection. This means that in the U.S., the most current data shows viral infection in 87 percent of the 1,343 samples tested in 2022.

The 87% average infection rate speaks for itself, however, it must be accompanied by explaining how the leaf samples were collected. The ADS testing program is called the "Clean Stock Initiative." The goal is to identify virus-free dahlia stock that growers believe to be clean, rather than find stock suspected to have a viral infection. Therefore, participants were instructed to send samples from only those plants they suspected (on visual inspection) to be virus-free. Of course, this raises the question of what the data would have shown if these samples had been collected randomly.

When new growers suspect they have a plant with a virus they often start pulling plants out or ordering test kits. They mistakenly believe that viruses in dahlias are rare and they need to stop the spread before their entire garden is infected. The reality is that unless they are growing a high percentage of first-year seedlings, the majority of their plants are already infected. As stated above, the plants in our gardens are, on average, 87% infected with some kind of virus.

Although most dahlia growers consider insects like thrips and aphids the primary vectors for viruses, if we step back and take a sober look at how we propagate modern dahlias, we humans are also culpable. Our desire to grow a clone of what we see online has us buying, selling, and trading stock far and wide. This commerce has spread viruses to every corner of the dahlia-growing world. When we sell or purchase a clone, we also purchase or sell all the viruses the cultivar has collected in its lifetime. For a hypothetical example, one of the most popular dahlia cultivars is 'Cafe au Lait'. Results from our local society reveal it is infected with the Tobacco streak virus (TSV). Knowing when or where the plant we tested picked up the virus is impossible. However, hypothetically, if it was infected in the same year it was hybridized (1969), then likely every single 'Cafe au Lait' in the world is similarly infected. In general, the earlier a new variety is infected before widespread distribution, the more likely it is that most of the stock in circulation is as well.

In contrast, dahlia seeds do not transmit RNA viruses. Researchers have not conclusively determined if DNA viruses like DMV transmit the virus through seeds. If we all grew dahlias from seed (like sunflower growers) and did not buy, sell, and trade tubers, the prevalence of viruses in our gardens would likely drop.

THE NITTY GRITTY OF VIRUSES

Viruses are microscopic organisms that cannot replicate themselves without a host. To reproduce, they invade the cells of their host and hijack healthy cells to produce more of themselves. Once inside, viruses use the phloem network (like arteries) to spread through the plant. As the plant's viral load increases, growers often see changes in their plants, like loss of vigor, slow growth, yellowing, streaking, wilting, spotting, curling, or bronzing of leaves. However, similar symptoms could also result from insect infestation, bacterial or fungal disease, too little light, extreme heat, soil that is too wet or too dry, herbicide use, root rot, nutrient deficiency, or too much fertilizer.

If you suspect a viral infection in all your plants growing in the same area simultaneously, the culprit is not likely a virus. Viruses typically affect different plants in different ways depending on the variety, the type of virus, the severity of the infection, and the plant's growth habit. Typically, in a patch of differing dahlia varieties, some plants would show viral symptoms while others would not. Some

VIRUSES CAN CHANGE DAHLIA BLOOM COLOR

Recent research has revealed that certain cultivars infected with Tobacco streak virus (TSV) undergo changes in bloom color. The virus has incorporated a portion of the plant's genome into its own, which can have effects on the plant beyond the typical symptoms of viral infection. Specifically, TSV can suppress a mechanism in the plant that regulates anthocyanin production, the pigment responsible for dahlia color. By inhibiting the plant's ability to limit anthocyanin production, the virus causes the plant to produce more pigment. This raises the question: why would a virus benefit from this adaptation? The answer lies in the fact that anthocyanin is more than just a pigment. It is also an antibiotic that helps plants defend against bacteria, fungi, nematodes, and herbivores. By increasing the level of anthocyanin in the plant, the virus is essentially boosting the plant's natural defenses against its competitors. Without bacterial and fungal competitors, the plant is a better host for the virus.

will be infected and yet be completely asymptomatic.

The most common indications of a viral infection are changes in the appearance of leaves. These are mosaic patterns, ring spots, and vein chlorosis (loss of chlorophyll). Mosaic is the most subtle symptom and appears as light and dark abstract patches on the leaves. These patterns can be random, and the light patches can be pretty subtle. Ring spots are easier to see. These can be well-defined, sharp, discolored rings or soft and subtle light green circles. Ring spots can also be accompanied by dead tissue inside the

Most of the cells produced by plants and animals become differentiated. The cells that make up our hair, skin, or bones only function for the purpose for which they evolved. Plants can make undifferentiated cells that when grouped together are called meristems. These cells are produced in different parts of the plant and await instructions to fulfill a particular function. Once activated, they can grow into a leaf, a root cell, or other structures as the plant dictates.

Meristem cells are activated when we pinch out our young dahlia plants. At each leaf axil, undifferentiated cells are waiting to be set in motion. The meristem cells stay undifferentiated as long as the main growth tip is undisturbed. When we pinch out that tip, however, the undifferentiated cells start growing new stems, resulting in a bushier plant.

Meristem cells are also at the root tips underground. The cells at the very ends of the roots form a cap, like a protective helmet, over the tip of the root. This protects the tissue in the root tip from abrasion or infection as it pushes its way into the soil. Through abrasion, the outer cells of the root cap are lost. However, just behind the root tip are fast-growing undifferentiated cells. Some grow into root tip cells to replace those lost through abrasion. Others develop into root cells behind the root tip. The growth of these root cells pushes the root forward and lengthens the roots.

Properly equipped laboratories can isolate meristem cells in a plant's growth tip to produce virus-free plants. This process is often referred to as tissue culture propagation. First, dahlia plants are grown at high temperatures. This forces the growth tip to multiply and "outrun" the viruses. Next, the meristem cells are harvested and reproduced in various growing mediums. Eventually, these tiny bits of plant tissue differentiate and grow into little plants with leaves and roots. Finally, these tiny plants are tested for viruses. Propagation through tissue culture is one way a variety infected with a virus can be "cleaned" or "cleared" of the virus. Unfortunately, using meristem cells to grow dahlia plants is not an option for the home gardener or the farmer-florist. This expensive technique can only be done in a lab with specialized equipment in a sterile clean room.

rings. Finally, vein chlorosis is the easiest symptom to spot. The center vein and diagonal leaf veins turn light green or yellow. Leaves can display more than one of these symptoms at once.

There are dozens of viruses known to infect dahlias. The only sure way to determine if a plant has a viral infection is to send a leaf sample to a lab or use an in-home test. Virus tests can give beneficial results; however, a negative test result for some virus strains doesn't always mean a plant is virus-free. For example, two viruses that infect dahlias, TSWV and Impatiens necrotic spot virus (INSV), are tospoviruses that don't spread evenly through the plant. Instead, tospoviruses concentrate in random parts of the plant tissue. We could get a positive result if the leaf sample was taken from an area where the virus is concentrated. However, if it was taken from a leaf where the virus is absent, the result would be negative, even though the plant is infected. This means that positive test results for a tospovirus are reliable but negative test results are not.

Reducing the prevalence of viruses is particularly difficult for those who grow on a large scale. For example, testing every plant if you grow 2,000 plants is not economically feasible. You could test a sample of one out of every 100 plants; however, that would give you no insight into the 99% of plants you did not test.

Dahlia leaves exhibiting virus symptoms.

Plants are typically infected with viruses through a wound, cut, or piercing from an insect's proboscis and the injection of their saliva. Thrips and aphids are the primary insect vectors. In thrips, the virus is acquired in the larval stage. This fact is critical to understanding virus spread.

Thrips larvae that feed on a plant with a virus will acquire it and become tiny virus "factories." Once acquired, they can transmit the virus throughout their entire life cycle. Only thrips that acquire the virus in the larval state can transmit a virus to plants. An adult that feeds on an infected plant and then hops to another plant will not acquire or transmit a virus.

Adult thrips that produce eggs do not share the virus with their offspring. Instead, the larvae must acquire the virus by feeding on infected plants when young. Since thrips larvae cannot fly, only larvae hatched on an infected leaf can acquire the virus and be a potential vector for other plants. Conversely, larvae hatched on uninfected plants will never acquire the virus and will never transmit it.

Both thrips and aphids have evolved to spread specific virus types. For example, Cucumber mosaic virus (CMV) and DMV are transmitted only by aphids. INSV, TSV, and TSWV are spread only by thrips.

The original plant source for a virus may not be a dahlia. Various ornamentals, vegetables, fruits, and annuals can be hosts for viruses. For example, TSWV can infect over 1,500 plant species. Plant hosts most commonly affected by viruses are tobacco, tomato, pepper, bean, potato, watermelon, chrysanthemum, iris, zucchini, calla lily, soybean, peanut, papaya, pineapple, lettuce, and impatiens.

One positive fact is that viruses don't live in the soil. Therefore, if a virus-infected plant is removed, another plant can be planted into the same soil without concern. Growers often observe that infected plants "grew out" of the infection. It may appear

that way, but once plants are infected, they will always be infected. More likely, when a plant rebounds from viral symptoms, it has to do with environmental changes. For example, the day and night temperatures are relatively cool when plants are young in the spring. With a juvenile root system and slow metabolism from the cold, it can be challenging for them to mount a robust defense against a virus. Under these conditions, young plants are often stressed, and the virus gets the upper hand.

This explains why we often see viral symptoms early in the season when plants are small. As the days lengthen and temperatures rise, plants have more energy and a more extensive root system. With less environmental stress and greater nutrient uptake from more robust roots, plants often get the upper hand on the virus. What appears to be a plant "growing out of it" is a more vigorous plant fighting off the viral symptoms. This plant response can be compared to how humans respond to viral infections. When we first acquire a nasty virus, we get sick with noticeable symptoms. Our head hurts, our nose runs, we get a fever, we have a sore throat, and we feel run down. Eventually, our immune system fights off the virus, and we get the upper hand. Finally, we feel well again, even though we still carry the virus.

For all practical purposes, once infected, there is no way for a home gardener or farmer-florist to cure or clear a plant of the virus; however, at great expense, private labs can generate virus-free stock from an infected cultivar. They grow plants at high temperatures causing the terminal growth bud to essentially outrun the virus. Undifferentiated meristem cells are then harvested and tested (see box on page 146). Those free of viruses are grown into tiny plants through tissue culture. Because dahlias are not heat-tolerant, this process is difficult, requiring special techniques and a bacteria-free clean room. There is one possible exception to the lifelong infection rule; researchers now believe plants infected with INSV can grow virus-free the following year after tubers are stored over winter.

The best thing a dahlia grower can do if they are unhappy with a plant and viral infection is suspected, is to dispose of the plant. Don't use any suspect plant material in compost or mulch. Instead, dispose of infected or suspect plants and tubers in the trash.

Some dahlia cultivars appear to be virus tolerant. They grow, bloom, and make tubers with vigor while showing no viral symptoms. For our local dahlia society, this appears true for 'Jomanda'. It consistently tests positive for TSV while asymptomatic, and its blooms very often win best-in-show awards.

Growers can purchase in-home virus test kits from Agdia Inc. of Elkhart, Indiana (agdia.com). These tests are available for five individual virus strains; TSWV (#39300/0005), INSV (#20501/0005), TSV (#25500/0005), CMV (#44501/0005), and Potato Virus Y (#41300/0005). These individual virus-specific tests are about $12 each, with a minimum purchase of five kits at the time of this writing. Agdia also offers a "comb" test (#25500/0025) that simultaneously tests for the first four viruses listed above. The comb test is about $20 with a minimum order of 24 kits. If you want to run a comb test, a minimum order with shipping is about $500.

The Agdia test kits have good instructions, which must be followed carefully for dependable results. When I am testing for either TSWV or INSV, I make one minor modification to their test procedure. These viruses are tospoviruses, as described earlier they do not spread evenly throughout a plant. Therefore, instead of testing a one-inch by one-inch (2.5 cm by 2.5 cm) square leaf sample as recommended in the instructions, I use two-half-inch by one-inch (1.25 cm by 2.5 cm) leaf samples from different parts of the plant. This gives me two samples from different sides of the plant and decreases the odds of a false negative result.

If one does want to conduct at-home tests, I recommend doing so in the fall, as the

Using two half-size leaf samples to test different sides of the plant.

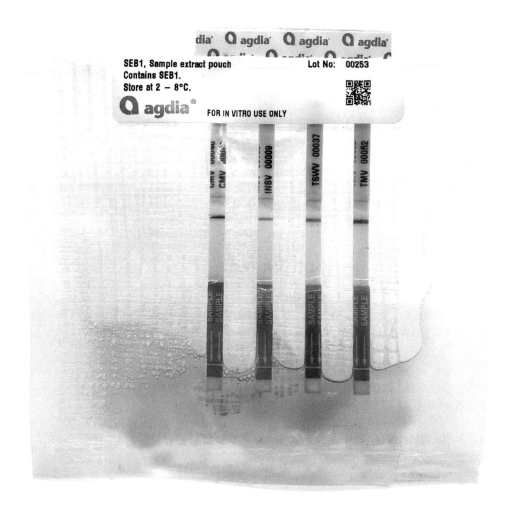

A negative Agdia comb test. Positive tests display two red lines instead of one.

tubers are being dug up. If we test plants in the spring or summer, those that test clean could become reinfected before digging and dividing tubers in the fall. In that case, we would be inadvertently saving infected tubers.

I do testing as part of my digging and dividing process. First, without cutting down the plant stems, I dig up the tubers with the full plant attached. I then examine the tubers. If they are diseased or not high quality enough to store, I will dispose of them with the plant. If the tubers look good, and I wish to keep them over the winter, I will take a leaf sample and test it. After 30 minutes, I have my test results. If the plant is infected, it gets disposed of,

and the tubers are not divided or saved. If the plant tests clean, I cut the stems and divide the tubers. This method of looking at the tubers before testing saves time and money. I don't end up testing plants with tubers that are not worth saving. I also don't save tubers from plants that test positive for viruses.

This testing regime must be done before frost has killed any plants because the at-home tests only work on living green leaves. If you wait until frost kills your plants and the leaves are black or brown, it will be too late.

Testing will reassure some growers, but it is costly and any action a grower takes as a result could be temporary. Even if we could afford to test every plant in our garden and remove every plant that tests positive, insects visiting our dahlia patch could potentially re-infect our "virus-free" plants. In addition, this theoretical scenario of 100% testing and removing all plants with viruses assumes no false negative tests. It also ignores the other 1,500 garden plants that carry viruses and may be growing nearby. This leads me to believe the goal of having a virus-free garden is unrealistic.

I've talked with growers who disposed of every plant in their garden upon discovering plants with a virus. Their strategy was to start fresh with all new stock. I understand their disappointment and their desire for a clean slate, however, it is likely that the plants they removed were over 80% infected, and they replaced them with new stock that was likely also over 80% infected. This is surely an oversimplification. All gardens are different. But at the moment, based on the best data we have, on average, dahlia stock in the U.S. is 87% infected. So we should expect well over half of any newly purchased stock to be infected.

This does not mean we should give up and do nothing. To avoid spreading a virus from one plant to another, the ADS recommends removing and disposing of any plants that one suspects are infected. They also recommend cleaning snips and cutting tools used between plants as it is believed that viruses can be spread when cutting blooms or dividing tubers. They recommend a solution of 10% bleach and 90% water.

On my farm, I observe my plants closely. If one is not thriving for whatever reason, I pull it out and dispose of it. It could be suffering from pest pressure, a variety that doesn't grow well in my climate, or it could be infected with a virus. Virus or not, I don't want unhealthy plants in my patch.

To lower the risk of viruses on my farm I spray horticultural oil and Captain Jack's Dead Bug Brew (certified organic) for insect control every ten days throughout the growing season. That adds up to over 20 applications in a season. Also, in addition to being a dahlia breeder, I am a cut flower farmer. Once a week, nearly all of the blooms are cut and sold. Since thrips love pollen and hide inside dahlia blooms, many insects are removed from my patch every week. Finally, as a hybridizer, 50% of my patch is planted in first-year seedlings. Researchers have found that with all but DMV, viruses is not transmitted through seed. That means a large percentage of my plants automatically start out virus-free each year.

Philippa Stewart of Justdahlias.

Philippa Stewart, England

Philippa Stewart of Justdahlias lives in Cheshire, England, with her husband Nigel. She is a long-time gardener with years of experience growing vegetables. Her garden in Cheshire is surrounded by potato fields. Dahlia tubers are similar to potatoes, which might explain why they grow so well in her high clay soil.

Philippa was always disappointed with her summer garden when the spring growth declined in July and August. She desired color that would brighten her garden into fall. One year a friend gave her a dinner plate dahlia, telling her it would bloom until October. After growing her first plant, she searched online and discovered dahlias come in various colors and forms. Like many of us, Philippa fell hard for dahlias.

Today she grows about 500 dahlia plants in five 25-meter (82-foot) beds. She sells cut flowers to florists and designers during the growing season but has more blooms than she needs. In 2018 she began experimenting with drying her dahlia blooms. The real push to dry flowers came during the pandemic. Weddings and events were shut down. There were few customers for Philippa's fresh blooms. So she decided to dry them. She now has a flourishing dried flower business with more customers each year. Philippa has an active Instagram account and a lovely website, complete with a gallery of all her dried dahlias.

Philippa's Website: justdahlias.co.uk
Philippa's Instagram: @justdahlias

Mixed dahlias.

9. DAHLIA PESTS

AS PREVIOUSLY MENTIONED, WE ARE not alone in our love of dahlias. Our fondness is shared by various creatures that climb, chew, poke, and slime their way through our plants and flowers. Pests vary by region and climate. What attacks your plants may not attack mine. In no particular order, here are some pests and remedies common to dahlias.

SLUGS AND SNAILS

Snails are one of the most destructive pests in the garden, especially when young plants emerge from the soil. The ubiquitous brown garden snail is a French import brought to California in the 1850s as a food source. Unfortunately, things got a little out of control, and now they are just about everywhere. Unlike insect pests, snails and slugs are mollusks and are closely related to clams and mussels. Both slugs and snails move by gliding along on a muscular foot, leaving behind a slime trail.

Like earwigs, these creatures are most active at night. They use rasp-like tongues to eat leaves, shoots, and any succulent plant parts. You can tell your plants have been eaten by slugs and snails when the leaf damage is around the edges of the leaves. Damage in the center of the leaves (small holes punched into the leaves) is typically a sign of earwigs.

Locate your dahlia beds far away from leafy hedges and bushes to reduce the potential damage from snails and slugs—a bed next to an ivy hedge is an invitation for slug and snail pressure. Snails and slugs can be harvested at night with a flashlight. Collect them in a plastic bag, seal them up, and dispose of them in the trash. At first, going out every night for a week is practical to bring the population in your garden down. After the first week, night harvesting can be done once or twice a week.

I have snails and slugs in my dahlia beds, and I use Sluggo Plus to keep them from chewing on my plants, mainly when the plants are small and just emerging from the soil. I sprinkle it on the ground as my new plants emerge, and then right on the leaves once the plants are up and producing leaves. As the plants grow, I reapply the bait on the leaves, buds, and leaf junctures. It's okay if some of the bait falls onto the ground. Try to keep as many of the pellets in the plant canopy as possible. Once the plants reach a certain size, slugs and snails live in the plant canopy, and spreading bait on the ground is not necessary.

Sluggo Plus sprinkled on young plants.

The active ingredient in Sluggo is iron phosphate. When ingested, it causes slugs and snails to stop feeding. It takes about seven days for them to die. Sluggo Plus also has spinosad, an insecticide that controls earwigs, ball bugs, and cutworms. Sluggo and Sluggo Plus are pet-safe and OMRI-approved for organic gardening. Snail baits work best if applied regularly in the late afternoon, just before snails and slugs come out to feed. In my garden, crows like to eat my Sluggo Plus. If yours is disappearing, it may you have similar bait-loving birds. I typically reapply my snail bait after a rain, as the moisture makes the pellets fall apart.

Here in the U.S., we don't have native hedgehogs. However, if you are lucky enough to live where hedgehogs roam, let them be. Hedgehogs are carnivores; they won't bother your dahlias but love eating slugs and snails. To attract a hedgehog to your garden, make a pile of leaves or a loose stack of firewood next to your plot.

They are nocturnal and like to curl up in a hiding spot during the day.

Emily Avenson, Belgium

For Emily Avenson of Fleuropean in Belgium, slugs appear in the early part of her growing season. To safeguard her young plants, she simply moves the slugs. At night, with a flashlight, she collects as many slugs as possible and relocates them far away from her garden. She calls this practice "re-homing." As her plants grow taller, the threat from slugs decreases, and by mid-July, her plants are large enough to fend for themselves.

EARWIGS

Wherever dahlias grow, earwigs seem to follow. With their large forceps-like pinchers, they are one of the more recognizable arthropods in the garden. They are tough little creatures because of their thick outer shell. Although they can damage our dahlias, they also play a

156

positive role in the garden by eating aphids. Earwigs winter in debris on the soil, and the female lays eggs in the spring. She tends her eggs until they hatch and feeds her young by regurgitating food like a bird. The young stay close to the mother, like baby ducks or chicks.

When my dahlias come out of the ground in spring, a bevy of hungry earwig nymphs start eating the leaves. Earwig nymphs look just like an adult, only smaller. Earwigs are nocturnal and chew on our dahlias in the dark. They can damage both blooms and dahlia leaves. Earwigs make many small holes in the center of the leaf, as opposed to edge damage caused by slugs and snails. To confirm you have earwigs on your plants, go out into the garden at night with a flashlight.

During the day, earwigs hide under leaves, wood, and mulch. Some gardeners trap earwigs by rolling pieces of corrugated cardboard wrapped with string or a rubber band to keep the roll tight. Others use a small rubber hose placed on the soil at night. In the morning, the hoses are collected and the earwigs get tipped out into a bucket. Some folks trap earrings with a small can of bait; a shallow tuna or cat food can sunk into the ground at soil level and filled with 1/2 inch (1.3 cm) of vegetable oil or fish oil will attract earwigs. Adding a bit of bacon grease will excite them even more. Once caught in the oil, they will drown.

Fortunately, Sluggo Plus is also effective for the control of earwigs. It is approved for organic gardening. I use it when my shoots break the top of the soil or when I plant out my cuttings or seedlings. I don't wait even one day before sprinkling it on the leaves of my tiny plants. If I forget to apply it, my seedlings could be eaten by the following morning. As your plants grow taller, reapply Sluggo Plus as needed. Sprinkling it in the leaf canopy, not on the ground, is essential. Plenty of it will fall on the ground without scattering it there intentionally. Remember, only Sluggo Plus controls earwigs.

The leaf on the left was chewed by an earwig.
The leaf on the right was eaten by a snail.

THRIPS

I often receive correspondence from frustrated growers with a picture of a deformed bloom, with one side open normally and the other half-closed. This condition is caused by thrips, a tiny (almost invisible) sap-sucking insect that pushes its proboscis into the back of dahlia buds. The toxin they inject causes blooms to be disfigured.

Thrips are so small it can be nearly impossible to see them in the garden. The best way to identify if you have thrips is to cut off a fully open bloom and bring it indoors. On a table, lay down a white sheet of paper. Turn your dahlia bloom upside down and knock it against the paper several times. If you see tiny little insects scurrying around, smaller than a hyphen, you have thrips.

Green Lacewing eggs for control of Whiteflies.

I use Captain Jack's Dead Bug Brew to control thrips. The active ingredient is spinosad, which is approved for organic gardening. Captain Jack's will also control bagworms, borers, beetles, caterpillars, codling moths, gypsy moths, spider mites, leaf miners, and tent caterpillars. Another product to control thrips is Monterey Bay Horticultural Oil, a concentrate that, once mixed with water, can be sprayed on the tops and bottoms of leaves. You can also spray it onto tiny buds to control aphids, leaf miners, leafhoppers, spider mites, scales, whiteflies, and mealybugs.

Here's how I was taught to spray my plants by an experienced grower. First, spray up close into every developing bud and partially open bloom because that's where insect pests tend to concentrate. The spray tip should almost touch the buds. Second, starting at ground level, spray the underside of all the leaves, working your way up into the plant canopy. Third, starting at the plant's top, spray the leaves upper sides, working your way down to ground level.

There are two other organic strategies for controlling thrips. First is the release of predatory insects. For example, Arbico Organics (arbico-organics.com) sells predatory mites that can consume up to twenty thrips larvae daily. The benefit of these predators is that the female mites lay eggs, and new larvae will continue hatching and devouring thrips on your plants. Second is the use of sticky traps. Research has shown that thrips are attracted to the colors yellow and blue. Arbico Organics sells yellow and blue sticky traps that can be hung high in the plant canopy to attract thrips and reduce their numbers.

Over the years, I have occasionally experienced a situation where a plant is so infested with thrips that I cannot turn the situation around. The plant will struggle to grow and will produce poor quality blooms. In this situation, I have resorted to a complete re-boot of the plant. I cut the entire plant nearly down to the ground, leaving stalks about 3 inches (7.5 cm) high. I spray the remaining stalks and any leaves with horticultural oil to kill any remaining thrips. The tubers underground generate new shoots that I protect from slugs, earwigs, and snails with Sluggo Plus. Those shoots quickly regrew into a full-sized plant and produce blooms and tubers like any other dahlia plant. If you choose this option, and you use overhead watering or live where you receive rain in the summer, be sure to cover the stalks with aluminum foil so water will not collect in the hollow stems. This time around, it is important to start a spray regimen *before* you see a new infestation.

The relationship between thrips and flowers is not new. Paleobotanists research the earliest examples of fossilized pollinators to pinpoint how long insects have had a symbiotic relationship with plants. In 2012 scientists in the Basque region of Spain found the oldest example of insect pollination to date, a 110 million-year-old pollen-laden thrip encased in amber.

WHITEFLIES

Whiteflies are tiny insects, less than one-tenth of an inch (0.25 cm) long. They suck sap and juices out of dahlia leaves. A heavy infestation of whiteflies can kill leaves and stress dahlia plants. Whiteflies also produce an exudate called honeydew, which can lead to the growth of harmful molds. They lay their eggs on the underside of dahlia leaves. You know you have them when a white plume takes wing when you brush against your plants. You can also look at the underside of your plant leaves. If you see a white smudge, that is evidence of whitefly eggs. These small insects reproduce quickly and, once established, are hard to fend off. Whiteflies go dormant in the winter but may be active year-round in warmer climates. Green lacewings are beneficial insects that eat whiteflies, and they can be purchased and released on your plants. They are available at Arbico Organics. You can also reduce whitefly infestation with a regular spray regimen of neem or horticultural oil. Spray once every ten days, and spray on the underside of the leaves (see boxes on pages 160 and 162).

APHIDS

Aphids are tiny soft-bodied yellow, brown, red, or black insects that are typically found in dense groups. They primarily feed on plant leaves and stems. They use their long slender mouth parts to suck fluids. The damage they inflict on dahlia plants includes stunting new shoots and, due to an injected toxin, the curling of leaves. Once dahlia leaves start to curl, controlling aphids is more challenging as the curled leaves give them places to hide. In addition to injecting toxins, as discussed earlier

Releasing mature Ladybugs for control of Aphids.

159

aphids can carry viruses from one plant to another.

Like whiteflies, these tiny arthropods produce a sweet sticky exudate called honeydew that attracts hungry ants—if you have an ant infestation on your plants, you likely have an aphid infestation as well. Aphids reproduce asexually at a rapid rate; a few can quickly become hundreds or thousands. If the aphids on your plants are concentrated on a single branch, prune that part of the plant, seal it in a plastic bag, and dispose of it.

Ladybug larvae.

One of the best ways to control aphids is to release predators that love to feed on them. Ladybugs and ladybug larvae are commercially available from many garden centers. They can be purchased hundreds at a time. Mist your plants with water before releasing them into the garden because bugs, like us, want food and drink all in one place. If our plants are dry, they may eat a few aphids and fly off in search of water, however, if your plants are wet, they will eat and drink in your garden and stick around. Why go anywhere else? Ladybugs are best released in the evening. Arbico Organics sells the eggs of other predatory insects (like wasps) that can be released on your plants. These predators hatch out hungry and will be happy to eat the aphids.

Ladybug larvae eat far more aphids than full-grown adults. A single ladybug larva can eat 400 aphids in two weeks as it goes through a growth spurt. Familiarizing yourself with the look of ladybug larvae is essential. They don't look anything like an adult ladybug. To me, they look like tiny alligators. If you see one in your garden, don't harm it, celebrate it!

Horticultural oil can also be sprayed on plants to control aphids. However, the application of oil only kills the aphids sprayed in that single application; it won't kill any later-arriving aphids. For this reason, it is imperative to apply

HORTICULTURAL OIL

Horticultural oils are made either from vegetable oil or mineral oil. Most of the standard big brands are mineral oil-based. The labeling of horticultural oil can be confusing. There are often references to "Dormant Oil" or "Superior Oil." Dormant oil is used in the winter when plants have dropped their leaves. Superior oils can be sprayed on a plant in winter or when plants have leaves. Check the label on the product you are using to ensure it can be applied when you plan to use it. Horticultural oil smothers and kills insects and their eggs.

Many of these oils are OMRI approved for organic gardening but can be harmful if inhaled. Use a mask and protective clothing when spraying horticultural oils. Follow the mixing direction on the product you use and apply oils in the morning or late afternoon when the temperatures are below 80 degrees (26°C). Never apply oils to a plant that is dry and under watered. It is a good idea to give your plants an extra water boost the day before you plan to spray.

Cucumber beetle.

horticultural oil several times. Be sure to use oil on leaf bottoms as well as the tops. You can see a short video of me spraying for aphids on the Kristine Albrecht YouTube channel. Look for video 138.

LYGUS BUGS (Western Tarnished Plant Bug) On the coast of California, lygus bugs are a constant challenge. Adults with flattened oval bodies are a quarter of an inch (.63 cm) long. They damage dahlia plants with their proboscis. If you have seen a strawberry with an indentation and a tight concentration of seeds, you have seen the effects of a lygus scar, sometimes called a cat face. Organic growers use insecticidal soap sprays. I have had some luck using a BugZooka tool (see below under cucumber beetles) on lygus. It takes time, but it is non-toxic and works well if your plot is not too large. Another way to

protect your blooms from being deformed by lygus bugs involves covering them with organza bags (various sizes are available online, see page 133). Covering a new bud and letting it bloom inside an organza bag is one way to preserve your blooms using a live-and-let-live approach. They are placed over a developing bud and are cinched tight with the provided drawstrings around the stem. Although effective, bagging each bloom is time-consuming.

CUCUMBER BEETLES

On my farm, the most common insect pest I see regularly are cucumber beetles. They look very much like a green version of a ladybug, light green with black spots. They also can display dark stripes instead of dots. They have an appetite for the young petals buried in unopened dahlia buds. When those blooms open, the ends of the petals are often chewed and scalloped. When I see these insects on my plants, I squish them; however, I have too many plants to make much difference. If you have just a few dahlia plants in your garden, simply squishing them might be the best control method. If you want fool-proof protection for your blooms, you can always bag them with an organza bag when they are in the bud stage.

Over the years, I have employed two strategies to fight cucumber beetles. The first requires no chemicals but does take time. It's a device called a BugZooka, a vacuum-based handheld bug catcher. It uses no batteries. You push down on the spring at one end and point the other end at the beetle sitting on your plant. When you press the button, tiny hinged doors open, suck in the bug, and close again. Push the spring again, and you are ready to catch another. You can walk through your plot and catch a few dozen before having to empty the chamber that holds the bugs. Cucumber beetles are very active when it is warm, but they move slower and are easier to catch in the morning when they are cold. They tend to hang out inside the disc center of our blooms.

I use the BugZooka on some selected plants, but my dahlia patch is too big to help all my plants. So instead, I control cucumber beetles with Captain Jack's Dead Bug Brew applications. I buy it as a concentrate, dilute it with water, and use a battery-powered sprayer to treat my plants every ten days. The active ingredient in this product is spinosad, OMRI-approved for organic gardening.

Galena Berkompas, Washington

Galena Berkompas of Micro Flower Farm in Vancouver, Washington grows organically and has developed several strategies for reducing cucumber beetle populations in her dahlia patch. First, she collaborates with her local bird population. Galena has erected multiple birdhouses on her property. As birds take up residence in

---

NEEM OIL

Neem oil is an extract from the neem tree grown in India. It has different effects on different chewing or piercing insects. When some insects ingest neem oil, it prevents them from molting, so they cannot mature. In others, neem oil prevents the laying of eggs. Still, others exposed to neem oil stop eating and starve. None of these effects are instantaneous. Reducing insect pressure with neem oil takes time and multiple applications.

Although neem oil biodegrades quickly, the seeds of the neem tree are poisonous, and one should wear a mask and protective clothing when using it as a spray, however, it is OMRI approved for organic gardening and is said to be safe for honey bees and mammals. Pure neem oil will not mix with water, so some suppliers add a surfactant to promote blending. If you buy pure neem oil, add a small amount of dish soap to encourage mixing. Follow the instructions on the product label.

---

her garden, they love feeding on the cucumber beetles right at their doorstep. One reason Galena has successfully attracted birds to her garden is the pond on her property. Birds are like us, they want to eat and drink at the same meal. They will tend to stick around if they have a reliable water source, however, you don't need a pond. Birds love birdbaths. They use them for drinking, washing, and socializing. Keeping your birdbaths full of clean water will encourage birds to stay in your garden.

Second, Galena uses Dwarf Amaranth around her dahlia patch as a trap plant. Given a choice, cucumber beetles prefer munching the amaranth over her dahlia plants. The high concentration of beetles on the trap crop gives her resident birds the perfect opportunity to grab an easy meal.

Finally, Galena sprays her dahlia leaves with Earth Juice Hi-Brix molasses (available at Arbico Organics) every ten days in July and August. She sprays less frequently in September and October when pest pressure is lower. When diluted with water and sprayed on plants, the natural sugars in molasses give plants added nutrition. Any spray that lands on the soil also benefits the underground microbes. In addition, it's believed that the sugars from molasses applications make sprayed plants less attractive to chewing insects.

SPIDER MITES

Spider mites are technically not insects. They have eight legs instead of six. They are small, about 1/32 of an inch (1 mm), and can be a variety of colors. They live on the bottom side of dahlia leaves, feeding on the leaf tissue. They are not related to spiders but received their name because of a silky web that they spin on the leaves.

Leaves infested with spider mites look mottled or stippled. Leaves can also display curled or burned-looking edges. In severe cases, the entire leaf can drop off from infestation. Spider mites thrive in warm summer temperatures above 80° F (27°C). Therefore, keeping your plants hydrated during hot spells is a good strategy for helping them mount a defense.

These little guys know how to reproduce. Newborn mites become sexually active after just five days of life. Their eggs hatch after only three days, and female mites can lay twenty eggs each day for several weeks.

If you find spider mites or webbing, remove and dispose of any infested leaves and consider starting a spraying regimen. Neem oil and horticultural oil kill adult mites, eggs, and larvae on contact. Be sure to spray under the leaves and in the leaf axils and repeat the spraying every three days until the infestation is knocked back. Spraying oils on plants should be done in the morning or evening. Never spray plants when the sun is high or temperatures are above 80 degrees (27°C). Biological controls can keep the population low once the mite population has been reduced. Arbico Organics sells several insect predators like lacewings, assassin bugs, and pirate bugs that can be released on your plants; they love to eat spider mites.

LEAF MINERS

Adult leaf miners are small black flies, often with a small yellow triangle on their backs. They lay their eggs inside dahlia leaves. When the larvae hatch, they feed on the tissue inside the leaf, between the upper and lower leaf surfaces. This feeding makes light-colored squiggly trails on the leaves. After a few weeks, the worm-like larvae mature, drop out of the leaves, and move on to another host.

Typically, leaf miner infestation does little damage to dahlia plants. A serious infestation can slow a plant down; however, the damage is usually minimal. The best thing to do if you see evidence of leaf miners is to cut off and dispose of any infested leaves. I see leaf miners in my garden in the early season but they're typically gone by mid-summer.

JAPANESE BEETLES

As the name implies, Japanese beetles are a non-native import to the United States and feed on over 300 species of plants. They were accidentally released in New Jersey in 1916 and have been marching south and west ever since. Adult beetles are about one-half inch (1.75 cm) long with copper-brown wing covers and a metallic green head.

Japanese beetle larvae overwinter in the soil eight to ten inches (20 to 25 cm) below the surface. As the temperatures warm the larvae move higher up in the soil and feed on plant roots, becoming a grub in May and June. Adult beetles emerge in late June and July and feed on both leaves and flowers. They eat the tissue between leaf veins, leaving a skeletonized leaf behind.

There are organic treatments for both grubs and adult beetles. You can find several of these at Arbico Organics. However, most dahlia growers who experience Japanese beetle damage tend to protect their blooms with organza bags as a physical beetle barrier.

Melissa Smith, South Carolina

Melissa Smith of Fraylick Farm in South Carolina experiences an invasion of Japanese beetles every summer. She bags about 80% of her blooms with organza bags to guarantee undamaged blooms for her florists and designers.

Heather Henson, Canada

Heather Henson of Boreal Blooms in Cold Lake, Alberta used organza bags for several years to protect her blooms from grasshoppers and thrips. However, she has not needed to use the bags for the last two years. With 40% of her garden now planted in perennials, life on her farm is more diverse and balanced. The perennial plants provide overwinter habitat for beneficial insects. Their seed heads provide food for local birds. As a result, the birds stick around and feast on the insects that used to feed on her dahlias. The changes she observes did not happen overnight; she has been tending her farm plot for seven years. Improving ecosystem health has been a gradual process that has brought balance and less work to Heather's farm.

Heather's experience of noticing subtle changes in the plants and animals on her farm has me thinking that we would benefit from greater context when we share our experiences online. Social media posts of plants damaged by insects are typically void of the greater context. How many years has the garden been cultivated? What is the surrounding land like? Has the soil been improved or amended? Has anything been done to encourage beneficial insects? The diversity of life on Heather's farm has me thinking deeper about the land and all the life on my farm.

Gabriela Salazar, Mexico

For Gabriela Salazar of la Musa de las Flores in the mountains near Mexico City, Japanese beetles arrive in May and June, at the beginning of the rainy season. They quickly start chewing on her plants and blooms, however, after two or three weeks, the beetles have gone. Gabriela takes a "live and let live" approach to the beetles and doesn't harvest many blooms when the beetles are active. Once they have gone, her plants recover, and her dahlia harvest resumes.

GOPHERS

At my farm, I am in a constant battle with gophers. They eat my tubers, take down plants, and make a mess of my beds. You know you have gophers when you see a fresh mound of disturbed soil. Another sign of gopher activity is an unexplained soft spot in the ground. Often the first sign I have a gopher issue is a wilted plant or a plant that has fallen over. Gophers love dahlia tubers. They are active year-round, although I see evidence mainly in the spring and summer.

The first line of defense against gophers is to guard the perimeter of your property. Even if the perimeter is far from your dahlia patch, that is the place to start trapping them. Once they reach your dahlias, their activity is disruptive, and catching them might disturb a lot of soil. Dealing with them outside the patch is preferable when you see a mound; you want to spring onto action.

I deal with gophers by trapping them. Trapping is clean and in keeping with my preference for organic gardening. I am always on the lookout for disturbed mounds of soil. If you spot multiple mounds in the garden, the freshest mound will show you the gopher's direction of travel. Therefore, you want to always set traps in or around the newest mound. I use three different gopher traps, because gophers come in different sizes. Gophers also seem to "grow accustomed" to different trap types, so using various traps leads to more successful catches. There is no "one size fits all" trap. I recommend buying all three traps if you are serious about ridding your garden of gophers.

My favorite trap for gophers is the GopherHawk (gopherlawk.com). It allows me to find the gopher tunnel and set a trap without shoveling dirt out of my beds. This system requires two tools: the wedge and the tube-shaped trap. The wedge is a long plastic pipe with a point on one end. It comes with a probe used to find the gopher's underground tunnel. You only need to purchase one wedge even if you buy multiple traps.

To set a GopherHawk, I gently push the probe into the soil 12 to 18 inches (30 to 45 cm) away from the freshest mound of dirt. When the probe hits a void in the soil, it feels different than solid ground, this lets me know I have found an active tunnel. I then push the wedge into the soil to make a vertical shaft into the active gopher run. Next, I push the trap down into this shaft. The inside of the trap has a spring with an outer sleeve. I pull firmly on the outer sleeve, which compresses the spring. The trap is now set.

Underground, inside the gopher tunnel, the GopherHawk has a snare and a sensitive trigger. When a gopher runs through the tunnel, the trigger activates the spring, catching the gopher around its middle. One of the things I like about this system is that there is a visible yellow indicator. Without digging or disturbing any soil, I can see whether or not the trap has sprung. This trap has very few false results. In my experience, if the trap is sprung, I have a 90% chance of catching a gopher. With other gopher traps, I'm lucky if the trap is successful 50% of the time.

My next favorite gopher trap is the "cinch trap." It comes in two sizes, a larger size for gophers and a smaller size for moles. In California, gophers are small, and I can use the small-sized trap. If the trap is getting sprung without success, I will try again with the larger trap. Using a cinch trap requires digging out the dirt mound around the freshest gopher hole. The hole must be large enough to insert the claw end of the trap into the gopher run, with the flat back end of the trap lying in the hole. I find setting the spring on these

A tuber clump almost completely eaten by a gopher.

traps difficult. I don't always have the hand strength to set it and resort to holding the trap on the ground with my foot while pushing back the spring and setting the trap. I then insert the claw end of the trap as deep into the run as possible. Because I don't want the flat metal end of the trap visible to the gopher, I will cover it with a bit of straw. It is easy to tell that the trap has been sprung by looking at the spring arm on the flat end. If the arm is in the two o'clock position the chances are good I have caught a gopher.

The third trap I use is the Macabee. This is the oldest design of the three I use. Coincidentally, it was invented in my childhood hometown: Los Gatos, California. The Macabee trap uses a simple spring jaw to catch its prey. It is smaller than the cinch trap and can be pushed further into the tunnel than other traps. Like the cinch trap, a hole must be dug in the garden to allow access to push the trap

into the gopher run. Because this trap does not have a wide metal plate on the back, we must attach a 16" (40 cm) length of string or chain to a ground stake. Then we secure the opposite end to the back end of the trap. This prevents a wounded gopher from pulling our trap deep into the run, where it would be lost forever.

Regardless of the trap I use, when I successfully trap a gopher, I reset the trap in the same spot and try again. There is often more than one gopher using these underground tunnels. I once caught three gophers in the same tunnel, one after another. You can see a short video of me using these three gopher traps on the Kristine Albrecht YouTube channel. Look for video 140.

166

Gabriela Salazar, Mexico

Gabriela Salazar of la Musa de las Flores in the mountains west of Mexico City has gophers that would love to eat her dahlias. She keeps them out of her dahlia beds using gopher wire installed underground. However, Gabriela installed a vertical wire curtain around her bed's edges instead of directly under her beds. This involved digging a 3-foot (one-meter) deep trench around the bed perimeter, inserting gopher wire into the trench, and backfilling with dirt. Because gophers burrow horizontally through tunnels in the soil to reach our plants, the wire curtain keeps them out of her beds. Instead of burrowing deeper into the soil to go under the wire, gophers stop at the wire and burrow in a different direction.

MOLES

Moles, like gophers, tunnel underground and make mounds, but they don't feed on dahlia plants because they are carnivores. Instead, they tunnel through the soil, looking for insects, worms, and grubs. While they don't eat our plants, they can damage them. Their shallow tunnels can pull soil away from tubers and roots. When roots and tubers lose contact with the soil, the health of a plant can go downhill.

Mole tunnels tend to be closer to the surface than those from gophers. Moles are fast burrowers, able to dig 150 feet (45 m) in a single night. They pile dirt into molehills, similar to gophers, except their mounds are farther apart. One way to tell if you have moles is to examine the dirt they pile up. Mole hills contain chunks of dirt. Gopher hills contain uniform, fine-grained dirt.

Mole traps and mole bait are available to rid your garden of moles. I don't use these. Instead, when I find a mole tunnel near my plants, I use my foot to compress the soil all along the tunnel. That puts the soil back into contact with my plant roots and tubers. Since moles don't feed on plants, once the soil is compressed, there is no lasting damage to my plants.

Four GopherHawk traps set in a dahlia bed.
Notice the undisturbed soil.

167

Some gardeners with a serious mole infestation make a mole barrier around their planting beds to keep the mammals out. To make a mole barrier dig a trench around your planting bed six inches (15 cm) wide and two feet (60 cm) deep. Then, fill the trench with 3/4 inch (2 cm) drain rock. When moles come tunneling along, they are stopped by the rock barrier.

RABBITS

Rabbits can be a destructive force in a dahlia garden. You know you have them if the plant damage is clean-cut. Unlike insects, rabbits don't leave ragged edges when they chew on your plants. Chicken wire fencing can help keep rabbits out of a dahlia patch as long as the wire is four feet (1.2 m) high and dug into the soil at least six inches (15 cm). Growers with dogs have reported success as the dogs keep watch and chase rabbits when they come near.

Galena Berkompas, Washington

Galena Berkompas of Micro Flower Farm in Vancouver, Washington has successfully foiled rabbits with a repellent called Liquid Fence. Rabbits don't like the smell of onions, garlic, and certain herbs. Liquid Fence is a concentrate made from eggs, garlic, sodium sulfate, and thyme oil. When diluted with water, it can be sprayed around the perimeter of garden beds. It is recommended that a second application be applied one week after the first. After that, it can be applied once a month. It can also be sprayed directly on individual plants in a landscape setting. One caution is that Liquid Fence is smelly, so be careful to avoid tracking it into your house. Galena has also found that rabbits don't like the smell of lavender.

GROUNDHOGS

The eastern United States is home to a large mammal commonly called a groundhog or a woodchuck. In truth, groundhogs are a type of marmot, the only marmot that lives at low elevations instead of in the mountains. Groundhogs are solitary creatures. If you have one in your garden it is likely to be alone.

Melissa Smith, South Carolina

Melissa Smith of Fraylick Farm in North Carolina has had hundreds of dahlias destroyed by a visiting groundhog. Groundhogs are large. They grow to over two feet (60 cm) long and weigh 13 pounds (5.8 kg). They are plant eaters and love the tender growth tip at the top of dahlia plants. Standing erect, they reach up to the top of the plant and pull it down toward the ground to eat the plant tops. In doing so, they inevitably snap the plant stem in half near the ground. A dahlia plant that has been taken down by a groundhog will not survive. It must be removed, or if there is enough growing season left, cut down completely and allowed to resprout.

The best way to deal with a groundhog in your garden is to trap it and relocate it. The proper tool for this job is a one or two-door live trap 36 to 42 inches (90 to 106 cm) in length. You can bait the trap with tender shoots and leaves from your dahlia plants. If that doesn't work, try cantaloupe or peanuts. Groundhogs are active in the morning and late afternoon. Therefore, that is the best time to set the trap. Be sure to bring the trap in at night, so you don't accidentally snare a nocturnal mammal you are not looking for (like a skunk). Once caught, the best plan is to relocate the groundhog at least five miles (8 km) from your dahlia patch. Choose an area with lots of wild foliage and some sheltered woods for cover. The better the new location is for the animal, the less likely it will want to make its home in another garden.

At right: the author's home garden.

'KA's Coral Sea'.

10. HARVESTING BLOOMS

HARVESTING AND CUT FLOWER CARE

SEVERAL SPECIES OF CUT FLOWERS (like roses) can be harvested when the blooms are closed. These can be shipped easily to florists and designers, where they will open after shipping. Unfortunately, dahlias are not like that. They don't typically continue to open after harvesting. As a result, they must be when cut fully open, when their petals are fragile and easily damaged. However, there are several techniques for harvesting dahlias to get them to their destination in excellent condition.

1. It is always best to water your plants well the day before you harvest them. That will give the blooms the hydration they need to look their best and last the longest. Dahlia exhibitors know this trick and always water well the day before blooms are cut for competition.

2. It is best to use your sharpest snips to harvest your blooms. Sharp snips will make a clean cut in the stem and allow precious water to flow up into the bloom through the stem. Dull snips crush the stem. Sharpen your snips using a sharpening stone.

3. The best time to cut blooms is in the morning when it is cool and they are well-hydrated. If possible, avoid cutting in the middle of the day as blooms carry field heat after harvesting. If it rained the night before and the blooms are carrying water, I turn them upside down after cutting and give them a gentle shake.

4. If you want blooms that have the best chance of a longer vase life, cut them on the immature side. The most mature blooms often have petals that go back to the stem and may only last for a short time in a vase. Immature blooms are less open

and will hold their hydration longer because the petals are held tightly together. As a result, they experience less evaporation. For many cut flower applications, slightly immature blooms last a day or two longer and hold up better for bouquets and table arrangements. You can identify a mature bloom by looking at the petals on the backside. These petals opened first and have been exposed to the sun and elements the longest. If those back petals are brown, shriveled, faded, or curled, that indicates a bloom that has passed its prime. Additionally, look for pollen in the center of the bloom. A bloom with visible pollen has switched to seed production and will give you a shorter vase life. Once a bloom has been pollinated, it starts producing ethylene, which encourages flower petals to fall off.

5. Where you make the cut on your stems depends on what the blooms are used for and how you have disbudded them. Florists and designers typically want 12 to 16-inch (30 to 40 cm) or longer stems. Longer stems give them maximum flexibility to use blooms for various purposes, like bridal bouquets or tall

arrangements. The length of each internode (the distance between the leaf axils) varies by dahlia variety. Because of this, I disbud my plants differently based on the variety. For instance, 'Cafe au Lait' has very short internodes so I typically disbud those plants down three leaf nodes.

In contrast, 'AC Ben' has long internodes and I will disbud them down only one leaf node. There is no "one size fits all" recipe for where to cut. Regardless of how far down you cut, it is always best to cut just above a leaf node. That tells the plant to branch and produce more blooms. If you are cutting for your own use and don't require a set stem length, I would cut just above the leaf node below the last spot you disbudded. If you have not disbudded, cut just above the leaf node that gives you your desired stem length. You can see short videos of me cutting blooms on the Kristine Albrecht YouTube channel. Look for videos 88 and 161.

6. It is best practice to strip off all the leaves from your stems just after cutting blooms. Leaves require hydration; if left on the stem, they will rob water from the bloom. In addition, dahlia leaves carry bacteria. If we don't strip the leaves from our blooms, bacteria can get into water-filled vessels and shorten vase life.

7. Any water-filled container you place your blooms into should be clean. This is true for a bucket or tub out in the field or a decorative vase in the home. If we empty a tub or a vase after use and don't wash it, we start the new blooms off with a bacteria-laden container. Before and after each use, I scrub my buckets and vases out with scouring sponges & dish soap. I often run my vases through the dishwasher on high heat after washing them by hand. If there is a ring of scum inside your vase, don't use it. Containers should be clean enough to drink out of.

8. Gently place your blooms in their buckets with enough room to rest undisturbed. Dahlia petals are fragile and easily damaged if they rub against each other. Avoid packing tubs so full of blooms that the petals are jammed together.

9. Blooms should be kept as cool as possible once cut and, ideally, cooled down overnight. If you are a cut flower farmer, building or buying a flower cooler will extend the life of your harvest. I keep my flower cooler at 40 to 42° F (4.4 to 5.5° C) If you don't have a cooler, keep your cut blooms out of the sun in the coolest spot you have that is out of the wind. If you'll be transporting blooms in a car after harvest, keep the blooms out of the sun and use the air conditioner to keep the car's interior as cool as possible.

10. Getting the stems into cool water after cutting blooms as quickly as possible is important. I don't recommend cutting blooms and laying them on the ground before setting them into the bucket. When I was new at growing dahlias, a show grower taught me that after cutting a bloom, it should be plunged into clean water within 30 seconds.

Once blooms are inside and on display in a clean vase, it is best to empty, rinse out, and refill the vase with cold, clean water every day.

Heat is the other enemy in keeping dahlias fresh. Keeping dahlias as cool as possible after harvesting is one of the most important things you can do to improve their life. Never leave a bucket of dahlia blooms in a hot car while you do errands. Likewise, inside a car keep them out of the sun.

Once arranged, never place a vase of dahlias in direct sun and keep them away from fruit bowls. Ripening fruit produces ethylene gas that ages the blooms and shortens vase life. For maximum life, you can put your blooms (in the vase) inside your refrigerator each night or outside if you have cold overnight temperatures.

TRANSPORTING DAHLIA BLOOMS

At some point, dahlia growers will need to transport their blooms in the back of a car or a van. We often forget how much movement there is on the seat of a vehicle until we have a bucket of precious blooms sitting beside us. Only then do we avoid potholes and crawl over speed bumps and driveway curbs. Dahlias don't like to rub against each other; too much rubbing damages the petals. No one knows this more than dahlia exhibitors—they have perfected methods to get their blooms from their gardens to the shows with minimal damage.

If you're traveling with a bouquet already in a vase, there is a quick and easy way to ensure the vase won't fall over in the car. Start with a cardboard box that is about 1/2 to 3/4 of the height of your vase. If your box is too tall, cut it down. On the box's top flaps, trace an outline of the diameter of your vase. Next, cut out the circle you traced on the top of the box using a razor blade. Cut your circle just a tiny bit bigger than the line you traced. Remove the cardboard circle from the top of the box, and you are done. You can set your box on the seat of your car or the floor of your van with the vase inside the hole you cut.

A vase supporter made from a cardboard box.

Me and Jan with tubs of blooms with Rigi Pot inserts for florists and designers.

If you have bulk dahlias to deliver and want the blooms to get to their destination in perfect condition you can use a system I learned from show growers in my local dahlia society. I start with a Rubbermaid Roughneck 3-gallon storage tote. They are widely available and are sold with a lid. For my purposes, the lid is not needed for transporting blooms. I use the lid, however, when these tubs do double duty as tuber storage containers in the winter. Into the tote, I insert an IPL Rigi Pot from Stuewe & Sons (stuewe.com). I buy the IP-110 or the IP-110U. These are designed for growing tree seedlings and are used by people who repopulate forests. When I insert the Rigi Pot into the Rubbermaid tote, it's a tight fit. I put one end of the Rigi Pot in first and pull on the tote handle while pushing down the other end of the insert. Part of the insert will stick up above the tote. That's fine.

Once the insert is in, I fill the tote with water about four inches (10 cm) deep and I'm ready to drop in my cut blooms. The Rigi Pots have 45 cavities that will hold the stems of my flowers. These cavities keep the blooms upright. Unlike blooms in an open bucket, the Rigi Pot openings hold each bloom individually. The key to avoiding having blooms rubbing each other is to arrange them carefully with different-length stems. For example, I will put a flower with a shorter stem next to one with a taller stem. The two stay upright at different heights and won't damage each other as they move. I can get a bloom in each cavity with smaller blooms or those with varied stem lengths, however, I will spread the flowers out with larger blooms and use only half of the available cavities.

When I transport blooms to a dahlia show I add extra rigidity to my bloom stems by pressing small squares of mattress foam down into each cell that holds the stem straight up. Using scissors, I cut up 1.5-inch (3.8 cm) foam pieces and wedge them between the cavity and the stem. This technique holds each bloom absolutely upright and rigid. If you want maximum stability and support for your blooms as they travel, a Rigi Pot set up with foam squares cannot be beaten.

As with any container you put your dahlias into, these totes and Rigi Pots must be clean. I have dozens of these totes with inserts. When my florists and designers pick up blooms, I want them to arrive in perfect condition at their shop or studio. So I send them on their way with my totes. The next time they pick up an order, they bring back the totes from the last pickup. When the totes come back, I remove the insert and thoroughly clean the tote and the insert. Every few weeks, I put the inserts in my dishwasher and give them a high-temperature cleaning. Keeping tubs, buckets, and totes clean and free of bacteria keeps dahlias fresh for days.

If you are traveling long distances with blooms in tubs, keeping them cool and out of the sun is essential. When I take blooms from my farm in California to a dahlia show in Portland, Oregon, I will travel for 12 or 13 hours through California's Central Valley. Summer temperatures there can be over 100° F (38° C).

To keep the blooms as fresh as possible, I put aluminum foil on the inside of the side and rear windows of my car. I secure the foil with blue painter's tape that comes off easily and doesn't leave sticky bits on the car. This blocks sunlight from striking the blooms and adding heat to the car interior. I also run the car's air conditioner the entire time, even when we stop for food or make a pit stop at a rest area. This cool environment benefits the blooms, even if it is a bit chilly for my passengers and me. We wear long underwear, down jackets, gloves, and wool hats to survive the long drive with the air conditioner on high, piling blankets over our lower bodies and legs. Such is the sacrifice one makes for keeping blooms cool and fresh so they will look their finest at the show! I'm pleased to say that I have had "best in show" awards after a full day of traveling using these techniques.

SELLING CUT FLOWERS

When I started growing dahlias, I never intended to sell cut flowers. Instead, I was growing for enjoyment and exhibition. Eventually, my focus turned to dahlia hybridizing. Because breeding dahlias is a numbers game, I found myself with thousands of fresh blooms every week as my dahlia beds expanded, so it made sense to sell them. How I did that changed over time. Here is my story.

I started with a roadside farm stand at the end of my driveway. My neighbors loved the fresh bouquets. My friends and I would cut blooms and make beautiful arrangements twice a week. Then, at 11:00 am, we would take the bouquets down the driveway, often to a long line of patient customers. The farm stand used the blooms we were harvesting and brought in income to cover farm expenses. It also provided me and my farm friends the opportunity to gather twice a week where we could work together, socialize, and do something we all loved. But as my breeding goals expanded I needed more free time; the 28 person-hours per week farm stand had to go.

In addition to making and selling arrangements, I sold tubs of blooms to local florists and designers. I would cut blooms on Sundays and Wednesdays and store them in the cooler for pick up the following day. Thursday pick-ups were always the largest. Design professionals who stage flowers for weekend weddings or events want their blooms on Thursday so they can sort and prepare them for the weekend. As my dahlia fields grew, so did the number of florists and designers I sold to. It was not uncommon to have 30–50 tubs of blooms go out on a mid-summer Thursday morning. However, taking custom orders from designers and giving them their desired colors, forms, and quantities required so much of my time and attention that my breeding program ultimately suffered. Also, cutting blooms twice a week did not allow me to

photograph and observe new varieties carefully; they were constantly being cut for weddings and events.

It took me several years, but I finally figured out how to sell my blooms while preserving time for my breeding program. I now cut blooms only on Wednesdays for Thursday pick-up. This is a big improvement; because the blooms stay on the plants longer, I can better observe and document them. I no longer take custom orders. My friends and I cut the blooms and makeup tubs of similar colors. I label each tub with a number and make a quick video. I text the video to my accounts, and they reply with a list of the tubs they want: first come, first served. The following day they pick up at a pre-set time. This new system balances my need to focus on breeding and the desire to supply organically-grown flowers to my community.

Melissa Smith, South Carolina

Melissa Smith of Fraylick Farm in South Carolina sells cut flowers from her 3,000 plants. In her hot climate, dahlia plants produce about half the blooms a similar plant would produce on my California farm. Like me, her florists and designers pick up their orders once a week on Thursdays. However, her harvesting routine is very different from mine.

Instead of cutting blooms in one day, Melissa harvests blooms every Sunday, Monday, Tuesday, and Wednesday. This allows her to cut as many blooms as possible as they gradually mature, storing them in her flower cooler which is kept between 38 and 42° F (3.3 to 5.5° C). By cutting over four days, she maximizes her opportunity to harvest sellable blooms before they pass their prime. With her lower bloom yield, cutting one day per week would reduce her sellable harvest and increase the number of blooms lost to deadheading.

At right: dahlias drying in Philippa's bathroom. Photo by Philippa Stewart.

176

Once her florists and designers pick up their orders on Thursday, she doesn't rest. She returns to her dahlia beds looking for blooms nearing maturity from her 'Cafe au Lait' and dinner plate varieties. Often these blooms will be too far along to be sellable the following Thursday. Rather than deadhead those stems, Melissa will cut the main blooms at the highest leaf axil along with the smaller of the two side buds. What is left is the largest side bud that Melissa promotes as the new main bloom. Instead of deadheading a full stem, she now gets a second chance to produce a sellable bloom down the road on that existing stem. The one exception Melissa has found to cutting blooms at their peak is 'Cafe au Lait'. In her climate, if she cuts them when they are mature, the blooms fall apart when her florists come for pickup. She cuts these blooms at about 40% open. She has found that this variety will continue to open in her cooler and be fully open when her customers arrive.

DRYING DAHLIAS

Philippa Stewart, England

Philippa Stewart of Justdahlias in Cheshire, England is an expert on drying dahlias. Her journey began at a flower farming workshop. One of the tutors mentioned they had managed to dry a few dahlias but had no success with the white varieties. Philippa began experimenting, and today, after drying thousands of blooms, white dahlias are her most popular color.

Philippa's dried dahlia blooms. Photo by Philippa Stewart.

A dried dahlia bloom.

For Philippa, harvesting for dried blooms is very similar to cutting blooms fresh. She typically cuts the stems down two or three leaf axils to give her customers at least a 12-inch (30 cm) stem. She then removes the leaves and the side buds, leaving just the main bloom and stem. Smaller blooms with shorter stems are also dried and are desired by people who make wreaths and flower crowns.

She started drying dahlias in a tractor shed with one open wall. It turned out to be too cold and damp, and the blooms molded. Starting over, she brought the blooms indoors, drying them inside her home. Philippa keeps her house on the cool side, between 60 to 68° F (15 and 20° C). She found it took two to three weeks to dry most varieties. The larger blooms take a bit longer. She has learned that contrary to what we might think, dahlias dry better at room temperature than in a warm or hot place. Flowers should never be dried in a location where they receive direct sunlight: the sun through a window will bleach out the vibrant color. Likewise, she has learned never to dry dahlias near a heater or radiator. Mild, consistent temperatures yield the best results.

The time it takes to dry dahlias varies depending on the humidity and temperature of the room you use. Philippa can tell when the blooms are fully dry by checking the stems, which stay hydrated longer than the blooms. If the stems are still a bit green, she leaves them hanging.

Philippa secures metal chicken wire onto her exposed wooden ceiling beams to provide a framework to hang her blooms indoors. She then hangs the blooms using a four to six-inch (10 to 15 cm) piece of stub wire (or floral wire) to make a small "S" hook. One end of the hook is pushed through the end of the stem. The other end of the hook is placed over the chicken wire. The blooms hang upside down. This causes the petals to droop toward the floor and then twist and curl upward. Philippa

tried drying blooms right-side up but the results were not as interesting. The petals flopped open and didn't have the same sense of movement as those hung upside down. Once the blooms have dried, Philippa takes them down, removes the wire "S" hook, and stores them right-side-up in buckets.

The biggest surprise when drying dahlias is the difference in color between fresh and dried blooms. Some varieties dry true to their color in the field, however, most do not. 'Kilmore' is a variety with a lemon and salmon blend. When dried, it is predominantly pink. Philippa has found that most orange varieties dry to a range of colors including burnt orange, red, and deep terracotta. 'Silver Years' grows on Philippa's farm as a white bloom with a pink blush that turns baby pink when dry. Burgundy blooms dry to black. The color changes gave some varieties she wasn't fond of, a second life. For instance, Philippa is not partial to variegated dahlia varieties. However, a supplier accidentally

Philippa's dahlia patch. Photo: Philippa Stewart.

'KA's Mocha Katie''.

sent her a tuber of 'Peppermint Splash', a light pinky purple and white variegated variety. To her delight, this bloom has the most beautiful muted and mottled colors when dried. It is now her favorite dried dahlia. The one color she steers clear of is mid-pink, as they tend to dry down to a dull purple.

One of the big surprises when drying dahlias is how tough and durable most of them are. We tend to think of dried flowers as being brittle and fragile. However, she has discovered there are exceptions to this rule. 'Karma Choc', for instance, is too fragile to make a good dried flower. 'Cafe au Lait', however, is a dried dahlia star, producing some of her most robust dried blooms.

Philippa found that the various dahlia forms produce mixed results when dried. Paying attention to the shape of the fresh flower is important. Water lily varieties dry well and display a wonderful sense of movement. Although growers often favor varieties with a high petal count, those with fewer petals tend to be more attractive as dried flowers. Open-center varieties also produce beautiful dried flowers. When using an open-center bloom, she harvests them before they are full of ripe pollen. Philippa has started saving seeds and growing her own seedlings. Most are open-center varieties; discovering how these unique blooms transform when dry is a sheer delight.

On occasion, a dried bloom will detach from its stem. Philippa has developed a simple method for re-attaching a wayward bloom using an 8 to 12-inch (20-30 cm) piece of stub wire. She bends one end of the wire to make a small hook. She then pushes the unhooked end of the wire through the center of the bloom and pulls the wire tight. This secures the wire and buries it out of sight in the bloom's center. She then holds the stem on the back of the bloom at a 45° angle and winds the wire several times around it. This simple fix holds the bloom securely to the stem.

Because the largest dahlias tend to separate from stems when dried, Philippa often uses this technique on the largest blooms even before drying them.

Philippa sells her dried blooms between November and April each year. They are a perfect way to continue selling dahlias through the fall and winter after the cut flower season has ended. As a rule of thumb, her dried dahlias sell for 10% more than fresh. Her dried blooms are popular with designers for mid-winter weddings and events. They have become so popular that in some years she is sold out by April. Because dried blooms vary so much in color, Philippa's website, (justdahlias.com) has photographs of every dried variety she sells. Buyers can see the dried flowers' true form and color before ordering.

Philippa ships dried dahlias in standard cardboard boxes. She has discovered that in addition to being sturdy, her dried dahlias can easily handle the jostling during shipping. First, she lays down a row of the longest-stem dahlias across the bottom of the box. All the flower heads are together at one end, with the stem ends at the other. She then places a layer of crumpled tissue paper over the dahlia stems.

On top of that, she places a second row of dahlias with the flower heads on the opposite side. After another layer of tissue paper, the final blooms get placed on top. Three layers of blooms are the maximum Philippa will ship per box. Once a final layer of newsprint or tissue paper is laid on the top row of blooms, she seals the box and shakes it. If nothing moves, she knows it is ready to ship. If the blooms slide around, she will add more crumpled paper.

Drying dahlias has created a second business for Philippa's blooms. For her, selling dried flowers is less stressful than selling them fresh. Promising a designer fresh flowers depends on fickle weather and the good grace that pests or diseases won't diminish the harvest. Selling dried flowers keeps Philippa within her comfort

Heather Henson's daughter Isla Rose with a dried bouquet.
Photo by Megan Timm of Brighter by Megan Photography.

zone. Instead of promising a future harvest that may or may not come to pass, she sells from her inventory of dried blooms. Luckily for us, Monty Don produced a TV story on Philippa and her dahlias. You can watch it online. Search for Gardener's World 2022, Episode 27. You will find the piece on Philippa 22 minutes into the show.

Heather Henson, Canada

Heather Henson of Boreal Blooms in Cold Lake, Alberta dries many of her dahlias. With a short growing season and harsh winters, designers use dry flowers for fall and winter weddings and events. Like Philippa, Heather dries her dahlias indoors. She uses her basement because, with the windows covered, there is no direct sunlight that could fade the colors. Because her basement has about 60 to 70% humidity in summer, Heather uses a dehumidifier to dry the air. She found that without it her dried dahlias turn brown.

Heather uses a standing wooden rack in her basement to dry her blooms. This same shelving rack holds grow lights and trays when she starts seeds. She bundles four to six flowers together with string at the ends of the stems. She then uses hooks on the rack to catch the string. Her bundles of flowers hang upside down until they are fully dry.

Dried flowers provide design work and income over the winter for growers in cold climates. Heather's customers buy beautiful dried bouquets that last all winter. Brides who use dried flowers can keep their bouquets and arrangements as a keepsake. Dried flowers for winter weddings are stress-free as the bride doesn't have to worry about the possibility of frozen or wilted flowers. The pricing for Heather's dried flowers is 30% higher than the equivalent fresh flowers.

DISPLAYING BLOOMS WITH PIN FROGS

When I want to bring individual blooms indoors to get a good look at them, the best tool is a ceramic vessel with a floral pin frog at the bottom. Pin frogs are an old-fashion device that allows you to secure the stem of a bloom onto the upturned pins so it will hold the bloom straight up in a vessel filled with water.

Dahlia growers in California who show their blooms are familiar with pin frogs because that's how blooms are staged at all California dahlia shows. In other parts of the country, blooms are staged alternatively in Oasis foam or crinkled-up plastic sheeting. I like floral pin frogs because of their durability and the opportunity to use them over and over, with no waste. At my dahlia society, when an older grower retires from exhibiting, they pass on their containers with pin frogs to the younger members. I regularly use an eighty-year-old container that I received from a retiring grower!

If you'd like to experiment with pin frogs, understand that they are not all created equal. Many of the inexpensive frogs available online have pins that are spread too far apart, making it impossible to secure a bloom that has a thin stem. Additionally, the pins should be at least three-quarters of an inch long (1.9 cm) to properly hold the blooms. Unfortunately, many of the inexpensive frogs have pins that are too short. There are two good sources online for quality pin frogs with closely-spaced pins. The first is EZ Pots (ezpots.com) which sells a limited selection of quality pin frogs in boxes containing 12 to 36 frogs at a reasonable price. The other source is Floral Genius (hhfshop.com). They sell pin frogs individually, but their specialty is round pin cup holders made of heavy metal. These small metal cups have a built-in frog and are so heavy they hold up blooms well, even though they are quite small. These metal cups are beautiful but

Using a "stem crutch" to hold a thin stem.

more expensive than buying pin frogs to add to an existing container.

The containers I use are cast-offs or second-hand. I shop at thrift stores or dollar stores for inexpensive glazed ceramic containers. The heavier and thicker the containers, the better. Some large blooms will tip over easily in a lightweight container but a nice heavy ceramic container will hold water and keep a large bloom upright (You can see me with a large bloom in a heavy pot on page 122). Next, I use a silicone sealer to secure a pin frog to the bottom of the container. It's nothing fancy, just the sealer you find at a hardware store that you'd use in a shower or around a sink. After ensuring my container and frog are clean and dry, I apply a generous amount of sealer to the bottom of the frog and press it onto the bottom of the container. I know I have used enough sealer if some of it squeezes out around the sides of the frog.

Some dahlia varieties have thin stems that will not stay upright, even with the best pin frogs. These thin stem varieties don't find enough purchase on enough pins to hold the bloom well. Fortunately, there is an easy trick to keep even the thinnest stem secure. First, I cut one-inch (2.5 cm) piece of an extra dahlia stem that is a bit bigger than my thin stem. The hollow opening in the extra bit of stem should be just big enough to accept the thin stem on my bloom. I then slide the extra stem over the bottom of my thin stem. Next, I use a pair of snips to trim the bottom of both stems together, leaving a 3/4 inch (2 cm) crutch at the bottom of my thin stem. Finally, I press both stems together into the tines of the pin frog. You can see a six-minute video of my containers and pin frogs on the Kristine Albrecht YouTube channel. Look for video 167.

Ceramic containers with pin frogs glued at the bottom.

11. Digging, Dividing, & Storing Tubers

TUBERS. TO DIG OR NOT TO DIG

FALL PRESENTS DAHLIA GROWERS WITH A choice: leave tubers in the ground or dig them up and store them over the winter. If you live in an area where the ground freezes, you have no choice but to dig up your tuber clumps every fall and store them safely until spring; if a dahlia tuber freezes it will rot. If you live in an area where the ground does not freeze, you have more options for handling your tubers over the winter.

There is no one right way to dig and divide tubers. Your decision rests on your personal goals, available time and energy, available storage spaces, and your particular climate. A grower without the time or physical ability has a good reason to not dig and divide tubers. They can pull out their tubers every fall, throw them away, and purchase new tubers the following spring. If their climate allows for it, they can simply leave tubers in the ground to re-sprout in the spring, without digging or dividing whatever.

Digging and dividing my tubers is an essential part of my dahlia culture. Here are ten reasons why I dig and divide my dahlias every year.

1. I want to multiply my tuber stock so I can sell them, give them to friends, or donate them to my local dahlia society. To accomplish this, my tubers must come out of the ground and be divided.

2. My farm has gophers. If I leave my tubers underground in the winter, I run the risk of loss.

At left: 'KA's Cloud'.

3. I am concerned about the possibility my tubers will decay if left in the ground. For example, a year of above-average rainfall could rot them.

4. Tuber clumps left underground multiply every year. It is not unusual for a clump left underground for a few years to develop 20 to 50 tubers on a massive clump. When those tubers sprout in the spring, they will give rise to a swarm of individual shoots competing for nutrients and sunlight. As the growing season progresses, the resulting tangle of foliage

187

will make an overcrowded plant more prone to powdery mildew. Such a plant will also produce smaller blooms.

5. I dig up my tubers every year and look at the health of each clump. If a set of tubers develops a disease, I want to dispose of it quickly. If the clumps are left underground, I have no way of assessing their fitness. By digging up the tubers, observing them, and dividing them, I can ensure all the varieties in my patch are healthy.

6. I live in a warm climate where winter daytime highs can get into the 70s (23-26 C). If I overwinter tubers in the ground, they might think a warm spell is spring and start to sprout. Once this happens, a cold snap will inevitably kill the new growth. These "false starts" in the winter would steal energy from my tubers.

7. I sell my blooms to florists and designers. I also show my blooms at organized dahlia shows. To do these things well, I need manageable and healthy plants that produce near-perfect blooms. Plants from a tuber clump left in the ground year after year will not perform at their peak.

8. I operate a no-till farm. A critical part of my soil preparation is growing a winter cover crop and then covering the chopped-down greens with a tarp in the early spring. This process would not be possible if I left my tubers in the ground; to successfully plant a cover crop, my field needs to be a blank canvas for sowing seeds, watering, and growing greens. In addition, the irrigation I use to grow my cover crop could rot my tubers if they were left in the ground.

9. By digging and dividing tubers, I am rejuvenating the plant tissue and have a better chance of keeping my varieties from degrading. Older plant material accumulates more mutations than young plant material. Plants are not that dissimilar to us. We are not as energetic at 70 as we were at 20. Tuber clumps left in the ground build up a mass of old plant tissue. This is more susceptible to mutation and lack of vigor than a plant grown from a younger single tuber. Each divided tuber is made up of plant material that is less than one year old. Digging and dividing tubers is a good regimen if we want to grow varieties year after year with less deterioration in quality or vigor.

10. I am a dahlia hybridizer, and I need to evaluate the quality of my new varieties. Therefore, I will only introduce a new variety that produces healthy tubers that store well over winter. Tubers left underground can not be analyzed for winter storage performance.

LEAVING TUBERS IN THE GROUND ALL YEAR

If you plan to leave tubers in the ground, at the end of the growing season cut your plants down to within two to four inches (5 to 10 cm) of ground level. The stalks of dahlia plants are hollow, like a straw. If the ends of the stalks are not covered, rain can collect inside them and could rot your tubers. A simple remedy is to cover the stalk ends with a small piece of aluminum foil. The foil will act as a waterproof cap, keeping the rain out. Growers who leave their tubers in the ground all winter often apply a thick layer of mulch up to a foot (30 cm) deep as insulation to protect them against any surprise deep freeze.

When your tubers sprout again in spring, you should consider thinning out the shoots that arise from each tuber clump. Tuber clumps underground all winter typically send up multiple shoots in the spring. If the forest of shoots is allowed to grow, the resulting dahlia "bush" will be overcrowded and have poor airflow, encouraging powdery mildew. By selectively cutting back most of the shoots and letting only two or three grow tall, you will have healthier plants and bigger and better blooms.

A giant tuber clump I left in the ground for four years.

Leaving tubers in the ground to sprout in the spring can be done with the precautions listed above, however, you may not be able to do it forever. Dr. Keith Hammett, a plant pathologist, and leading professional plant breeder studied species dahlias in the wild that are never dug up. Following several years of tubers overwintering and re-sprouting in the spring, he observed that dahlia plants eventually die. The undivided tuber mass finally expires and the plant then regrows from seed.

You can see a short video of a tuber clump I left in the ground for four years on the Kristine Albrecht YouTube channel. Look for video 146.

WHEN TO DIG UP TUBERS

You can dig up your tubers after your plants have been growing for a minimum of four and a half months (135 days). I typically dig and divide my tubers between late September and early November because the weather is pleasant. My tubers have been in the ground for plenty of time,

189

A tuber clump with three prominent eyes in the center of the image.

the soil is easy to work, and the rains have yet to start. If I waited for frost I would be digging up my tubers unpleasant cold and wet weather.

It is commonly recommended to wait a week after the first hard frost to dig up tubers. Some growers believe that frost has a beneficial effect on tubers and help them store better over the winter. Yet, dahlia growers in warm tropical climates successfully dig, divide and store their tubers without frost. The experts I talk to agree that frost is irrelevant concerning tubers. Instead, dahlias are triggered by the summer solstice to fortify their tubers. When the nights start getting longer, dahlia tubers are given priority. See more on this topic under Dahlia Myths on page 225.

If you live where the ground does not freeze, you can leave the tubers underground all winter and dig and divide them in the spring using the soil as a winter storage medium. An advantage of this approach is that tubers dug up in spring can have more pronounced eyes. Sometimes, they even have immature sprouts. However, it can expose your tubers to gophers, ground-dwelling pests, and rot.

To use this underground storage method, cut the stems of your plants off about two to four inches (5 to 10 cm) above the ground in the fall and cover the hollow stalks with aluminum foil to keep out the rain. If your tubers develop new shoots during the winter, you can cut them off at ground level. After the last frost (April 1st

190

in my climate), dig up the tubers and divide them as you would in the fall. Allow 8 to 24 hours before planting to allow cut wounds on individual tubers to heal. Keep your tubers dry and out of the sun while waiting for the wounds to heal. Tubers do not need a prolonged resting period between digging and planting.

Melissa Smith, South Carolina

Melissa Smith of Fraylick Farm in South Carolina digs up her tubers in November. She doesn't wait for frost. In her climate, frost may not come until later in the year. She cuts her plants down to the ground one or two weeks before she digs out the tubers. She's found that this waiting period makes the eyes on the tuber crown easier to see.

DIGGING UP TUBER CLUMPS

In the fall, our plants have shifted gears. They are now producing very little new foliage, and flower production has tapered off. This is the time of year when dahlias are making seeds and bulking up the tubers underground. Six weeks before I plan to dig up my tubers I slowly wean them slowly off of water. You can read about this process in the section of this book about preparing for the end of the growing season on page 130.

When I am ready to start digging, I cut my plants down to within six inches (15 cm) of the ground and dispose of the old foliage. Although it is tempting to cut down all the sorry-looking plants in the garden at once, I only cut down those I have time to dig up that day. Immediately after cutting my plants, I transfer my plant tags from the soil to the cut-off stalks. The tags I use are made of thin plastic, and I force them down into the cut stalk, where they

stay nice and snug. I only cut down the plants I can process in one day for three reasons. First, once a mature dahlia plant is cut down, the remaining hollow stalks will collect water and lead to rot. Second, when a dahlia plant is cut down, the plant wants to regrow. If it is cut down a week or two before digging, it will put its energy into making new shoots and leaves, draining energy from the tubers. Finally, in my climate, the eyes on the tuber crown are easier to see on a freshly cut plant; they tend to shrink back just a day or two after the plant is cut down.

Once your plants have been cut down, you can start digging up the underground tuber clumps. Although it looks like rough and ready work, digging and handling tuber clumps should be done with care and finesse. Tubers can be fragile, especially the narrow necks where the tuber body

Using a cordless multi tool to cut down dahlia stalks.

191

Digging underneath a tuber clump.

connects to the crown. They are most vulnerable when they come out of the ground and lose the support of the soil.

Using a shovel or digging fork, I dig straight down on all four sides of the plant stalks, about 12–16 inches (30–40 cm) away from the central stalk, and rock the tool back and forth to loosen the soil around the tubers. A shovel has some advantages because it provides more support for the tubers and leaves a cleaner wound should it cut through a tuber. Once the soil has been loosened on all sides, I slide the shovel gently underneath the tuber clump and slowly force it upwards. If I have a digging partner, we lift the tubers simultaneously with our shovels from opposite sides. Next, I gently remove any large clumps of soil or mulch and turn the whole tuber mass upside down to drain any water inside the stalks.

If your shovel accidentally makes a clean cut through the body of your tuber, that's actually okay. As long as the remaining tuber body has a neck and a crown, it will sprout again in spring. If, however, your fork makes a hole in the tuber, I suggest using a knife to cleanly cut off the damaged section, leaving some tuber body, neck, and crown intact.

Lifting tubers out of the ground with the plant tag.

192

Washing tubers on an elevated metal mesh.

Next, I will set up a washstand to clean my tubers. I use a simple wood frame with hardware cloth (wire mesh) on one side. The frame rests on a plastic five-gallon planting pot or two saw horses. These makeshift platforms lift the work surface off the ground at a comfortable height. Next, I wash the soil off my tuber clumps using a spray nozzle on a garden hose. The spray should be forceful enough to clean the tubers but not so aggressive as to damage them. After they are washed, I immediately divide them. It is essential that once divided, the individual tubers are set in a shaded spot to dry for 8 to 24 hours, depending on size. Avoid drying tubers in direct sun as it can promote shriveling.

Galena Berkompas, Washington

Galena Berkompas of Micro Flower Farm in Vancouver, Washington digs up her dahlia tubers in late October and early November. However, as a mother of four young children, she doesn't always have time to divide them right away. Instead, she stores her unwashed tuber clumps on open shelves in her flower cooler at 40 to 42° F (4.4 to 5.5 C). They stay in the cooler until she has time to divide them. In her naturally humid climate, her tuber clumps stay hydrated without shriveling.

Philippa Stewart, England

Philippa Stewart of Justdahlias in Cheshire, England digs her tubers up in early November or after the first hard frost, whichever occurs first. She takes her tuber clumps into a shed where she rests them upside down on the floor for three weeks. This drains water from the hollow stems. After their rest period, Philippa shakes off loose soil, trims off small roots and broken tubers, and packs the clumps into banana boxes with the tubers nestled in wood shavings. In her area, these shavings are sold as horse bedding. Her goal is to arrange the tuber clumps in the boxes so they don't touch each other. For Philippa, wood shavings are an ideal storage medium because they are lightweight. She is a one-person operation, and banana boxes full of tubers get heavy if filled with a heavier medium.

She stores the boxes over the winter in an outbuilding attached to her home. Because

193

one wall of the shed adjoins her house, the temperatures never drop below freezing. The shed has wooden shelves to receive the banana boxes. Philippa is careful not to store tubers on the concrete floor. If she needs the floor space, the boxes sit above the floor on a wooden pallet. Philippa divides the tubers in spring before planting.

Lorelie Merton, Australia

Lorelie Merton of Florelie Seasonal Flowers in Bungaree, Victoria does not wait for frost before digging up her tuber clumps. Some years she will experience a fall frost; in other years dahlias need to be dug before the frost occurs. She cuts down her plants gradually in preparation for digging. First, she will cut just the top third of her plants. One week later she cuts down another third of her plants, leaving them one-third of their original height. One week later, she cuts her plants to the ground, leaving a six-inch (15 cm) stalk to make handling the tuber clumps easier. After waiting another week, Lorelie will finally dig up her tuber clumps using a garden fork. She uses this three-week, step-by-step approach because she has found it

encourages dormancy in her tubers and results in better over-winter storage.

Once Lorelie starts digging up her tubers, the process will take about a month. After scraping off loose soil, the tuber clumps are set upside down in labeled crates and taken inside a shed. Lorelie does not wash her tuber clumps. Instead, she focuses on getting her 8,000 clumps out of the ground. The priority is gathering tubers before the approaching rains make the ground too wet.

Once all her tubers are dug up, Lorelie divides the tuber clumps. Because so many tuber clumps are stored in her shed, the humidity is high enough that they don't dry out while waiting to be divided. To avoid rot, she activates a fan in the shed to keep the humidity from climbing too high.

She divides her tuber clumps unwashed and sterilizes tools between clumps using Metho, an industrial alcohol used for cleaning and disinfecting. She prefers Metho over a bleach solution for three reasons. First, the alcohol doesn't irritate her skin the way bleach does—after

Making a horizontal cut with the multi tool to remove the green stalks.

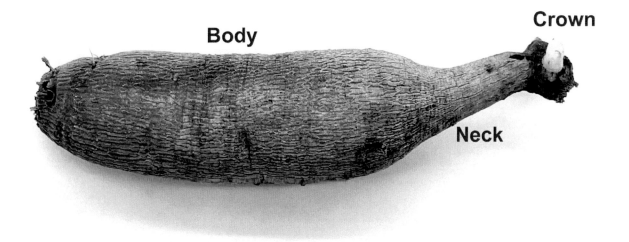

Body

Crown

Neck

A viable tuber must have a body, an intact neck, a crown and an eye.
This tuber also has a young sprout at the crown.

dividing 8,000 tuber clumps and sterilizing with bleach, Lorelie's hands would take months to recover. Second, the alcohol solution does not damage her clothes. Third, the alcohol evaporates quickly and doesn't rust her tools.

Emily Avenson, Belgium

Emily Avenson of Fleuropean in Belgium digs up her tubers after her second fall frost. She does not wash them but simply shakes off loose soil and places them into nursery crates. She adds no storage medium. Once crated, her tubers are moved to a basement room connected to her home, providing an ideal environment for over-winter storage. Emily divides her tuber clumps into smaller clumps at planting time when the eyes on her tubers are more prominent. She does not divide her clumps into individual tubers.

DIVIDING DAHLIA TUBERS

Regardless of the size or shape, a dahlia tuber must have four essential parts to grow a new plant in the spring: a body, an unbroken neck, a crown, and an eye. If your tuber is missing any of these, it should be discarded. Some tubers have a neck and a crown; however, the body has a

sharp cut-off edge. As mentioned earlier, this can result from a shovel strike; most of the time this won't affect the tuber's viability. but while a tuber with a partially cut body should grow just fine, any tubers with broken necks should be discarded. Finally, a tuber must have an eye to sprout in the spring.

The process of dividing clumps of dahlia tubers is not 100% efficient. Even the most experienced growers successfully save and store only a percentage of the tubers that come out of the ground. When first dug, some tubers will be missing eyes or be rotten, damaged, or otherwise unfit to keep. The same goes for tubers after storage: some rot, dry out or turn out to be missing eyes. The number of viable tubers you can save for storage is varietal as well. On rare occasions I have saved over twenty good tubers from a single tuber clump; however, if, on average, you retain three to five tubers from each clump, consider your efforts successful.

Tubers come in all shapes and sizes. These factors do not determine the resulting plant's health, vigor, or bloom quality. I have grown beautiful plants from tiny, ugly, and odd-shaped tubers. Tuber shape and

The tip of the snips point to an eye on this tuber crown.

size vary by variety. Some dahlia varieties regularly produce plump, round tubers, while others produce tubers that are long and thin. One caution when it comes to very thin and small tubers (thinner than a pencil): they are more likely to dry out during winter storage. If you want to keep very thin tubers alive over winter I suggest wrapping them in plastic wrap.

Some growers dig up their tubers in the fall, store them as whole clumps over the winter, and then pull them out in the spring to divide. These growers find dividing in the spring easier because the eyes swell. I divide my tuber clumps in the fall because they take up less room in my small temperature-controlled shed. Once I have reduced my tuber mass to just the viable individual tubers, I can organize them and fit them into my storage space. This strategy also allows me to know how many viable tubers I have to plant and sell —I don't have the option of waiting until spring to inventory my tubers.

I divide my tuber clumps on a table covered with an absorbent cotton bath towel. As described above, I rinse my freshly dug tubers just before dividing them. The towel catches moisture and allows me to shake off any lodged dirt or mud. I work with only one tuber clump at a time. Having multiple varieties on the table invites trouble; it's too easy to mix up the varieties, especially if you get distracted while working. I place my tuber clump on the towel. Next, I place the plant tag into a greenhouse flat and set it on the table. As the individual tubers are separated from the clump, I place them into the flat—thus their tag stays with them during the entire dividing process.

First, I look at the top of the clump for the easiest tubers to remove. Those are the tubers that are connected to the top of the stalk that clearly have an eye. I use Silky Teflon Garden Scissors sold by Hida Tool Company in Berkeley, California (hidatool.com). I make a pie-shaped cut, pushing back into the stalk, releasing my

196

first tuber. If the tail of the tuber breaks while dividing, I cut it off with my snips. I don't trim off the roots at the back end of the tuber because they give the tubers a better head start at planting time. I continue cutting pie-shaped cuts in the stalk around any eyes, releasing individual tubers from the clump. Remember, each tuber must have an eye on the crown to be viable.

Once all the easily accessible tubers are removed, I usually encounter mud and dirt in the center of the clump, so I will return to the wash station for another rinse. Once back at the table I locate and release the remaining tubers that have eyes. Many tubers in an average tuber clump will not have eyes and need to be discarded. In my experience, about 10% of the time a single eye on a tuber crown will be shared by two or three tubers. In this case, saving several tubers together with a fused crown and one eye is fine; there is no requirement that dividing yields only individual tubers.

It can be challenging to handle and divide a tuber clump if it is large and heavy. In that case, I will cut the clump into sections. To do this, I make a horizontal cut to remove the old plant stalk from the tuber mass. This section of the clump (the part above ground during the growing season) is thick and woody. Cutting through with a pair of garden shears or scissors can be challenging.

Instead of shears, I use a cordless oscillating multi-tool. It has a serrated blade that vibrates back and forth and easily cuts through the woody parts. I use a 2.5-inch (6.3 cm) wide blade made for cutting wood. This tool has made a profound difference in the ease and speed of my tuber dividing. It also saves me from

Making a pie-shaped cut to release a single tuber.

197

hand injuries and muscle soreness after a long day of dividing. I use a DeWalt 20V multi-tool; however, many other manufacturers sell these tools. If I was not using a multi-tool, I would make this first cut using long-handled pruning loppers.

To divide a large tuber clump into sections, I cut vertically down through the center of the stalk with the multi-tool dividing the clump into two pieces. This opens up space and gives me a better view of the eyes on the tubers. Sometimes I will divide these two sections in half, resulting in four total sections. I make these cuts only after determining where best to cut without damaging any visible eyes. You can see a couple of videos about dividing tubers on the Kristine Albrecht YouTube channel. Look for videos 89 and 156. You can find a video on dividing pot roots by looking for video 157.

The mother tuber is easily identified and should be discarded. Notice that three tubers on this partial tuber clump were chewed by gophers.

If you have trouble identifying the eyes on the tuber crown, there is an alternative dividing method. Using a knife, scissors, or a multi-tool, make two opposing vertical cuts in the central stem of the tuber mass (the shape of an X). This will transform your tuber clump into four smaller clusters. Each "quartered" section might contain two or three tubers. There is a high probability of having at least one eye in each quarter. By dividing a clump into four parts, you increase your tuber supply without having to identify individual eyes or divide individual tubers. Each quarter section will be planted individually in spring, just like a single tuber. If you are new to dividing tubers and don't have someone experienced to help you, this quartering method could be your ticket! The upside of this method is not having to identify eyes. The downside is that you will have to store more bulky tuber sections over the winter and there is a possibility that one or more sections may not have an eye. You can see a short video about finding tuber eyes on the Kristine Albrecht YouTube channel. Look for video 92.

If your tuber clump is from a plant grown from a tuber (not a cutting or a seed), you should see the "mother" tuber nestled within the clump. This original tuber propagated the plant before the new tubers formed around the stalk. The mother tuber can typically be identified by its darker skin or by the visible variety name written on the tuber. Sometimes it is in poor shape and rotting. When you have finished dividing all the viable tubers, I recommend disposing of the mother tuber. It used its energy to generate a plant and a host of new tubers. Its job is done.

Once divided, tubers need to be dried for 8 to 24 hours. This allows the cutting wounds to heal over; if tubers are stored while wet they can develop mold on the cut surfaces. I spread the tubers in a single layer in their

I dry my tubers on a table with the tuber crowns hanging off the table edge. This helps the crowns dry completely.

greenhouse flat and move them into a shady outdoor spot or indoors to dry. Don't let these tubers dry out longer than 24 hours, as they will start to shrivel. If your tubers are very small, a four to six-hour drying period is usually enough. Check them often for shriveling or softening. Even though we refer to this step as a drying-out period, we are not looking to take moisture from the tuber. We are only looking to heal the cutting wounds and dry the skin so the tubers can be labeled for storage. Keep the plant tag in the flat with the tubers during drying. If you have too many tubers to spread out in one flat, use a second flat and split the tubers between them. Be sure to add a second plant tag to the new flat. I would refrain from spreading tubers out with other varieties on a table. In my experience, it is easy to get the varieties mixed up.

After drying, the tubers need to be labeled. There are two ways to do this, individually or by the container. For individually marking tubers, I have used three different types of pens: a black Sharpie, a garden marker, or a surgical marking pen. Surgical markers are designed for hospitals to write surgical instructions on human skin. The surgical pens I use are made by Viscot and are available online. I typically don't label tubers individually because I divide three to four thousand tubers each year. Instead, I put my tubers into plastic shoe boxes with a single label on the outside. Varieties are not mixed. Only one variety goes into each box. Because the label on the outside of the box can get dislodged, I place a plastic plant tag with the variety name inside each box as a backup. If in the spring, I choose to sell tubers or donate them to my local dahlia society, I will label each tuber individually at that time.

I'm a big believer in learning from books and videos; however, dividing tubers is best understood by working alongside an experienced grower. I learned to divide tubers from growers in my dahlia society, who had been dividing tubers for 40–50 years. If you are new to dividing tubers and have a dahlia society nearby, join in for one-on-one instruction from a seasoned grower. Having an expert looking over your shoulder and showing you the right moves up close is the best way to build confidence and become proficient yourself.

TUBER STORAGE

One of the most common dahlia questions I hear is, "how should I store my tubers over the winter." Unfortunately, there is no one answer because the best techniques and materials will depend on your climate and your available storage facility. After years of trial and error, I have developed a

THE DAHLIA HOTEL

A friend who grew up in Sweden told me that the most Swedish city dwellers live in apartments and do not have access to a basement or a garage. Even though Sweden is far to the north with cold winters, most people have access only to heated spaces in their homes, making storing dahlia tubers over the winter difficult. That's where the "Dahlia Hotel" comes in. Someone in Sweden has started a business renting out space in a climate-controlled environment for dahlia growers. For a fee, growers check their tubers into the Dahlia Hotel for a nice cool winter rest.

system that works well for me. Your job is to experiment and find what works for you in your climate.

Storing tubers successfully over the winter is about controlling temperature and humidity. Tubers cannot tolerate freezing temperatures. If you live in a cold climate, protecting them from temperatures below 32° F (0° C) is critical, or they will die. Likewise, if your storage space regularly gets above 50° F (10° C), your tubers will struggle to remain dormant until spring. Humidity is a bit like Goldilocks and the Three Bears. You want the moisture level to be not too wet nor too dry, but "just right." Too much moisture can rot or mold your tubers. An environment that is too dry will cause the tubers to shrivel up. A good target humidity level is 90% or slightly above. I recommend buying an inexpensive hygrometer to keep an eye on your humidity levels. In addition to the proper temperature and humidity, tubers like those conditions to be consistent. A storage space where temperatures rise and fall during the day or over the weeks is not as good as one that stays at a constant temperature all winter.

I live in a warm climate. I can experience 75° F (24° C) daytime highs in December and January, and no room or barn on my property is cool enough to consistently keep my tubers dormant at 42° F (5.5° C)

At left: Arrangement and photo by Emily Avenson.

through the winter. Therefore, I store my tubers in an insulated shed held at 42° F (5.5° C) with an air conditioner and a Coolbot controller (storeitcold.com). I didn't build the cool shed just for tubers. It is used in the summer as a cut flower cooler. Growers in cold climates have the opposite problem. They use space heaters in their storage sheds to keep their tubers from freezing on the coldest nights.

I haven't always had an insulated shed with an air conditioner. For years I searched around for cool locations where I could store my tubers. For several years I stored them in the crawl space under my house. This was not ideal. The crawl space never got cool enough, so my tubers sprouted early. It was also uncomfortable and difficult to check on the tubers as the crawl space was small. One year I stored my tubers in an old refrigerator. That worked well until the refrigerator stopped working and all the tubers rotted! Refrigerators tend to dry out the air inside them, so tubers stored this way must be wrapped in plastic or sealed in boxes with a moist storage medium. One year I stored my tubers in a shed that was in constant shade. This was less than ideal as the unseasonably warm winter days raised the temperatures too high and many of my tubers sprouted early.

One of the most common mistakes I see new growers make is using their garage for tuber storage. It is a rare garage with a consistent internal temperature of 42 to

201

45° F (5.5-10° C) and a high level of humidity. Many of our garages feel cool in the summer; however, if the house furnace is located in the garage, it will heat up considerably when the furnace is running. In colder climates, most garages can get below freezing, killing stored tubers. In warmer climates, garages, particularly those with a south-facing wall, get too warm in the winter for proper tuber storage.

Strategies for keeping tubers at the proper humidity depend on your location. I live in a relatively dry climate. I store my tubers in slightly moist peat moss and monitor them regularly, adding small amounts of moisture as needed. My friends in the Pacific Northwest have too much humidity in their storage sheds. They store tubers in dry sawdust and use dehumidifiers to keep the tubers from rotting.

Finally, good tuber storage requires consistent monitoring. I check my stored tubers every three weeks. I open the boxes, check the moisture levels, and look for rot or shriveling. If my storage medium gets too dry, I add a teaspoon of water and check again in a week. If the medium is too wet, I crack open the box lid and let some moisture evaporate. What is important here is getting in the habit of examining tubers all winter long. You can see a short video of me checking my tubers on the Kristine Albrecht YouTube channel. Look for video 127.

I learned how to store my tubers from long-time dahlia growers in my area. There is no substitute for the wisdom of a local grower who has tried everything and settled on what works for your particular climate. If there is a dahlia society in your area, that could be a rich source of tuber storage advice.

Finally, we may all encounter a variety that does not store well. If you have tubers from a variety that did not survive winter storage, it may not be your fault; the culprit is usually the size and shape of the tubers. Varieties that make small and thin tubers can be tricky to store. These tubers, sometimes as thin as a pencil, have trouble retaining moisture and tend to wither and die in storage. With these tubers, I use plastic wrap. I start with an 18-inch (45 cm) piece of wrap. I place the first tuber at one end and wrap around the tuber once. I then turn the ends in, set another tuber next to it, and wrap it around once. Using this method, I can wrap several tubers in one piece of wrap. This method ensures that the tubers inside the wrap are separated by a layer of plastic. If they were all wrapped together and touching each other, one rotten tuber could spread rot to all the others.

Some growers use plastic wrap for storing all of their tubers. This saves space because a storage medium is not required. This reduction in bulk allows some growers to store their tubers in an old refrigerator kept between 40 and 45° F (4.4 and 7.2 C), which would be prohibitive with most bulky storage methods. In addition, plastic wrap does an excellent job of holding the tuber's natural moisture in dry climates. Likewise, plastic wrap keeps excess climatic moisture from getting into the tubers in wet climates. For these reasons, it can be a practical storage solution for many climatic conditions. It is not used universally by growers because it is time-consuming and challenging to recycle or reuse.

HOW I STORE TUBERS IN MY CLIMATE

I have tried several tuber storage mediums over the years, including vermiculite, plastic wrap, and peat moss. I finally settled on peat moss for storing most of my tubers for four reasons. First, it is acidic. That acid environment discourages the growth of mold and fungus that can rot tubers. Second, it is faster than plastic wrap and not as dusty as vermiculite. Third, it is reusable each year. I store my peat moss in 32-gallon (121 L) garbage cans with lids between winters. Finally, peat holds moisture which is critical in my dry climate.

PEAT ALTERNATIVES

I store my tubers over the winter in peat moss. I purchased it years ago and reuse it each year. It has been the best storage medium I have found for my climate. However, more growers are choosing to avoid peat. In parts of the world, peat is banned or being phased out of commerce.

One peat alternative I have experience with is vermiculite. Agricultural vermiculite is a mineral mined from the earth and baked at high temperatures. The baking process makes the mineral expand like an accordion. This is what gives vermiculite its ability to absorb and hold moisture.

Vermiculite was the storage medium I used for the first several years I grew dahlias. It worked well in my climate but was dusty and sometimes irritated my skin. Vermiculite is not acidic like peat, so it does not have the same anti-fungal properties.

I buy peat moss in the largest vacuum-sealed bag available at my local garden center. When I get home, I unpack it into a 32-gallon (121 L) garbage can. It's been compacted, so first I break it up and fluff it up with a shovel. Next, I determine the moisture level in each load of peat because it can differ. What I am looking for is peat that is slightly moist to the touch, but not dripping wet. If the peat is too moist I leave the lid off the can for a few days to dry it out. If it is too dry I add some water a little at a time as I mix it. Sometimes the moisture level is just right and doesn't require any adjustments.

I store my tubers in inexpensive plastic shoe boxes I buy at my local dollar store. I like them because they are a perfect size, stack well, and are see-through, so I can easily see condensation inside the boxes. At the bottom of each box, I lay down one inch (2.5 cm) of peat moss. I then nestle in enough tubers to fill the bottom of the box. I keep the tubers from touching each other. This will prevent one decaying tuber from spreading rot to the others. Next, I add more peat until the first layer of tubers is covered. I then add another layer of tubers and add more peat on top. I repeat this process until the last tubers are 1.5 inches (3.75 cm) from the top of the box. I then cover them entirely with one inch (2.5 cm) of peat moss, leaving a half inch (1.25 cm) of air space. I do this to protect the top layer of tubers from getting wet if condensation drips from the inside of the box lid. Should there be an excess of moisture dripping, it will land on the peat and soak up the extra moisture instead of dripping directly on a tuber.

I then label the box with the variety name, adding a backup plant tag with the variety name inside the box. Finally, I put the box into a temperature-controlled shed with the box lid sealed tight. The plastic boxes full of tubers get stacked into my cool shed at a temperature of 42° F (5.5° C). I have a humidity monitor and keep the humidity between 90 and 95%.

Storing tubers successfully involves regular monitoring. If I see a box with condensation inside, I open it. If there is more condensation inside the box lid, I know the moisture level is too high. In that case, I put the lid back on the box slightly askew, allowing some moisture to escape. A sampling of those boxes without condensation inside will also get opened. Next, I brush aside some peat moss and pull out a tuber for inspection. I'm checking to see if it is firm and not shriveling. Shriveling is the first sign that the peat is not moist enough. If the tuber is firm, I return it to its box, put the peat back in place, and secure the lid. Ideally, stored tubers stay as firm and hydrated as the day we put them into storage.

If, while checking the boxes, I find tubers that are shriveling, it is usually because the

The first layer of tubers nestled into peat moss.

The first layer of tubers being covered with more peat moss.

Tuber varieties are kept in separate boxes. Each box is labeled.

Boxes full of tubers going into refrigerated storage.

peat is too dry. I will add a teaspoon of water to the peat, close the box lid, and check again in a week. If I find one box with shriveled tubers, I will check all the boxes in storage, assuming there may be more with similar issues. While checking my tubers, I am also looking for any that have rotted. A rotting tuber could affect the other tubers in the same box. If I find a soft and rotted tuber, I will dispose of it along with the peat moss surrounding it. You can see short videos of how I store my tubers on the Kristine Albrecht YouTube channel. Look for video number 98.

Melissa Smith, South Carolina

Melissa Smith of Fraylick Farm in South Carolina lives in a more humid climate than mine. Because winter temperatures are too high for storage in her garage or shed, she stores tubers over winter in her flower cooler as I do. She keeps them between 40 and 45° F (4.4 to 7.5° C) all winter. However, her climate is naturally humid, typically at about 90%. So instead of adding moisture to keep the tubers from shriveling, she reduces the moisture level in her storage boxes by storing tubers in dry peat moss. This dry material absorbs excess moisture and keeps her tubers from rotting.

Galena Berkompas, Washington

Galena Berkompas of Micro Flower Farm in Vancouver, Washington has a cool and humid climate. Unlike me, she doesn't need to add extra moisture to her storage medium. Galena divides her tubers and lets them dry in the shade or indoors for a day before storing them. She treats the cut scars and any shovel wounds with cinnamon before storage. Cinnamon is a natural anti-fungal agent that disrupts fungal cell membranes. She packs her tubers into plastic bags filled with dry vermiculite and stores them in her flower cooler between 40 and 42° F (4.4 to 5.5° C). In her climate, the humidity in her cooler stays between 90 and 99%. Because

vermiculite is dusty, Galena wears a respirator whenever she works with it.

David Hall, England

David Hall of Halls of Heddon in Northumberland, England digs up his tuber clumps in November, washes them with water, and dries them upside-down on open benches in a glasshouse for three to five days. His November temperatures are usually relatively mild, and the humidity is high enough that the tubers won't dry and shrivel. He then turns the clumps right-side-up and trims off the smaller roots and broken pieces.

He lines the benches and shelves in his glasshouse with aluminum foil under a thin layer of compost. His tuber clumps are set on top of the compost, where they remain in the open until the end of December. He does not pack them away in boxes or crates. In early January, he turns on heat mats that warm the tubers in preparation for making cuttings. While the temperatures outside are between 39 and 41° F (4 and 5° C), the tubers inside are warmed to about 64° F (18° C). He does not mist the tubers or provide any additional moisture during this time. The native humidity is enough to keep the tubers from drying out.

Because David is using his tuber clumps to make rooted cuttings, they are out of the ground for a much shorter time than they are for most dahlia growers. That is because making cuttings is a winter activity long before the weather outside is appropriate for planting.

Heather Henson, Canada

Heather Henson of Boreal Blooms in Cold Lake, Alberta digs up her tubers in mid-October, after Canadian Thanksgiving. She dries them on top of the soil for 48 hours before collecting them for storage. During this drying period, her tuber clumps are inside a high hoop tunnel and kept from freezing with propane heaters. Heather doesn't wash her tubers because, in mid-

Unnamed 'KA's' seedling.

'KA's Rosie Jo'.

October, any water sprayed on the tubers or the ground would turn into a sheet of ice. Instead, after drying, the unwashed tuber clumps are placed in Rubbermaid tubs filled with spruce wood shavings. Heather drills small holes in the tubs to give them a bit of airflow. The tub lids keep moisture in so the tubers won't dry out.

Her tubs are stored in a heated garage at 41° F (5° C) for the winter. Heather checks the tuber clumps occasionally. If a tub seems too wet, she will loosen the lid allowing some moisture to escape. She will add a small amount of water if a tub appears too dry. Heather uses spruce wood shavings because they are a renewable resource, available at her local feed store, and inexpensive. In the spring, Heather reuses the shavings as bedding for her chickens.

She brings the tuber clumps out of her garage four weeks before her projected planting date and places them on shallow trays. She uses greenhouse flats, but metal roasting trays also work. Next, she partially covers the clumps with wood shavings or potting mix moistened by a light sprinkle of water. Finally, the trays are placed indoors in a warm sunny spot. The increased heat, light, and moisture causes them to sprout. She then moves her sprouted tuber clumps out into the field and divides them as she digs her holes and plants them. Dividing tuber clumps once they have sprouted takes the guesswork out of identifying eyes on tuber crowns. If one has the space to store whole clumps, this technique could be helpful for newer growers who often find it challenging to identify small eyes on freshly-dug tubers.

Heather grows 400–500 dahlias each year but does not sell tubers. Therefore, she doesn't need to multiply her tuber stock each year. If she dug and divided all her tuber clumps, she would have far more tubers than needed. Instead, Heather digs up only the number of clumps she estimates she will need the following spring. The rest are left underground. In her climate, the tubers left in the soil will freeze. When the ground thaws out, they will rot and break down, feeding the organisms in her soil. I envy Heather's ability to do this. In my warm climate, if I don't need a tuber clump, I have to remove it, or it will re-sprout in spring. Heather's sub-freezing temperatures allow her to leave the soil undisturbed, feed her soil organisms, and save labor.

Lorelie Merton, Australia

After dividing her tuber clumps in the fall, Lorelie Merton of Florelie Seasonal Flowers in Bungaree, Victoria stores them unwashed in crates filled with potting mix. Her crates have ventilation holes on the sides and no lid on top. Tubers are nestled into the potting mix and kept moist with an occasional sprinkle of water from a watering can. Lorelie originally moistened her stored tubers using a spray bottle. However, she stores as many as 30,000 tubers, and pumping the spray bottle all day left her with sore fingers. Without lids on her storage crates, Lorelie and her helper Hannah keep a close eye on their tubers and wet them down when needed so they won't dry out.

In years past, Lorelie stored her tubers in sawdust. It was inexpensive and readily available, however, she found it a bit hydrophobic. It resisted taking on sufficient moisture. She has found the potting mix easier to work with and better at absorbing and maintaining a constant level of moisture.

Lorelie's farm is visited by mischievous birds who delight in pulling up plant tags in the soil. For this reason, she uses sturdy copper tags secured at eye level on the tops of metal poles. Once her tubers are dug, divided, and stored away, the copper tags from the field go inside her tuber crates to identify each variety. When storing tubers, it is important not to rely on paper or cardboard. Rodents and insects love to chew on paper goods.

Gabriela Salazar, Mexico

Gabriela Salazar is in the mountains west of Mexico City. After a five-month blooming season, she digs and divides her tubers in November. After her tubers dry for a day or two, she packs them in vegetable crates filled with dry peat moss. The tops of the boxes are covered with a metal wire mesh to protect against hungry mice. She then stores her tuber crates in a dark and cool shed. She does not use an air conditioner or a cooling system. The natural humidity in her mountain climate keeps her tubers from drying and shriveling. She checks on her tubers once a month to ensure they are not rotting or drying out.

HOW PLANT CARE AFFECTS TUBER GROWTH

Most growers consider that their plants will always produce robust tubers for propagation the following season. However, good tuber production is not a guarantee. It is greatly affected by how we care for our plants all season.

To understand tubers, we must explore how our plants produce and use nutrients. Fundamentally, every part of a plant is either a "source" or a "sink." Sources are plant parts that make sugars and amino acids, the nutrients plants use to function and grow. Sinks are the plant parts where those nutrients are used or stored. The plant's sinks compete for precious water and nutrients.

When first planted, before the start of photosynthesis, the mother tuber is the future plant's only source. The starch it holds is converted to sugar and amino acids that fuel the growth of first shoots and leaves. Once photosynthesis starts, leaves replace the original tuber as the plant's primary source. Instead of nutrients flowing from the tuber, they start flowing from the leaves. These nutrients build new stems, branches, leaves, flower buds, and, ultimately, a new set of tubers underground. With all of these sinks in competition, the plant must prioritize where its energy goes.

Once blooms start to open, they become the plant's most demanding sinks, especially pollen production in the disc center. Sexual reproduction is the plant's ultimate goal. Ensuring robust pollen and stigma production takes precedence over everything else.

The bloom's sink demands become even stronger after pollination when the seed head forms. Producing seeds takes a massive investment of nutrients from a plant. If the plant is giving priority to blooms, seeds, and seed head production, what plant part is losing in this competition? Tubers. Tubers get the share of nutrients that are left over when the plant has ensured its blooms and seed heads get what they need.

So, if our dahlia plants are giving buds, blooms, and seeds, the highest priority, how can we encourage our plants to divert energy to tuber production? Simple. We lower the plant's floral sink by disbudding, cutting blooms, and deadheading. Disbudding is described in detail on page 114, but in short, it removes the two smaller side buds on every bloom. Because dahlias typically form three floral buds at each node, disbudding eliminates two-thirds of the floral sink on our plants, freeing up nutrients for tuber production. If growers do nothing else, simply disbudding will make for better blooms and more robust tubers.

Dahlias are called cut-and-come-again plants. That is not just a description of how they work. It's also a prescription for how we should care for them. The more we cut our blooms, the lower the floral sink, and the more energy goes to tuber production. One of the most important things we can do for tuber growth is deadheading mature blooms. Because the largest sink is pollen and seed production, we invite poor tuber production when we allow mature blooms to go to seed.

A robust tuber clump from a plant that was disbudded, cut from, and deadheaded.

This does not mean we can't collect seeds or hybridize with our plants. It just means we should do so in a planned way. For example, we should remove any spent blooms we are not using for seed production and only leave intact those we plan to collect seed from. I see the results of lowering the floral sink on my farm. I'm a cut flower farmer. In peak season, after a day of cutting, only a few dozen mature blooms may be left on my 1,800 plants. I also disbud all my plants, both stock varieties and new seedlings. As a result, my tuber clumps are typically robust.

In contrast, I have a friend who grows many of the same varieties as I do on a plot nearby. However, this grower doesn't cut the blooms or disbud them. Instead, blooms are left for display on the plants. I am dazzled by the display of flowers at all stages of maturity when we visit this plot. It is a beautiful sight. At the season's end, however, the plot yields tubers that are small and few in number. In addition, they often store poorly over the winter. My friend's floral sink demand is so great there is little nutrition left for the lowest priority sink: tubers.

I recently heard from a grower disappointed by the few tubers he was able to harvest from plants he grew from cuttings. I asked about his dahlia care and discovered that the plants in question were planted only for tuber production, not for blooms. As a result, these plants were treated differently than all the other plants in his plot. He never cut the blooms, he never disbudded, and he never deadheaded. His only interest in those plants was harvesting tubers, so he ignored the plants and left them on their own all season long. Without realizing it, he sabotaged his own goal.

Like all things related to dahlias, tuber production is also based on the variety you grow. Some varieties make lots of tubers and others make very small or very few tubers. If you are growing a poor tuber producer, cutting blooms, disbudding, and deadheading will help. However, tuber production could still be meager based on that variety's particular traits. Of course, there are other factors that also lead to more robust tubers. I briefly describe some here.

SOIL

The better your soil, the more nutrients your plants can take up and the more excess nutrients they can devote to tuber production. I recommend a soil test in the fall and amending your soil based on any deficiencies the test reveals.

SUNLIGHT AND WATER

Dahlias need at least six hours of sun per day. Dahlia plants use light to make sugars and amino acids necessary for tuber growth. Therefore, a plant struggling in low light will underperform in producing blooms, seeds, and tubers. Likewise, water is needed for photosynthesis. Without water, dahlias won't generate enough nutrients to produce healthy tubers.

MULCH

Mulch your soil to retain moisture and water your dahlias regularly. A good layer of mulch will also discourage weed growth which will compete with your dahlias and rob plants of the energy needed to make tubers.

DISEASE AND PESTS

If a plant has been negatively affected by pest pressure or the leaves are covered in powdery mildew, it will struggle to produce excess nutrients. A weakened plant will put its limited nutrients into flowers and seeds, not tubers. I recommend spraying your plants early in the season with horticultural oil to keep powdery mildew, aphids, and thrips at bay. I spray every 10 days. Start spraying before you see mildew, when your plants are about 12 inches (30 cm) tall.

VARIETY

Every dahlia variety has a unique blend of genes from its two parents. As a result, this unrepeatable variety has a unique form, color, and bloom size. This combination of genes also determines how well it produces tubers. Some varieties, like 'Cafe au Lait', produce lots of tubers, while others don't.

TUBER CHALLENGES

SPROUTING

What happens if, over the winter, your tubers develop long white shoots that look like a bag of sprouting potatoes? This occurs when stored tubers are too warm or exposed to too much light. To "sleep" all winter, tubers must be stored in a dark place at 40-45° F (4.4-7.2° C).

The best thing to do if your tubers sprout is to cut off the shoots leaving 1/8 of an inch (.31 cm) on the tuber and get them into a cool, dark environment. You can often store them in the crawl space of a house, in an unheated basement, or in a root cellar. If none of those places are available or cold enough, you could keep them in your refrigerator or a refrigerator in your garage. They might all fit in a dormitory-sized refrigerator if you have just a few tubers. If you store them in a refrigerator, be sure to seal them in a plastic container with a lid that fits tight. Ensure your storage medium is moistened with a small amount of water, and regularly check on the tubers.

SHRIVELING

Due to time constraints, a grower sometimes digs up their tubers, throws them in a pile, and leaves them for several days to weeks. When they check on them again, they might find shriveled tubers. This happens especially in warmer climates. Shriveling is a result of the tubers drying out. Tubers typically have the proper amount of moisture they need to get through the winter and send up a shoot in the spring. They can do this without any added water. If kept too warm or dry, however, they will lose their moisture to the environment and shrivel. Tubers don't always come back from being severely dried out; however, you can usually save a slightly shriveled tuber. In this instance, I would get them into storage boxes with a lid and moistened storage medium. I would bring them to a dark, cool place at 40-45° F (4.4-7.2° C). After a week, I would check on them, and if they have plumped up a bit, I would continue storing them as is. If they haven't plumped up, I'd add a teaspoon of water (for a shoebox-size container) and check them again in a week.

An alternative method to help shriveled tubers get through the winter is to wrap them in plastic wrap and store them in a cool, dark place. Again this should be somewhere close to a constant 40-45° F (4.4-7.2° C) as possible. One good strategy for shriveled tubers is to divide your stock in half. Wrap half in plastic wrap (described on page 202) and place the other half in a moist storage medium. This way, you give your tubers two different treatments to help them survive. If one method fails, hopefully, the other method will succeed. Don't throw out a slightly shriveled tuber. They can spout perfectly well in the spring.

FREEZING

Dahlia tubers cannot tolerate freezing temperatures. If your tubers freeze in storage, there is nothing you can do; they are damaged beyond saving and will soon turn mushy. If you suspect your tubers have frozen but are unsure, place them in a storage medium and into a dark, cool place that stays consistently at 40-45° F (4.4-7.2° C). Check on them in a week. If they are mushy, they froze. If they are firm, they may still be viable.

TUBER SIZE AND COLOR

Tubers come in all shapes, sizes, and colors. Some are large and long. Others are

Tuber size and color can vary.

Tuber color also varies by variety. Most of my tubers are light brown. However, I have some varieties that produce very light tan tubers. One of my varieties, 'KA's Rosie Jo', often produces slightly red tubers.

LENTICELS

I include tuber lenticels here under the subject of challenges because often growers believe they cause harm when, in fact, they are harmless. Lenticels are small raised scars or scabby-looking bumps that can form on the outside of a tuber. They arise when a tuber sits in soil that is saturated with water. The lenticels are small air holes that allow a tuber to exchange gases when underwater. Lenticels look bad, but they will not interfere with the functioning of a tuber.

short and round. The shape of your tubers will not affect how they perform. The only time size is an issue is if a tuber is so thin that it may not have enough moisture inside to survive winter storage.

A dahlia tuber with lenticels. Photo by Paula Fisher.

Me with an 'Aggie White' bloom.

'KA's Mocha Maya'.

12. Common Dahlia Questions

CAN YOU PLANT THE ORIGINAL TUBER AFTER TAKING CUTTINGS?

A tuber stores energy for producing shoots that will turn into plants. If a tuber produces two or three cuttings, that tuber still has enough reserve energy to be planted in the ground and grow a healthy plant. However, I throw tubers out once they have produced ten cuttings. This is because, after so many cuttings, it is in a weakened state, and any sprouts will typically be too thin and small to grow into a robust plant.

WHEN SHOULD I PINCH OUT MY YOUNG PLANTS?

If your variety produces large or giant blooms, you will want to pinch them out after three leaf pairs. For smaller or medium bloom varieties, pinch your plants after four to five leaf pairs. For more on this, see page 109.

WILL I HAVE FEWER BUDS OR BLOOMS IF I DISBUD?

The answer is yes for the total number of buds but if we are talking about mature blooms, the answer is no. This is because the secondary buds bloom later than the central bud, so the two secondary buds will be closed when you cut the mature central bloom (and the secondary buds come off the plant with it). Florists and designers usually remove these immature buds. Some will use them for other purposes like boutonnieres. Removing the secondary buds during disbudding does not reduce the number of mature blooms you can cut. However, if you like the immature buds in your arrangements, you may not want to disbud your plants. More on page 114.

IS IT NORMAL THAT ONLY ABOUT HALF MY PLANTED TUBERS SPROUT?

There are many reasons a tuber won't sprout after three to four weeks underground, including rot, gophers, or no viable eye on the tuber crown. In addition, a tuber could be too dried out to sprout or have a broken neck. I recommend digging up those tubers that are not sprouting and looking at what is happening. If there is a sprout, but it's just slow growing, you can replant the tuber. If rot is found (the tuber is soft when squeezed) and part of the tuber is still firm and healthy, it could be saved. Cut off the rotten portion and replant the tuber. For this method to work, the tuber neck and crown must be intact and firm, and there must be a viable eye. Soil temperature and moisture also play a role in how fast a tuber will sprout. Soil temperatures of 50 to 60 degrees F (10 to 15 C) are best for sprouting tubers. Likewise, soil that receives tubers must be moist. Planting a tuber in very dry soil will not result in a sprout.

WILL MY TUBERS GROW A STRONGER PLANT IF I DIVIDE THEM INTO SMALL CLUMPS RATHER THAN INDIVIDUAL TUBERS?

While a small tuber clump won't necessarily make a stronger plant, there can be advantages over single tubers. First, if dividing tubers is new to you, there is a greater possibility you will get an eye with a small clump than separating a clump into individual tubers. Second, if your clump has only one eye, all the tubers on that clump will provide energy to get the plant off to a good start. Third, if one of the tubers in your clump rots, the other tubers will support the growth of your small plant. Finally, if you have gophers in your garden, a cluster of several tubers can survive a gopher attack better than an individual tuber.

'Bloomquist Alan'.

WILL DAHLIAS GROWN FROM A SEED MAKE BLOOMS JUST LIKE THE PARENT?

Not likely. Dahlias grown from a tuber are clones—the blooms will look just like the parent plant the tubers came from. Dahlias grown from seed are unique and unrepeatable. Like a litter of puppies, they can be completely unlike their parents, differing in size, shape, or color.

HOW LONG SHOULD I WAIT TO DIG UP TUBERS AFTER CUTTING DOWN MY PLANTS?

The short answer is not long…one or two days at most. It is best to leave your plants intact until you are ready to dig the tubers out. Then cut down the plants the day of digging or the day before you dig. This ensures that rain will not collect inside the hollow stems and potentially rot your tubers. It also ensures that if digging is delayed there won't be time for your plant to re-sprout and take energy from the tubers underground. More on page 189.

WHY DO MY SEEDLINGS PRODUCE OPEN-CENTER BLOOMS?

There are two primary reasons that seedlings produce open-center blooms. First, open centers are a dominant trait in dahlias. The original species dahlias from Mexico and Central America have open centers. Second, suppose the seeds you are germinating were open-pollinated by bees. In that case, they have a very high likelihood of being open-centered. Bees instinctively seek out the most accessible flowers to gather nectar and pollen. Those will always be the open-center varieties. Closed-center dahlias are hard for bees to access because the pollen is hidden.

IF I AM NOT GROWING FOR CUT FLOWERS, SHOULD I STILL DISBUD?

This is a personal decision. I recommend disbudding even if you are not a cut flower farmer or a dahlia exhibitor. Disbudded blooms are bigger than non-disbudded blooms. Also, the attention you give your plants while disbudding will provide you insights into their health and status. When I disbud, I inevitably find deformed buds that need to be removed and insect pests I can eliminate. Finally, disbudding your plants eliminates two-thirds of the floral "sink," resulting in better tuber production. There is more on this subject on page 114.

WILL PLANTS GROWN FROM SEED MAKE BLOOMS AND TUBERS THE FIRST YEAR?

Yes, dahlia plants grown from seed will produce blooms and make tubers all in their first year. If tuber production is a priority, consider being vigilant about disbudding, cutting blooms often, and deadheading your plants.

WHAT IS THE WHITE POWDER ON MY DAHLIA LEAVES?

Dahlia plants in many climates become infected with powdery mildew on their leaves. It is an airborne fungus that is very difficult to avoid. Growers with infected plants have done nothing wrong. The spores of this fungus are in the air just about everywhere. Starting a spray regimen with horticultural oil early in the season will discourage the mildew and reduce the total mildew load. In addition, stripping the lower leaves of mature plants will increase the airflow and reduce powdery mildew. Read more about powdery mildew on page 139.

WHY IS MY TWINE SAGGING?

Twine made from natural materials like cotton, jute, or hemp will stretch when wet. They may be tight when installed, but sag as they pick up moisture from the air or rain. I recommend using a 1/8" (3.5 mm) polypropylene twine for corralling dahlia plants because it does not stretch and can be used over and over, year after year. Baling twine also works well.

CAN I CUT MY IMMATURE SEED HEADS OFF THE STEM AND HAVE THEM RIPEN INDOORS IN A JAR OF WATER?

Making seeds for the next generation is the most energy-intensive task a dahlia plant will undertake in its short lifetime. The plant feeds the developing seeds sugars, amino acids, hormones, and starches. When we cut a seed head from the plant, those nutrients and energy sources are severed. Putting a severed seed head in water may keep it hydrated, but it won't provide it with the energy and nutrients it needs to make healthy seeds.

WHY ARE THERE ANTS ON MY PLANTS?

Aphids are tiny arthropods that produce a sweet sticky exudate called honeydew that attracts hungry ants. So if you have an ant infestation on your plants, you might have aphids. Read more about aphids on page 159.

WHAT IS THE AVERAGE FAILURE RATE WHEN PLANTING TUBERS?

In my experience, planting tubers has a ten to twenty percent failure rate. The most common failure is tuber rot. In addition, some tubers never sprout because they do not have an eye (growth bud).

DO I HAVE TO DIG UP MY TUBERS EVERY YEAR?

I recommend digging up your tubers yearly, but if you want to leave them underground over the winter, you can, as long as they won't freeze or rot in your climate and you don't have gophers. If you plan to leave tubers underground for the winter, I recommend cutting your plants down to within two to four inches (5 to 10 cm) of ground level. The stalks of dahlia plants are hollow, like a straw. If the ends of the stalks are not covered, the rain will collect inside them and could rot your tubers. Covering the ends of the stems with an aluminum foil cap is an easy way to keep water out.

WHY ARE MY PLANTS SHORTER THAN OTHERS I'VE SEEN?

There can be several reasons that a dahlia plant does not grow tall. First, it could be varietal. Some varieties don't grow tall. 'Cafe au Lait' is a good example. In my garden, it is always one of the shortest plants. Second, it could be poor soil or a lack of essential nutrients. A soil test would answer that question. Third, it could be that the plant is struggling due to pests or a lack of water or light. Fourth, plants that experience high summer temperatures will grow shorter than those in cooler climates. Finally, it could be from root competition if the plant is located near a big hedge or planted near a tree.

MY PLANTS NEVER BLOOMED. WILL THE TUBERS BE VIABLE NEXT YEAR?

Yes, dahlia plants may not bloom in a single season because they were planted late, they were planted in the shade, or because of a cold summer. This will not affect the viability of the tubers dug up at the end of the season. Provided they have viable eyes, they will produce plants the following year.

WHY ARE SOME OF THE SPROUTS FROM MY TUBERS RED OR PURPLE INSTEAD OF GREEN?

Some dahlia varieties have darker stems caused by the chemical anthocyanin. This is the same chemical that makes the color of dahlia petals. So it is normal to have dark reddish or purple dahlia sprouts.

WHAT IS THE BEST MULCH FOR DAHLIAS?

Mulch is a local product. The best mulch in your area may differ from what is best elsewhere. Ideally, an inexpensive agricultural byproduct near you can be used as a mulch to keep moisture in the soil and retard weed growth. In my area, the best mulch is rice straw. The mulches you want to avoid for dahlia beds are wood chips and hay. Wood chips absorb nitrogen from the soil as they break down, and hay has seeds. Wood chips work fine in perennial landscapes that are never disturbed (around evergreen trees and shrubs) but not in dahlia beds where the soil gets disturbed at least twice a year.

WHILE DISBUDDING, CAN I ALSO REMOVE THE LEAVES CLOSEST TO THE BLOOM?

I have often been asked this question. It feels right because when you harvest a bloom, you will ultimately strip off the leaves, so why not save time and do it while disbudding? You don't want to do this. In addition to water, it takes sugar, amino acids, and hormones for our plants to produce a bloom. Plants are efficient in how they use their resources. Instead of transporting nutrients to the bloom, our plants use the leaves closest to each bloom as the primary nutrient source. If we strip the leaves closest to the bloom when it is in bud form, we will eliminate their primary energy source, and the resulting bloom might suffer.

WHAT IS THE DIFFERENCE BETWEEN COMPOST AND MULCH?

Compost is made of organic matter that is in various states of decay. It can be made from manure, plant material, food scraps, or lawn trimmings. Compost needs a proper balance between green and brown material for the decomposition process to be complete. Mulch is simply any material that covers the surface of the soil. It need not be decomposed. Most mulches are made from organic matter like leaves or straw.

WHY DO SOME OF MY WHITE DAHLIAS TURN BROWN?

Color in dahlia petals serves many functions for the plant. One of those is as sunscreen to protect the next generation of seeds. What our eyes see as white petals is actually an absence of pigment. That lack of pigment makes white dahlias susceptible to sunburn, especially in hot weather. One remedy for browning petals is to shade white dahlias during the hottest part of the year, using tall stakes and shade cloth or with umbrellas. I use a 30% blocking shade cloth over my white varieties.

I PLANTED IN 4-INCH (10 CM) POTS. SHOULD I STORE THE POT ROOTS INSIDE THE PLASTIC POTS OR REMOVE THEM BEFORE WINTER STORAGE?

Either method will work. I typically store my pot roots in their 4-inch (10 cm) plastic pots. Then, I use a silver Sharpie felt pen to write the variety name on the black pot. I also use a black marker to put the name on any tuber parts that broke out of the pot. If the plastic pot falls off in storage, I can still identify the variety.

WHY DO YOU SOMETIMES PLANT IN SMALL SINK POTS?

As a dahlia breeder, I pull out and discard over 95% of the first-year seedlings I plant in mid to late season. By the season's end, the only seedlings left growing will be the small percentage I wish to keep and grow again. As a result, I plant my seedlings very close together. If those seedlings were planted in the ground, their roots would intertwine. This would make removing them difficult and disturb their neighboring plants' roots. Growing the first-year seedlings in small plastic sink pots allows me to remove them easily. You can see a short video of me looking at first-year seedlings and removing unwanted plants on the Kristine Albrecht YouTube channel. Look for video 165.

CAN I PLANT A TUBER IN A FOUR-INCH SINK POT JUST LIKE A SEEDLING?

Yes, if the tuber is small enough to fit in the small pot. If you want to try this, I recommend settling your tuber down into high-quality potting soil in your small pot and planting the pot with the top rim at ground level. If you have a tuber that will not fit into a small pot, you can move up to a larger pot and achieve the same result.

WHAT IS A FIRST, SECOND, OR THIRD-YEAR SEEDLING?

When a dahlia seed is germinated and planted, it grows into a unique plant. Unlike a plant from a tuber or a cutting, plants from seeds do not look exactly like the parent plants. The first year a plant from seed is grown, it is called a first-year seedling. If the breeder digs and stores its tubers and grows them the following year, those plants are called second-year seedlings. Second-year seedlings are clones of the first-year seedling and are grown a second year to allow the breeder to observe their good and bad traits. A third-year seedling is a clone from tubers saved from the second-year seedling. Sometimes it takes many years of regrowing and observation before a seedling is named and introduced as a new variety.

CAN YOU GROW A COVER CROP WITH TUBERS LEFT IN THE GROUND?

I have never tried this, so I can't speak from direct experience. I always remove my tubers before planting a cover crop. Here is the challenge I see with this plan. Growing a cover crop requires irrigation. Adding water into the soil could rot the tubers below. If you leave tubers in the ground, you want to keep the soil as dry as possible to avoid rot. Keeping the cover crop wet enough to grow and the tubers dry enough to avoid rotting could be challenging.

WHY DOES MY FULLY DOUBLE DAHLIA VARIETY NOW MAKE OPEN-CENTER BLOOMS, AND WILL THE TUBERS MAKE OPEN-CENTER BLOOMS NEXT YEAR?

The answer depends on what exactly is going on with your plant. First, the most common reason a fully double variety makes open-center blooms has to do with the time of year. It is not uncommon for a fully double variety to make open center blooms at the season's beginning and end. Fully double blooms have their best form in midseason. If the reason for the open centers is the time of year, the tubers will most likely produce fully double blooms the following year.

DO YOU DRY YOUR TUBERS BEFORE STORING THEM FOR THE WINTER?

I dig up, wash, and divide my tubers in one day. Then, I let them dry for 8 to 24 hours (depending on tuber size) and pack them up for storage the following day.

WHY DO SOME BLOOMS ONLY OPEN ON ONE SIDE AND NOT THE OTHER?

If you have a bloom that only opens on one side, it is likely caused by an insect pest rather than a genetic defect. In my garden, that is usually thrips. Insects can insert their proboscis into the back of the bloom when it is in bud form. They inject their saliva, which liquefies the cells inside the bud, making it easier to suck out the plant juices. Unfortunately, their saliva is toxic to the plant and damages the bud. When the flower ultimately blooms, the damaged part does not open.

Deformed blooms caused by toxin injection from thrips.

Unnamed 'KA's' seedling.

13. COMMON DAHLIA MYTHS

We live in a time when we are flooded with information. It can be hard to separate the good information from the bad. Here are a few persistent dahlia myths I'd like to address.

PLANTS GROWN FROM CUTTINGS WON'T PRODUCE BLOOMS OR TUBERS IN THE FIRST YEAR.

Growing from cuttings is the preferred method of propagating dahlias for many show growers. It is becoming more common among newer growers who want to multiply their stock or extend their growing season. However, there are two big misconceptions about cuttings. One is that plants from cuttings will not bloom in the first season; this is false. The second is that plants grown from cuttings will not make tubers; this is also false. Dahlia plants grown from cuttings thrive and bloom just like a plant grown from a tuber.

Sometimes a tuber clump from a cutting has a different shape than plants grown from tubers. While it is not always true, the clump stem can be thicker and the tubers themselves smaller. When dividing clumps with thicker stems, I include more of the stem with each tuber to ensure I capture an eye. Sometimes the tubers from a cutting are more compressed into a solid mass. This configuration can make dividing each tuber more challenging.

Like all dahlia characteristics, the size and number of tubers vary by variety. Tuber production is also a function of whether or not a grower disbuds, cuts often, and deadheads spent blooms. The more a grower does these three things the better tuber production will be. You can see a short video of tubers from plants propagated from cuttings on the Kristine Albrecht YouTube channel. Look for video 125.

A HARD FROST IS REQUIRED BEFORE DIGGING UP TUBERS.

There is a widespread belief that we should not dig up tubers until a week or two after a killing frost. This always puzzled me because dahlia growers in warm or tropical climates never get frost. They dig and divide tubers just fine. I dig and divide my tubers months before any frost because, in my location, frost comes after the start of our rainy season. I prefer to dig and divide tubers when the weather is mild and dry rather than cold and wet.

I asked Dr. Keith Hammett, one of the world's dahlia experts, about frost and tubers. He replied that "Tuber production is a consequence of day length. Frost is irrelevant. Day length is the determinant."

Our dahlia plants respond to day length. The days start growing shorter at the summer solstice (June 21st in the Northern Hemisphere and December 21st in the Southern Hemisphere). In response, our plants increase the energy they put towards tubers. So I start digging and dividing about 75 to 90 days after the summer solstice. There is nothing wrong with waiting for frost. Many growers routinely wait for frost and then successfully dig and divide their tubers. But contrary to popular advice, it's not a requirement.

ROOTING CUBES USED WITH CUTTINGS INTERFERE WITH TUBER PRODUCTION.

This is a common comment on social media. This myth proposes that the spongy rooting cubes will somehow thwart, deform, or retard the production of tubers underground. This is false. I've grown over 8,000 cuttings in rooting cubes. At the end of each season, my

'KA's Mocha Jo'.

cuttings make whole, robust tuber clumps with no sign of damage or deformation from the rooting cubes. Robust tuber production depends mainly on the grower's habits and actions like disbudding and deadheading, not the rooting cube (See the section in this book on how plant care affects tuber development on page 210). I sometimes rip small unused parts of a rooting cube off before repotting a cutting into potting soil, because the rooting cube takes time to decompose, and I prefer having less of it in my soil.

DAHLIA TUBERS NEED A LONG REST PERIOD BEFORE REPLANTING.

It is often said that once a dahlia tuber is dug up and divided, it needs a significant rest period before it can be replanted or used in a cutting bed. I have seen several numbers thrown around. Some say tubers need four months of rest. Others say they need three weeks of rest.

The truth is dahlia tubers do not require any rest period. If you had a heated greenhouse or an indoor growing area with enough artificial light to keep dahlias alive over winter, you could dig and divide tubers in the fall and replant them the same day. A fresh tuber is prepared to sprout and produce a new plant immediately. The number of days a tuber takes to re-sprout depends on the cultivar, temperature, and moisture.

WHEN DIVIDING TUBERS, THE WOUNDS FROM CLIPPERS REQUIRE TREATMENT WITH CINNAMON, SULFUR, OR OTHER CHEMICALS BEFORE STORAGE.

While dusting tuber scars with sulfur, cinnamon, or other powders is quite common, it is not necessary. For almost two decades, I have cut my tubers apart, let them dry for a day, and put them into storage without other treatments. I have a very high success rate for overwintering tubers using this method. Dusting a tuber with sulfur or cinnamon cannot hurt; however, I have seen no evidence that it is required for winter storage.

SPRAYING PLANTS WITH WATER ON A HOT DAY WILL BURN THE LEAVES.

Unfortunately, this is a common myth that is quite persistent. Dahlia plants love to be showered with cooling water on a very hot day. This will not burn their leaves. On the contrary, it will protect leaves from drying and burning in the heat.

SEEDS FOR BLUE DAHLIAS CAN BE PURCHASED ONLINE.

Every species of flower has a color in its palette that is missing. Sweet peas don't make yellow flowers. Dahlias don't make blue flowers. To achieve a true blue color, the anthocyanin compound delphinidin must have six hydroxyl groups. The anthocyanin in dahlias has only five hydroxyl groups, which is why dahlias can be mauve, purple, or lavender but not true blue.

Online ads showing true blue dahlias are fake. These images have been digitally altered to look blue. If you purchase these seeds and grow them out, you will not grow a blue dahlia. Sellers have plausible deniability because seeds never grow precisely true to the parent plant. The seller can say, "Each seed is unique, and there is no guarantee you will get a blue dahlia." In 1846 the Caledonia Horticultural Society of Edinburgh committed to a 2,000-pound prize for the first person to hybridize a true blue dahlia. The award was never claimed. Although the prize no longer exists, 2,000 pounds in 1846 is worth $27 million U.S. dollars today. Get busy, people!

Mixed dahlias.

Making friends at the farm.

Keith Hammett, New Zealand

Dr. Keith Hammett, QSM lives on ten acres in the countryside near Auckland, New Zealand. He has been a leading dahlia grower, thinker, author, and breeder for over sixty years. His love of plants started as a British teenager. At age 15, he joined his local horticultural society. By chance, a British champion dahlia exhibitor lived in his neighborhood and agreed to mentor him. Keith became an accomplished dahlia grower and exhibitor. His interest in garden plants translated into a keen interest in biology classes at school. At university, Keith received a botany degree and moved on to study for a Ph.D. While his interests were in plant breeding, the professor who taught it had a teaching style that didn't suit him, so he switched his focus and received his Ph.D. in plant pathology. That program was a good fit, allowing him to grow dahlias, sweet peas, and other plants in the university botany gardens.

Plant pathology took him to New Zealand during a boom in commercial horticulture, particularly the growth of the Kiwi fruit industry. Dr. Hammett had been breeding plants as a hobby back in England and it became an occupation while working on a project to commercialize Pepino Melons. He never stopped breeding plants, and today Keith tends a garden of 800 to 1,000 second-year dahlia seedlings in the warm, semi-tropical climate of New Zealand's North Island. In addition, a nearby farm grows 10,000 to 20,000 first-year seedlings as part of his breeding program. It is often said that breeding dahlias is a numbers game. His large number of seedlings gives him better odds of success than most breeders, but his approach is not random. He has specific goals for his crosses and selects his parent plants carefully.

What sets Keith apart from most other dahlia breeders is his aesthetic choices when selecting new cultivars. For decades he bred dahlias for exhibition. Like most breeders in the late 20th century, varieties were selected to conform to pre-set show standards. The bloom form and purity of color were paramount to winning at dahlia shows. The beauty and diversity of the plant foliage were not valued traits and were not included when dahlias were shown at an exhibition. He likes to refer to the varieties he used to grow for a show as "balls on sticks."

At left: Dr. Keith Hammett in his dahlia patch with his cat "Skitty."
Photo by Trina Woolmore.

Keith might still be breeding dahlias for exhibition had he not visited Mexico in 1989 to observe species dahlias growing in the wild. There, he was struck by their graceful, informal single blooms and the diversity of their foliage. His breeding goals changed. One result of this change is his Mystic series of cultivars with dark foliage. He then developed several dark-leaf collarettes called the Dream series.

When breeding for exhibition in the past, Keith felt like a technician or an engineer. Today he feels more like a visual artist focused on the possible instead of the preordained. The show varieties he used to grow now look too formal and out of place in the garden. Instead, he is looking for varieties that have a more natural appearance.

Keith's garden practice has also changed over the years. Early on, he relied on chemical inputs for plant nutrition and pest control. Over time he has come to view many garden practices and inputs as contributing to planetary pollution and degradation. Today he has more of a live-and-let-live approach to growing his plants. He largely lets his plants fend for themselves. He feels an affinity for the farmer-florists and their approach to organic gardening. He believes it is the best path forward for our planet. Rather than "how to grow dahlias," he now focuses on "how dahlias grow."

Growers new to dahlias may believe they were always as popular as they are now. However, Keith reminds us that not so long ago there was a time when they were despised. He quotes a short poem that says: "Hurrah, hurrah, the frost is here, and the dahlias are dead." Dr. Hammett credits the renewed interest in dahlias largely to cut flower farmers who desire cultivars with new colors and forms. Flower farmers are interested in muted and antique colors that historically have been rejected by show breeders. He believes this influx of growers with a new perspective is healthy for the dahlia community.

Today, Dr. Hammett continues to breed dahlias and sweet peas. He is currently working on breeding sweet peas for scent, which is what they are known for. However, the scent has not historically been a trait that breeders have selected for.

In addition to dahlias, Keith has a love of cats. He was the chairman of one of two cat registries in New Zealand for a time. He also showed cats at one time. However, as with flowers, he questioned whether the show bench was in the animals' best interest. He has observed that some breeding trends with dogs lead to poor health in some breeds. For him, the closer a species is to the wild forms, the more aesthetically beautiful he finds it. He has never ventured into breeding cats because he would have difficulty parting with the kittens.

Keith is on Instagram: @drkeithhammett
He also has a website at: www.drkeithhammett.co.nz

14. DAHLIA CULTURE

DAHLIAS: PAST, PRESENT, AND FUTURE

IN 1788 THE FIRST DAHLIA TUBERS WERE sent from Mexico to the Royal Botanical Garden in Madrid. At the time, they didn't attract much attention. Species dahlia blooms were small and simple flowers with eight petals. The dahlias sent to Spain were a tiny part of a trove of plants sent from the Americas. Spanish botanists shared dahlia tubers and seeds with botanical gardens in other European countries.

In Mexico, various species of wild dahlias grew in small pockets at various altitudes. They did not have the opportunity to cross-breed, as they grew in isolation from each other. In addition, the various strains of species dahlias in Mexico had different numbers of chromosome pairs (ploidy), so even if they were close by, they couldn't cross-breed. Serendipitously, once in the botanic garden in Madrid, two species dahlias crossbred. It is believed these were *D. coccinea and D. pinnata* (both tetraploids). Seeds from these crosses were sent to the botanic gardens in the major capitals of Europe, where the best examples were further crossed. Within thirty years, plant breeders turned the open-center species dahlia (with eight petals) into several doubled cultivars.

By 1828 dahlia plants were selling for as much as $25 in England ($657 today). The first dahlia exhibition was held in Germany in 1836 during a medical and scientific convention. There were 6,000 dahlias on display, representing 200 cultivars. From those early successful hybridizations, dahlia diversity continued to increase.

Dahlias arrived in England in 1802 and were quickly featured in botanical magazines. The National Dahlia Society in England started in 1881, followed by the German Dahlia Society in 1897. The American Dahlia Society (ADS) followed in 1915, with its first show inside the New York Museum of Natural History. In 1921 the Royal Horticultural Society (RHS) in England published the first official book that divided dahlias into 16 different classes. In 1925 the fledgling ADS adopted the RHS classification standards, and so began the modern era of growing show dahlias based on pre-set standards of form and color. Some early U.S. show varieties in the 1910s and '20s were 'Jersey Beauty', 'Lulu Patty', 'Jody Gregory', 'Yankee King',

'Southport Pride', 'Little Playmate', and 'Woodland Peach'.

'Jersey Beauty' was introduced in 1923 after receiving a bench score of 98, reportedly the highest ever given to a new dahlia cultivar. In the U.S., the 1920s marked the high-water mark for the popularity of dahlias. The Great Depression in 1929 followed by World War II reduced the number of dahlia growers; gardeners were encouraged to grow food rather than flowers during these formidable world events.

The website dahliaaddict.com tracks the availability of 3,100 dahlia cultivars in the U.S. and reveals that only one variety listed above, 'Jersey Beauty', is still available today. This is not surprising. Dahlias are loved for their staggering diversity and variability. That diversity results from dahlias being octoploids, with four sets of chromosomes from each parent. They also have transposon elements, or "jumping genes." These are segments of DNA that can move or "jump" from one location to another within the genome. While this gives dahlias great diversity, it also can lead to instability. Dahlia varieties are often lost through mutation in a matter of years or decades. As a result, it is rare to grow a dahlia today that was grown by our grandparents.

There are some exceptions. 'White Aster' is a dahlia cultivar introduced in 1878 and is still grown and available for purchase today. 'Little Beeswings' was hybridized in 1909 and by 1997 was grown by just a single U.S. grower. Since then, it has been multiplied and is now available from several suppliers. 'Stoltz von Berlin' (Pride of Berlin) was first introduced in 1884 when Germany was in the vanguard of dahlia breeding. It is still grown today and is available from a few suppliers. The variety 'Thomas A. Edison' was introduced in 1929 and is still growing in the U.S. It was named after the genius inventor with his approval. Edison was himself an accomplished horticulturist and plant breeder.

Long-lasting dahlia varieties are on the minds of scientists working to sequence the dahlia genome. With funding from donors through the ADS, Dr. Virginia Walbot of Stanford University, Dr. Alex Harkess, and doctoral candidate Zach Meharg of Auburn University and HudsonAlpha Institute for Biotechnology in Alabama are working to sequence the

VARIETY & CULTIVAR

Dahlia growers typically call the various plants they grow varieties. Technically speaking, "variety" refers to naturally occurring plants in the wild. These wild types, also called species dahlias, have a botanical name with a genus (like *Dahlia*) and a species name (like *coccinea*). Botanists always use upper case for genus and lower case for the species name (*D. coccinea*). These variety names are in Latin and are always italicized. There are currently 42 recognized wild dahlia species.

In contrast, a cultivar is a term used to describe a plant that is bred or found in a cultivated area like a farm, garden, nursery, or park. The word cultivar comes from combining the first few letters of the word CULTIvated with the first few letters of the word VARiety. To ensure that cultivars are not confused with varieties, their names are not in Latin. They are capitalized, and they are not italicized. They also have single quotes around them. 'KA's Cloud' is a proper cultivar name.

Unless we grow the native species dahlia from Mexico, we all grow cultivars, not varieties. So, technically, we should be referring to our cultivars, not our varieties, however, because of widespread popular usage, I use these two words interchangeably in this book.

THE LANGUAGE OF FLOWERS

In the mid-1800s, an unspoken language flourished that was based on flowers to communicate emotion. In England and America, flowers were a secret way to express feelings that proper etiquette did not allow in polite company. Each flower species had a symbolic meaning inspired by literature, legends, and cues from the flowers themselves. For example, Baby's Breath symbolized purity and innocence. Camellias symbolized longing. Chrysanthemums expressed condolences. The Daffodil symbolized unrequited love. Hyacinth symbolized forgiveness. Lavender symbolized distrust. Nettles symbolized cruelty, and Oaks symbolized bravery.

Young women in high society would deliver flowers to friends, lovers, or relatives to express feelings they could not express in words. Sometimes women would wear or carry a particular flower to send a coded message of affection, sorrow, or desire to those who shared the language of flowers.

By WWI, this practice faded, but today, flowers still carry messages of love or sorrow. Visiting a cemetery reveals that flowers are common on headstones and monuments. Flowers lift our spirits, and we want to see them during times of grief. One of the most common headstone carvings is of ivy. In the language of flowers, ivy symbolizes fidelity and attachment. Ivy vines wrap themselves around trees. Even if the tree dies, the vine can remain entwined. It is a fitting symbol of the attachment the living have to those who have departed. There is another reason ivy is common on headstones. It is easy to carve. Asking a stone carver to make ivy leaves is an affordable request.

The dahlia is also perfect for a headstone. It symbolizes eternal love and commitment. As perfect as those sentiments are, dahlias are rare on headstones. They have too many petals, making them expensive to carve. Only the wealthy could afford to pay for a craftsman to reproduce a bouquet of dahlias. Therefore, most people chose ivy, daisies, or iris on headstones because of their simplicity. As a result, finding dahlias on a monument is rare indeed.

dahlia genome and assemble the dahlia family tree. They are interested in why some early cultivars like 'White Aster' are still grown after 140 years while others have disappeared. The final results of this effort will not be known for several years because assembling a full sequence of an octoploid species is a huge task. However, as the work progresses, we may learn the secret as to why some dahlias have stood the test of time while others have not.

Dahlia growing and dahlia breeding followed a predictable pattern through the 20th century. First, breeders focused on breeding cultivars that would win awards at dahlia shows. Next, growers rushed to buy varieties that proved to be show winners. The emphasis for breeders was on blooms with perfect or near-perfect form and bright, pure colors.

As I write this book, dahlias are experiencing a resurgence in popularity. This is the result of several factors. First, the growth in the number of farmer-florists has introduced dahlias to a new audience. For decades florists and designers purchased flowers from wholesalers. Because dahlias are fragile, don't ship easily, and don't hold up when out of the water, wholesalers often did not offer them. If a florist or designer had access to dahlias, it was usually based on a relationship with a local grower. Today, the availability of dahlias for cut flowers, weddings, and events has increased as florists and designers are starting to grow their own dahlias.

Farmer-florists can grow varieties they and their clients love without relying on a wholesaler. Vase life is not a barrier because they can cut their blooms a day or two before a wedding or event. Farmer-florists love dahlias because they are easy to grow, produce copious blooms, wow their customers, and yield tubers that multiply their rootstock. A farmer-florist with a few rows of dahlias can offer clients flowers they will rarely see in florist shops.

As brides, event planners, and cut flower customers become familiar with the beauty of dahlias, they also want to grow them. This new interest in dahlias was a prelude to 2020 when COVID-19 shut down workplaces, and people started working from home. Travel and family gatherings came to a halt, and the home-bound sought out new hobbies. Gardening boomed during the pandemic. A generation of people who had never worked in the soil discovered the joy of growing flowers. They started looking on social media for what flowers they could grow. Dahlias are social media eye candy and fit the bill perfectly.

We have seen a flood of new dahlia growers in the last few years. However, these new growers differ from the show growers who came before them. Growers who show their dahlias strive to produce blooms that match strict standards. Dahlia shows are similar to dog shows. If you plan to show a prized beagle at a dog show, it had better look like the standard set for its breed. Showing a cross between a beagle and a dachshund will not win any awards.

The evaluation standards set by dahlia societies place the highest value on bloom form. The form is the shape of the dahlia bloom and its petals. On a scorecard of 100 total points, the ADS gives 30 points to the bloom form. The highest marks are given to perfectly symmetrical blooms that conform to the petal and bloom shape set for that particular flower form. Irregular or misshapen centers, wayward petals, asymmetrical blooms, or petals that curl or twist are undesired characteristics (for most forms) at a dahlia show.

Color is the second most important value on a judge's scorecard. The ADS assigns 20 points to color. The emphasis here is on pure, uniform color. While there are classifications for variegated petals and bicolor varieties, a quality show dahlia will exhibit a purity of color without streaking, blotching, or veining.

The other qualities that show judges evaluate are:

-Substance (10 out of 100) denotes the bloom's freshness, luster, and strength.

-Stem quality (10 points out of 100) to ensure that stems are not crooked, damaged, or weak.

-Foliage (10 out of 100) with points for uniformity, size, and symmetry.

-Bloom position (10 out of 100) should be at 45° off the stem for most varieties. Down-facing, side-facing, or up-facing varieties are scored poorly (for most forms).

The priority for show blooms explains why farmer-florists are often on the hunt for non-show dahlia varieties. A farmer-florist whose customer is a wedding designer or a bride will likely have a different set of priorities when looking for blooms. In 2023 Jessica Becker of the Ohio Dahlia Society formed a cut flower committee of the ADS to explore the idea of engaging with cut flower farmers and designers who

A foggy morning in the dahlia patch.

are not interested in growing dahlias for exhibition. I am a member of that committee along with other cut flower farmers and hybridizers.

One of the committee's first actions was to send out a survey to 24 U.S. dahlia growers who focus on florists, events, wholesale, CSAs, flower subscriptions, and agritourism. The survey revealed that 87% of respondents rated color as one of the top three most important traits when securing dahlia varieties. Florists and designers also want dahlias that are <u>not</u> uniform or symmetrical. Perhaps the most popular wedding dahlia is 'Cafe au Lait', which can produce front-facing blooms and wildly varied petal shapes and colors.

Many of the show varieties also meet the needs of florists and designers. Some examples include 'Jomanda', 'Peaches-N-Cream', 'Clearview Peachy', 'Cornel Bronze', 'Rose Toscano', and 'KA's Rosie Jo'. However, designers and florists often desire dusty, muted, and antique colors that show breeders have discarded for decades. Farmer-florists are now starting to breed their own dahlias and are bringing to market new varieties that reflect their desire to expand the dahlia color palette.

The rising interest in dahlias in the 21st century has lifted all boats. Dahlia societies have increased their membership. Interest in showing dahlias has grown. However, with the popularity of dahlias on social media and the explosion of new farmer-florists, highly desired varieties are scarce due to high demand and short supply. Today, when a supplier opens their catalog in December or January, they often sell out of the most popular varieties in a matter of minutes, if their website doesn't crash first.

The website dahliaaddict.com helps us understand the current situation. This site has a Trivia page that lists the 50 most-searched-for varieties. Out of this list (at the time of writing), four are suitable as show varieties. The other 46 produce blooms desired by florists and designers. The challenge to those who sell dahlias is that tuber propagation has yet to match this avalanche of interest. Unfortunately, it can take years to build up enough tuber supply to meet demand. Tuber suppliers are now realizing how large the market has grown for varieties that florists and designers want.

To make matters worse, several of the most searched-for cultivars were introduced only in the past few years. That means there is not enough stock to meet the high demand. As a result, growers are paying higher prices for tubers and have to wait several years before receiving the rare varieties they covet.

We have been here before, and it was even crazier than today. There was a "dahlia frenzy" in the 1920s, just before the 1929 Great Depression. A single tuber of the most popular variety, 'Jersey Beauty', went for $25 in the late 1920s, the equivalent of $439 today.

THE AMERICAN DAHLIA SOCIETY

The ADS started in 1915 and now has 70 independent local societies under its umbrella. The ADS is a nonprofit organization that stimulates interest in and disseminates information about dahlias at dahlia.org.

The ADS produces the *Classification and Handbook of Dahlias*. This booklet lists all the dahlia cultivars in the U.S. performing well at ADS-sanctioned shows across the country.

The ADS supports research, particularly leaf testing of dahlia viruses. Each year the ADS Virus Project based at Washington State University tests leaf samples from tuber suppliers and dahlia society members from across the country to track the prevalence and changes in virus infection. The ADS also supports the Dahlia Genome Project, a multi-year project to sequence the dahlia genome based at

Auburn University and HudsonAlpha Institute of Biogenetics in Alabama.

HOW DAHLIA VARIETIES ARE NAMED AND INTRODUCED

Once a breeder identifies a new variety with promise, they grow it for several years to ensure that its desirable traits are stable. A new dahlia is typically given a reference number during the early phase of evaluation (typically three to five years). However, as it gets closer to the time of introduction, breeders usually give their varieties a name.

Dahlia names run the gamut from serious to whimsical and historical to contemporary. In the U.S., there are just a few rules or guidelines for naming dahlias, in an attempt to ensure a level of uniformity:

1. Names should be in a language other than Latin so they won't be confused with botanical names.

2. Dahlia names should be capitalized to differentiate them from botanical names represented in lowercase letters, for instance, the species dahlia, D. brevis. This rule distinguishes dahlias bred by humans (cultivated varieties), such as 'Hollyhill Black Beauty', from those with Latin names originating in the wild.

3. Cultivated dahlia names should be bracketed with single quotes when referred to in print.

Beyond that, breeders have discretion on how they name their introductions. While it is advantageous to keep names short (and spare growers the chore of writing long names on tubers), that logic is not universally followed. The ADS allows 22 characters for each cultivar when publishing their Classification Handbook. Therefore, any variety with more than 22 characters will have its name truncated. A search of over 3,100 varieties on dahliaaddict.com turned up two varieties with the longest names. 'Happy Single - First Love', and 'Twyning's White Chocolate', are each 25 characters long.

The National Dahlia Society in the U.K. has more strict rules for naming varieties. Established in 2004, they are as follows:

1. Names shall use words in languages other than Latin. This rule will keep a cultivar from being confused with a wild species.

2. Names should not include the words: dahlia, variety, cultivar, group, hybrid, maintenance, mixture, selection, sport, series, strain, improved, or transformed.

3. Punctuation marks shall not be used with the following exceptions: apostrophe, period, comma, exclamation mark, hyphen, forward slash, and backslash.

4. Names cannot exaggerate the merits of a plant.

So, for example, 'Unbelievably Great Red', or 'The Biggest Bloom', are not allowed in the U.K.

Dahlia names fit a few basic patterns.

PREFIXES

Some breeders use an identical prefix at the beginning of their variety names. This allows growers to tell instantly who introduced that variety. It also ensures that the varieties from a single breeder will be listed together when looking at alphabetical lists. For example, Barry Davies uses the prefix "Barbarry," a blend of his name and Barbara, his wife. Barry's varieties start with Barbarry, like 'Barbarry Drum'. Rich Gibson, uses the prefix "20th Avenue" after the street he lives on. I also use a prefix; all my varieties start with "KA's," like 'KA's Cloud' or 'KA's Mocha Maya'. KA are my initials with the apostrophe "s," signifying that those varieties are mine. Similar to naming a restaurant "Joe's Barbecue."

Unnamed 'KA's' seedling.

COLORS

Perhaps the most common way a new cultivar is named is by inspiration from a color or a feeling. 'Alabaster', 'Apricot Puree', 'Terracotta', and 'Blackjack' are all dahlias named for their color. Likewise, 'Strawberry Cream', 'Just Peachy', and 'Ketchup & Mustard' all refer to foods of a particular color. Unfortunately, with varieties named this way, the breeder is, often, over time, forgotten.

SPONTANEOUS INSPIRATION

The most common form of variety name is a spontaneous inspiration that does not establish the cultivar as one in a series from a particular breeder. For example, 'Jungle Man', 'Take Off', 'Wicky Woo', and 'Pulp Fiction' may have just popped into a breeder's head or were suggested by a friend.

TRIBUTES, FRIENDSHIP, REMEMBRANCES, GRATITUDE

Some dahlias are named in honor of someone or something the breeder admires. 'Thomas A. Edison', 'Winston Churchill', and 'Doris Day' are examples of tribute names. Sometimes, a breeder will name a variety after someone they admire who has passed away. For instance, my variety called 'KA's Papa John', is named after my dad. When I see the plant growing, I think of him.

'18th Surgical Hospital' was named by John Kreiner, a helicopter pilot in Vietnam. In 1966 he was shot in the foot, and the doctors and nurses at that hospital treated him. At a reunion in San Francisco with his fellow Vietnam pilots, the group visited the Dahlia Dell in Golden Gate Park, and that's when he got the idea to have a dahlia named for the hospital.

The variety 'For Robin' was named by San Francisco hybridizer Lou Paradise. His friend Pat asked him to name a dahlia to remember comedian Robin Williams shortly after his tragic death. Pat was a roommate and a good friend of Mr. Williams.

Some varieties are named for people in a breeder's life, like the varieties 'Amy K', 'Maggie C', or 'Tyler James'. For example, my cultivar 'KA's Mocha Katie' is named after a floral designer I work with. While walking through my seedling patch, she was the first to recognize that seedling's beauty and promise. Sometimes, a husband, wife, mother, or father will pay a breeder to name a variety after a loved one. I know of a few cultivars named after loved ones in exchange for donating to a dahlia society. The variety 'Dori T' is named after the wife of a donor to the ADS genome project.

SPORTS

There is a loose "gentleman's agreement" for naming a sport. In botanical terms, a sport is a new variety that spontaneously arises from a mutation on a branch or sector of an existing variety. With dahlias, a sport can also arise in a single tuber in a tuber clump. An example of a sport would be white blooms spontaneously growing on a branch of a variety that produces yellow blooms. Typically a sport will have blooms identical in form and size to the original but display a new color. It's not easy, but an experienced breeder can take a cutting, grow it out over winter, save the tubers, and grow and save the sport if it proves stable. The "agreement" for naming sports is that the new name will reference the original. A few examples of sport names are:

- 'Mary's Jomanda' is a sport of 'Jomanda'.
- 'White Charlie Two' from 'Charlie Two'.
- 'Dave's Kiss' is a sport of 'Aurora's Kiss'.
- 'Cornel Bronze' is a sport of 'Cornel'.

There are times, however, when the gentleman's agreement breaks down. For example, the dahlia 'Bryn Terfel' is a giant red informal decorative. It is a cultivar from New Zealand. A breeder in the U.K. captured a beautiful bronze sport from 'Bryn Terfel' and named it 'Aggie White'.

Likewise, 'Ivanetti', 'Isabel', and 'Caitlin's Joy' are all sports of 'Cornel' without a reference to the original variety.

Suppose you are curious about the varieties each breeder has introduced. You can buy a copy of the *Classification and Handbook of Dahlias* from the ADS. In it, you will find the last name and nationality of the breeder for every listed variety. This lists dahlia cultivars currently active and successful at the dahlia shows across the U.S. and Canada. Because this list mostly show flowers, it leaves many new varieties out, including those mainly valued as cut flowers. To broaden your search, you can refer to the "World Dahlia Directory," with over 64,000 varieties from around the globe. You can find it at dahliaworld.co.uk/dahliadirectory.htm.

Once a new variety is grown for several years by a breeder, and they are satisfied it meets all their quality standards, there are several paths toward introduction. Some breeders will share tubers with friends, hoping the new variety will be grown, multiplied, and eventually become popular. Other growers will sign a contract with a tuber supplier to be the primary sales outlet for their new variety. Finally, some breeders will create an online store and sell tubers of their new variety themselves. As a new variety is grown and images of it circulate on social media, there is often a higher demand for it than available tubers. It can take several years for the supply of a new variety to catch up with demand.

Breeders who focus on varieties for exhibition often send tubers directly to growers they know have a winning track record at dahlia shows. These breeders want their new varieties to win awards at dahlia shows; this usually increases demand for tuber stock. For these breeders, it matters less to sell a lot of tubers than it does to get tubers into the hands of the best show growers. Breeders of show-quality varieties will often submit their new varieties to the ADS trial gardens (see next page). They can count on high demand for the new introduction if they score well.

HOW VARIETIES ARE LISTED IN THE ADS CLASSIFICATION HANDBOOK

Every year the ADS publishes its *Classification Handbook of Dahlias* (CHD). Using a series of codes, the CHD lists each dahlia's name, ADS classification number, bloom size, bloom form, bloom color class, hybridizer name, and the year of introduction.

I am often asked by new breeders how cultivars get listed in the CHD. There are three paths to inclusion. The first is to have a variety win at least two blue or higher ribbons at an ADS-sanctioned show in the U.S. or Canada in a single year. A ribbon higher than blue indicates "best in class" or "best in show." One can earn these two ribbons at one or separate shows.

To continue to be listed in the CHD in subsequent years, the cultivar must win at least three blue or higher ribbons in the following two years. For example, if a new cultivar wins two blue ribbons in the first year but receives no blue ribbons in the next two years, it would be dropped from the CHD. It would be re-listed if it won two blue or higher ribbons in the fourth year. Hybridizers whose varieties meet the criteria do not need to petition the ADS for inclusion in the CHD. Each year the ADS Classification Chairperson tallies the scores from across the country and automatically includes (or de-lists) varieties.

The second path into the CHD is to achieve a score of 85 points or higher at an ADS trial garden. There are seven ADS trial gardens in the U.S. and Canada. Breeders with new cultivars can send three tubers or (in some cases) cuttings to these trial gardens, where they are grown and evaluated over an entire season. They are located in varied climates to determine how varieties grow in different conditions. Each new cultivar is scored on a scale of 100 points based on form, color, foliage, stems, growth habits, bloom production, and bloom position. New varieties scoring 85 points or higher will be added to the CHD. To stay in the CHD, each variety added by the trial garden score must win two blue or higher ribbons the following year or three blue or higher ribbons in the next two years.

Once the dahlia season has ended, scores from all the trial gardens are collected and tallied by the ADS and sorted into seven different classes of bloom size and type. The Trial Garden Committee averages the top three scores for each variety. The cultivars with the highest average score in the seven classes are each awarded a Derrill Hart Medal. This is the highest honor given by the ADS for a new introduction. Through a rigorous and competitive season-long process, they are recognized as the best new show varieties of the year. Following the announcement of the medal winners, show growers often rush to purchase them.

The third and final path to earning a listing in the CHD is through a seedling "bench score." ADS-sponsored dahlia shows have a special section for the evaluation of new seedlings, the bench score. A team of senior judges evaluates three blooms of a new seedling on a scale of 100. They consider blooms for color, form, stems, foliage, bloom position, and substance (substance refers to how firm, fresh, and crisp a bloom looks). Unlike the trial gardens, judges have only blooms to evaluate, not plants, so they cannot judge based on bloom production or growth habits. Having a new variety bench scored at ADS shows can be more accessible for breeders who have only a few tubers of their new variety. Instead of sending off 21 tubers to the various trial gardens, a breeder needs only a few plants to produce blooms for a bench score at a dahlia show. Any new cultivar with a bench score of 85 or higher at an ADS show is listed in the

CHD. Every year, at the end of the season, all the bench scores from across the country are tabulated. Varieties that score an 85 or higher at three or more shows in one year are eligible to receive the Lynn B. Dudley Medal. Like the Derrill Hart Medal, seven Dudley Medals are awarded in each class to the seven highest-scoring new varieties evaluated on the seedling bench. As with the recipients of the Hart Medal, introductions that win a Dudley Medal are often the most desired new cultivars for show growers.

While winning blue ribbons, entering the trial gardens, or bench scoring new varieties can all lead to inclusion in the CHD, these various paths are different. At a dahlia show, each bloom is competing for blue ribbons against others, and your nearly-perfect flower could be beaten by one that is just slightly better. On the other hand, scoring in a trial garden, or having a seedling bench scored has no competitive component. A cultivar that receives a score of 85 does not have to prove itself compared to any other entry.

Finally, the ADS publishes the Composite Listing every ten years. This large volume lists all the dahlias that have been listed since 1976. The most current volume covers every cultivar that appeared between 1976 and 2016. Therefore, if you can't find information about a dahlia in circulation but is not in the current CHD, you will likely find it in the most recent *Composite Listing*. Both volumes are available from the ADS at their website: dahlia.org. Once there, click on "Store."

DAHLIA FORMS

For exhibition growers, the number of recognized dahlia forms (flower shapes) is dependent on your country. In the U.S. the ADS recognizes 29 dahlia forms. Because images and descriptions of dahlia forms have appeared in many other books on dahlias, I won't repeat them here. If you wish to see each form's official ADS. definitions along with images, see the ADS website at dahlia.org/wp-content/uploads/2018/02/UnderstandingDahliaForms.pdf.

THE DAHLIA GENOME PROJECT

For 13 years, I served as the President of the Monterey Bay Dahlia Society, a group of about 60 dahlia growers on the Central Coast of California. I was tasked with lining up speakers for our meetings. We are fortunate to have a well-known dahlia expert 40 miles away at Stanford University. Dr. Virginia Walbot is a biology professor specializing in corn genetics. She also maintains a dahlia garden at the university and uses dahlias, with their diverse forms and colors, to teach undergraduates about inheritance and plant genetics. Over the years, she and her students have experimented with dahlias. I had heard that she had a presentation on the science of flower color; in 2016, I invited her to one of our meetings to present her talk to our society.

Our group is typically pretty chatty. Members of the society have known each other for a long time, and our meetings were partially about socializing and catching up. The room grew quiet however once the lights went down and Dr. Walbot started speaking. With each progressive slide, our members became increasingly engrossed in the genetics of the pathways that produce color in dahlia blooms. As her presentation ended, she had a final slide, her dream slide. It expressed her desire that someday the dahlia genome would be sequenced. She explained that the only sequenced flower genomes were those that have significant commercial value, like roses and sunflowers. While dahlias have a lot of enthusiastic growers, there are no large commercial interests that would foot the sizable bill for sequencing. In other words, it would require private funding support.

That slide took me down a path that I am still on today. I had recently retired from a career as the Development Director of a Montessori school. Over eighteen years, my colleague and I raised $8 million in donations. I thought that Dr. Walbot's fundraising dream was achievable and I decided to try and help make it happen. First, we discussed the project timeline and how much money would be needed. Not being a scientist, I was surprised to find out that the project would take many years. By the time the project is complete, we will have been working on it for about a decade.

Sequencing the dahlia genome is a huge task and requires hundreds of thousands of dollars. Fundraising to complete the job is a big part of the effort. On the scientific side, the dahlia genome is large compared to other plants and animals. Modern dahlias are octoploids, with four sets of genes from each parent. All of these extra chromosomes add complexity to the dahlia genome. Scientists compare the size of each genome using "base pairs." A base pair is a tiny bit of DNA that forms a rung on the DNA ladder. Most plants have a genome of between 100 and 900 million base pairs. Strawberries (another complicated octopoid) have 813 million base pairs. The human genome consists of 3.2 billion base pairs. Each component of the dahlia genome is over 4 billion base pairs, thus as an octoploid with eight total components, the dahlia genome is a 32 billion base pair species. The sheer size of the dahlia genome requires more time to document and more time to analyze and assemble into a usable data set.

I am often asked what it will mean for dahlia growers and enthusiasts once the genome is fully sequenced and assembled. Not much will likely change in the first couple of years after completion. However, as the mechanics of sequencing DNA gets better and the costs associated with genomics drop, dahlia breeders will have access to data that could significantly improve our breeding programs. Here's a hypothetical example of just such an effect:

Kristine, Dr. Walbot, and one of her students at Stanford University in 2017.

Let's say I have a variety (we will call it variety A) that I like for its color; however, I want offspring with a different form. Variety A is an informal decorative form. I want to breed a variety with this same color but with a stellar petal form. I could cross variety A with all the stellar dahlias I can find. This may or may not get me closer to my goal. Because dahlias are packed with so many genes, the form each variety displays often differs from the offspring. My effort of crossing variety A with several potential parents is a game of chance, with many rejects on the way and no guarantee of success.

Once the dahlia genome is sequenced and assembled, there will come a time when I can submit leaf samples to a lab for an inexpensive genetic scan. The cost per variety is estimated to be less than $10.

Using our example above, I could send in 20 samples of potential mates for variety A and let the lab know I am looking for the genes resulting in the stellar petal form. This process will be similar to "23andMe" or "Ancestry," which we use to identify our human family tree. The lab will send back results showing which samples have the best chance of giving me the stellar form I desire. I could then make crosses with varieties more likely to give me what I'm looking for. Because breeders don't see the results of crosses for an entire year, this genetic screening could speed up the development of desired new varieties, helping breeders find these genetic needles in the haystack.

The ability to send in samples for screening could also provide the first significant steps in controlling the effects of viruses in dahlias. Dahlia viruses have been with us for centuries, and there is no cure for a plant with a virus. Several dahlia varieties appear to have a high tolerance for viruses and grow and perform well even if infected. In the future, geneticists might be able to determine which gene or genes confer this tolerance. Breeders could submit samples to determine which potential breeding parents carry the genes for virus tolerance. I can imagine an entire group of new varieties that are virus tolerant and asymptomatic.

For scientists, a reference genome will mean dahlias will be included in more scientific research. Scientists conducting genomic research on a particular plant species often include research on closely related species. The parallel track gives them greater insights. Often a specific gene and its function can't be determined in the target species, however, it may be successfully identified in the parallel species. If the two species are close relatives, the gene in question is likely in the same location on a particular chromosome. Locations on chromosomes are similar to street addresses in a neighborhood. In closely related species the order of genes is the same, just as the order of street addresses would be the same on parallel streets.

The closest relative to dahlias are sunflowers. Dahlias and sunflowers are both native to North America and share a wild habitat. The two plants originated only a few million years apart. Sunflower researchers, who enjoy substantial research funding for this worldwide oil crop, have been waiting for a genome from a close cousin to compare to sunflowers. Once the dahlia reference genome is complete, dahlias are expected to be included in future sunflower research. For instance, if a scientist wants to search for the sunflower gene that may provide tolerance to higher temperatures, they would likely do parallel research on the dahlia genome.

Dr. Walbot collecting leaf samples at my farm.

In the process, they may discover what gene accounts for heat tolerance in dahlias.

Dr. Walbot and I worked quickly in those early days. There were just two of us, and we were excited to get started. We both committed to working as volunteers without compensation. This allowed 100% of donations to go directly to the work. Although Dr. Walbot and I were excited and enthusiastic, we knew this project needed to be under the auspices of the ADS. When looking for gifts, it is a benefit to donors to have tax deductibility through a non-profit organization.

To get started, I approached the ADS. Its mission includes spreading information and promoting the development of dahlias. The ADS Board agreed it was a project they should support. There was no professional fundraiser on the ADS Board, so I was appointed to the Board's Finance Committee, responsible for Genome Project fundraising. We established a goal of $50,000 to achieve our early objectives. After six months we reached our first fundraising goal in late 2016. The following year Dr. Walbot received permits from the USDA to import seeds collected from wild dahlias in Mexico.

In October 2017, Professor Walbot and her colleague Tim Culbertson collected dahlia leaf samples and seeds in Jalisco, Morelos, and Queretaro, Mexico. Professor Eduardo Ruiz Sanchez assisted them at the University of Guadalajara, along with botanists from the University of Morelos in Cuernavaca, Mexico.

In early 2018 I grew species dahlia seeds from the Mexico trip so scientists could have fresh leaf material. Leaf tissue was sent to a sequencing lab for RNA transcriptomes, an inexpensive way to start organizing the dahlia family tree. In the summer of 2018, Dr. Walbot, Tim Culbertson, and I traveled to Washington state to collect leaf samples from the gardens of Martin Kral, Wayne Lobaugh, and Brad and Rosemary Freeman. We were assisted by Professor Alex Paradez from the University of Washington.

In the fall of 2018, Dr. Walbot collected samples from several modern dahlia cultivars for RNA sequencing. Varieties sampled were 'Mexico', 'Jomanda', 'Rhonda', 'Thomas A. Edison', 'Emory Paul', and 'Pam Howden'. When Dr. Walbot shows up at my farm to take leaf samples, she arrives with stainless steel canisters of liquid nitrogen. The temperature inside the canister is -109 F (-78 C). Samples are carefully taken, documented, placed in labeled envelopes, and dropped into the cold canisters.

Later in 2018, samples from 15 species dahlias and 11 modern dahlias were sent out for RNA sequencing to Novogene, a sequencing lab in China. The result of the RNA sequence was a surprise. The modern, fully double dahlias and the smallest species dahlias (open center with eight petals) are genetically indistinguishable. This means that modern and species dahlias spring from one shared gene pool. This is like what we know about domestic dogs—there is one shared gene pool with a wide range of characteristics.

As 2018 came to a close, a new scientist joined the effort: Dr. Alex Harkess, a plant biologist and National Science Foundation Plant Genome Initiative Postdoctoral Fellow. During his fellowship, he collaborated with Professor Walbot's lab, and she knew about his keen interest in floral evolution. He is now a Faculty Investigator at the HudsonAlpha Institute for Biotechnology in Huntsville, Alabama, the largest genome sequencing lab in the U.S. Dr. Harkess is also an Assistant Professor in the Department of Crop, Soil, and Environmental Science at Auburn University in Auburn, Alabama. Dr. Walbot founded the Genome Project and did the initial ground-breaking work. She chose Dr. Harkess to see the project through the subsequent phases, which will result in a fully assembled reference genome.

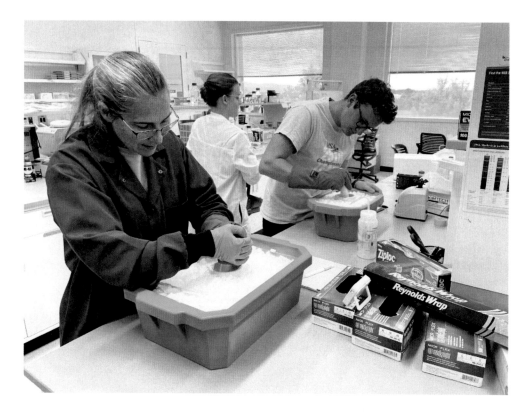

PhD student Zach Meharg and colleagues in the lab at HudsonAlpha.
Photo by Dr. Sarah Carey.

In 2019, Dr. Harkess and I started planning the second phase of the Dahlia Genome Project. This phase would require years of painstaking work by humans to recheck the automated initial assembly done by computers. The human assembly has always been understood to be the most time-consuming and expensive part of the project. Dr. Harkess compares this challenge to putting together a billion-piece jigsaw puzzle without a picture on the box. Making things even more complex, because modern dahlias are octoploids, imagine the box has eight complete sets of pieces all jumbled together. Some puzzle pieces are double-sided, and 85% of the pieces look identical. Finally, many of the pieces don't even belong to dahlias. Sequencing plant material drags in DNA from fungi, bacteria, and viruses. These "foreign" puzzle pieces must be identified and thrown out of the mix. In the past, assembling the puzzle was done painstakingly by hand. Fortunately, today computers are programmed to recognize patterns in DNA fragments through computational biology to produce a draft assembly, making human assembly more efficient. Even with computers, figuring out what strings of DNA go where is a challenge that will take years to complete.

At the 2019 National Dahlia Show in Grand Rapids, Michigan, Dr. Harkess gave a presentation explaining what it means to sequence a genome and how the project should progress. Specifically, he expressed the need for a talented graduate student who could do the lab work for the full assembly while working toward a Ph.D.
When his talk was over, a young man approached and told him that, stimulated by the presentation, he was considering applying to the program. His name was Zach Meharg.

One result of moving the project to HudsonAlpha in Alabama is that my farm was too far away to grow plants for the project. Using ADS membership lists, I searched for experienced dahlia growers within driving distance of the lab. Marcie Holt in Ringgold, Georgia, came to our aid. She is an experienced grower and agreed to grow the varieties Dr. Harkess would need for sampling. I sent her plants and tubers, both modern varieties and species dahlias. I had two other growers across the border in Alabama grow backup plants as a precaution.

After accepting Zach Meharg as a new graduate student, he and Dr. Harkess started growing the dahlias at their facility. In addition, they collected samples from 800 varieties at the ADS National Dahlia Show in Wooster, Ohio. Six hundred specimens have been sequenced to help put together the dahlia family tree. The variety used for the final reference genome is 'Edna C'.

The pace of work on dahlias at HudsonAlpha has picked up with Zach working full-time on the project. The work of understanding a species' genome is not a straight line. It involves discoveries from several angles.

One such project that Zach is working on as I write this book is exploring the genetic differences between sports and their parent plants. Recall that a sport is a dahlia bloom that is identical in form to the parent plant but displays a different color. Sports could provide a shortcut to understanding which genes are responsible for flower color. Searching the entire genome for color formation would be difficult. However, because a sport is genetically identical to the parent plant except for the genes controlling color, it might be possible to find those genes with a simple comparison.

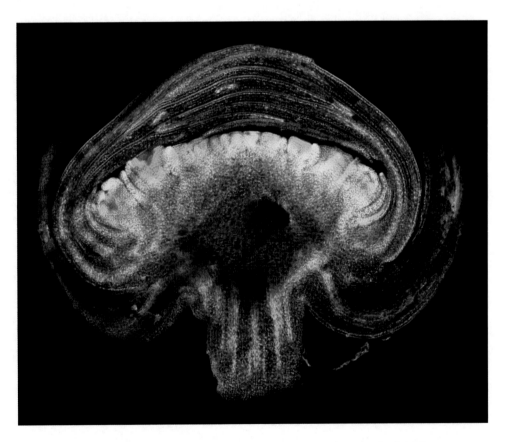

A dahlia bud seen through a confocal microscope. Photo by Zach Meharg.

In March of 2023, Zach and I hosted a Zoom meeting with several U.S. hybridizers to gather up tubers and cuttings of sports and their parent cultivars. Zach will grow these plants in his greenhouse and take leaf tissue samples. He will then perform low-pass (inexpensive) sequencing to assemble a data set. Special software will then look for differences between the parent and the sport. With luck, we may soon know which gene or genes control color variation in dahlias.

Studying sports is an example of looking for subtle differences between two data sets. An opposite strategy would determine what is similar in data sets. For example, Zach wants to know what genes control the floral forms in dahlias. What makes a cactus dahlia take that unique form? To answer this question, he intends to sequence multiple samples of a single form. Then, using software, he will compare several data sets of that form with those of another form, for example, cactus dahlias compared to informal decorative dahlias. By identifying what genes are common to the cactus form samples and different from the informal decorative samples, we may soon learn what genes control floral form.

Another area of interest is at what point in the growth of a dahlia bud, does it differentiate into its final floral form? If we dissected dahlia buds as they emerge at the tip of the stem, we would see undifferentiated meristem cells. As the bud develops, those cells differentiate and ultimately build the floral form we recognize as a particular dahlia form (like water lily or collarette). To look into a developing bud, Zach uses a laser-powered confocal microscope. This device allows scientists to see inside tissue with great clarity and depth of field. Using the microscope, Zach may be able to determine when the cells inside the bud start to differentiate. He can then collect RNA from the bud tissue. When switched on, genes produce RNA that encodes the proteins that carry out the genetic instructions. Identifying the RNA present when a bud starts differentiating may lead back to the genes that determine floral form.

After many years of hard work to sequence the full dahlia genome, the project is now exploring the above-mentioned experiments and many more. By 2025 we should have a fully assembled genome. A few years later, breeders like myself may have access to data similar to human genetic data derived from 23andMe today. That data could guide our future breeding goals and techniques. The ADS maintains a web page on the Dahlia Genome Project at dahlia.org/docsinfo/genome-overview/more-info-about-the-genome-project/.

THE SCIENCE OF DAHLIA COLOR

Dahlias produce their many colors from a pigment called anthocyanin. Only plants can synthesize anthocyanin, providing color to a wide spectrum of plant stems, leaves, flowers, and fruits. Blueberries and purple cauliflower get their color from anthocyanin. The display of reds, oranges, and purples in fall tree foliage comes from anthocyanin. The diversity of colors is what most of us love about dahlias; for us, dahlia color is a visual delight. However, for dahlia plants, color plays many different roles.

First, anthocyanin is an excellent sunscreen. Color in dahlia petals protects the flower, and the reproductive organs inside, from damaging ultraviolet radiation. When new growth shoots appear on a plant or tree, they are often red or purple. Anthocyanin protects vulnerable new cells. When leaves start photosynthesizing, they turn green and mask the anthocyanin beneath. Fall colors in leaves are the result of unmasked anthocyanin colors after photosynthesis has turned off for the season and green chlorophyll is broken down and recycled by the plant.

Second, anthocyanin serves plants by attracting pollinators. Bees and other pollinators have unique forms of color vision. The bright petal colors we love also guide bees and flies to the center of the bloom, where the next generation of seeds is pollinated.

Third, anthocyanin is an antibiotic. It deters the growth of some bacteria and fungi to help the plant stay healthy.

Fourth, anthocyanin is bitter and serves the plant as a deterrent for chewing insects and other herbivores like deer. Picotee is a color pattern in dahlias where flower petals have an edge color darker than the petal body. This could serve the bloom as an insect deterrent since most chewing insects start on the petal edges. The bitter anthocyanin in the darker edges may protect the petals because of its bitter taste.

Fifth, anthocyanin serves dahlia plants by making colors that appeal to the human eye. Dahlia growers select the most beautiful varieties to propagate and cross-breed. In the competition for survival, the most desired colors and color combinations ensure they will continue to be grown and multiplied.

Without getting too technical, I want to describe the process of anthocyanin synthesis in our dahlia plants as explained to me by Dr. Walbot.

The color we see in dahlia blooms results from a ten-step anthocyanin-producing chemical process as the flower bud develops. However, genes can mutate and stall the color pathway at various steps. When this happens, the flower color is the result from all the accumulated steps until the stall. The pigment will be yellow if the pathway is stalled after the first step. We see a lot of yellow flowers in nature, confirming that a mutation that stalls the pathway at the first step is common. The pigment is colorless if a mutation stalls the pathway at the second, third, fourth, or fifth step. Flowers with colorless pigment our eyes see as white. In nature, after yellow, white is the most common flower color.

The remaining intermediate steps in the pathway result in light pink flowers. If the process continues almost to the end of the ten steps, a glucose molecule is added, giving blooms the beige color we see in 'Cafe au Lait'. Until this point, all of the chemistry has taken place in the cytoplasm, the main part of the cell. The final tenth step involves a pump that moves the developing anthocyanin from the cytoplasm into an acidic vacuole within the cell. Deep colors can be formed only when this final step into an acid environment is complete. This step generates colors like purple, red, peach, apricot, coral, orange, burgundy, and dark pink. These colors result from the addition of the glucose molecule, and the addition of diverse sugars, acids, and other cellular molecules. Each addition alters the final color. Thus, there is not just one shade of pink, purple, or fuchsia, but many.

Several dahlia varieties rely on more than chemistry to resolve the final pigment in their flowers and stems. The intensity and hue of pigmentation in some varieties are determined by exposure to sunlight. In some varieties, light promotes or inhibits anthocyanin production as color is being produced. You can do a simple test for this in your garden. Choose a variety with deep colors like purple, red, orange, or dark pink. Cover an immature bud with aluminum foil when the bud is tight, and the colored petals inside are not yet visible. Form the foil, giving the bud room to open and bloom. Also, ensure it is tight around the stem below the bud to block out all light.

Leave the foil cover on the bud until it opens inside into full bloom. This can be difficult to determine since you can no longer see the bud through the foil. I take the guesswork out of this by tying a small string on a neighboring bud at the same stage of development. When the bud with the string is in full bloom, I know the bud under the foil is likely in bloom too. Next, I remove the foil and see what color the flower is. In my garden, about 90% of varieties are not affected by developing in darkness. About 10% of varieties produce blooms of a different color when maturing under foil. If a variety changes color when covered in foil, we know that sunlight triggers anthocyanin production to reach the tenth step and make a deep color or make a dark color at the petal edges (called picotee). Two varieties that change color when developing in the dark are 'Valley Porcupine' and 'KA's Blood Orange'. These would be good choices for experimentation if you are interested in trying this in your garden.

If you do this experiment in your plot, you will notice something unusual. The blooms that mature under the foil are typically 20% smaller than the neighboring blooms that mature in the light. This surprised me at first. I could understand that the color would change without exposure to sunlight, but why would the bloom size be affected too? It turns out that the photosynthesizing parts of a plant closest to a bloom provide most of the energy needed for bloom production. The green sepals that cover the immature bud are the closest photosynthesizers to a bloom. As the bloom opens, those green sepals provide nourishment and energy to the developing bloom. When we cover a bud with foil, it is not only the petals that are in the darkness. The sepals are in the dark too; they can no longer provide energy for the developing bloom. As a result, it will not grow as big and full as its counterpart in full sun.

Light exposure at critical periods is responsible for blooms with petals that change color from the base to the tip. 'Ketchup and Mustard' is a variety with red petal bases and yellow petal tips. This results from the petal tip's exposure to sunlight during a photosensitive period as the bud starts to open. Protective green sepals shield the inner-most parts of the emerging petal from light. As a result, only the ends of the petals receive light during the photo-critical period. This light stops the petal tips at the first step, which makes them yellow. In contrast, the shaded bases progress to the final step and make red pigment.

'KA's Peppercorn' is a bicolor variety. It has red petal bases with white petal tips. Exposure to light is an inhibitor for this variety that keeps the petal tips stuck at the second, third, fourth, or fifth steps in anthocyanin production (resulting in a lack of pigment that we see as white) as the petal bases progress to step ten and make red.

Bicolor varieties are easy to experiment with. Before the petals emerge, cover a tight bud with aluminum foil, making sure the cover is large enough so the bud can open and bloom. The foil must be tight against the stem below the bud to block out all light. As described above, I tie a string to a nearby bud of the same size. Without exposure to light during the photosensitive period, blooms that are typically bicolor will produce blooms of one color.

Some dahlia varieties have deep color on almost all of their petals, with just the bases of the innermost petals displaying a contrasting color, often yellow. This is evidence of a variety that has a longer photosensitive period for the development of deep color. Instead of being photosensitive for a day or two, these varieties might remain sensitive to sunlight for a week or more. This results in nearly all the petals developing deep color, with only the lowest parts of the innermost petals displaying a contrasting color. This is because the base of the innermost petals was shielded from light the longest. These varieties can also be covered with foil when in bud form. If, for instance, we have a dark pink variety with yellow petal bases in the center, we might see a fully yellow flower if the bud was covered with foil, excluding all light as the bud developed.

After discussing these light experiments, I often get questioned about the offspring of a plant where the light was withheld as the bud developed. The most common question is whether or not seeds or tubers collected from the bloom or plant with altered color will carry the alterations to the next generation. The answer is no. To understand why we need to explore the difference between genotype and phenotype. Genotype describes the set of genes that determine the characteristics of a variety. This is the genetic map that it has inherited from its two parents. The genotype is what makes each variety unique. It is the plant's genetic "blueprint." Phenotype is the plant's physical appearance. It is the outward appearance that we observe in our gardens. Phenotypes are influenced by both a plant's genes and the environment. Phenotypes can change based on climate, temperature, soil, sunlight, and the care a plant receives. Plants do not pass on their phenotype, only their genotype. For example, a variety that normally produces a five-foot-high (1.5 m) plant might only grow to be three feet tall (.9 m) if it does not receive enough water. Five feet (1.5 m) is the plant's genotype. Due to its growing circumstances, three feet (.9 m) is the plant's phenotype. That plant will pass on

A split image of two blooms (an unnamed 'KA's' seedling with picotee petal edges). The bloom on the left was covered with foil and developed in darkness.

A split image of two 'KA's Blood Orange' blooms.
The bloom on the left was covered with foil and developed in darkness.

its five-foot-high (1.5 m) genotype to the next generation.

There is only one very rare exception to this rule of inherited traits, the inheritance from a sport (described on page 241). A sport is a single bloom or a section of a plant that spontaneously mutates and produces blooms different from the rest of the plant. If a plant sports and produces a bloom of a different color, that difference is caused by a genetic mutation. That mutation produces a new genotype. So, if we have a plant that produces red blooms and generates a single white sport, the seeds produced by that white bloom will pass its traits to the next generation.

Sometimes a sport affects only one-half of a dahlia bloom. In this case, a bloom can be half red and half white. Seeds collected from the white half have a different genotype than the seeds from the red half. However, as stated before, sports are rare. I have only seen one sport on one of my plants in my years of growing over a thousand plants each year. It should be said that not all unusual blooms are sports. Some dahlia varieties are notorious for producing blooms with a spectrum of colors and patterns. These varieties are genetically unstable and keep growers guessing when producing blooms.

It is not only blooms that use light as a pigment trigger. Dahlia varieties with purple pigment in their stems can also require light to make stem pigment. You can observe this by looking under leaves and branches on your plants with pigmented stems. The underside of the branches will often be pale green because they are shaded and do not receive direct sunlight. Likewise, the stems will often have a streak of light green just below branches and leaves because those areas were shaded. Growers with purple stem varieties can do a simple experiment with aluminum foil to see the effects of shade on pigment. This is a great experiment to do with children. Wrap a 1/2 inch (1.2 cm) wide piece of foil around a young stem so no light can get through. Leave it in place for ten days. When you remove it, you may see the stem under the foil is green, not purple. Many of the green streaks and spots we see on our purple stem varieties result from random shading.

The stems of varieties with purple stems are often green in the areas where they are shaded.

Covering a purple-stem often changes the stem color.

'Unnamed 'KA's' seedling'.

256

'KA's Apricot Jam' & 'Bloomquist Alan'.

Mini Sweet Dahlia Muffins.

TUBERS AS FOOD: A RECIPE

At a dahlia society meeting years ago a member made deep-fried dahlia chips (like potato chips). Like most things deep-fried, they were pretty tasty. Over the years, however, I have tried preparing dahlia tubers in different ways but was never satisfied with the results—until I used them as a substitute in a recipe for sweet potato muffins. Now, one of my favorite things to do at a dahlia society gathering is to bring a plate of dahlia tuber muffins. They always capture the imagination of those assembled, and since they are so tasty, there are never any leftovers. What a great way to use tubers that I am culling anyway! A bonus of this recipe: it is vegan.

SWEET DAHLIA MUFFINS

Makes 12 muffins
20 minutes of prep time
30-minute cook time

Ingredients:

1 cup (220 g) packed brown sugar
3/4 cup (180 ml) vegetable oil. Additional oil is needed to grease the muffin tins, or use paper muffin cups
1/2 cup (125 ml) applesauce
2 cups (300 g) washed, peeled, grated, and drained fresh dahlia tubers (not old or shriveled)
1/2 cup (125 ml) soy, oat, or almond milk
1 teaspoon lemon juice
2 cups (250 g) all-purpose flour
1/2 cup (71 g) chopped walnuts
1 teaspoon baking powder
1 teaspoon baking soda
1 teaspoon salt
1/2 teaspoon ground cinnamon

Preparation:

1. Preheat the oven to 375° (190° C).
2. Fill a 12-cup muffin pan with paper muffin cups or grease the metal cups liberally.
3. Skin and grate the washed dahlia tubers (as fresh as possible) with the finest grater you have. Squeeze out any excess water.
4. Using a hand mixer, combine the brown sugar, oil, and applesauce in a large bowl for two minutes.
5. Add the grated dahlia tubers, plant-based milk, and lemon juice and stir until combined.
6. Whisk together flour, walnuts, baking powder, baking soda, salt, and cinnamon in another bowl. Add the wet ingredients and hand mix until fully mixed. Don't over-mix.
7. Spoon the batter into the muffin cups.
8. Bake for 30 minutes or until an inserted toothpick in the center of the muffin comes out clean.
9. Remove from the pan and cool on a rack.

DAHLIA TOURISM

Once you fall in love with dahlias, there is no end to the enjoyment of seeing them growing in various gardens. Here is a list of worldwide destinations where you can see dahlias. If you cannot travel you can look these places up online and enjoy them in photographs. If you do plan to visit any of these sites, please check with each location before making travel plans. Garden visitation and the timing of events can change over time.

BELGIUM

BRUSSELS
The Flower Carpet is a bi-annual temporary display of begonias, dahlias, and other blooms on the main square in Brussels in front of the Grand Palace. Using over 1 million flowers, this living tapestry measures 253 feet by 79 feet (77 x 24 m). It is produced every other August by over 100 volunteers. This spectacular display lasts from the Thursday opening ceremony to the following Sunday. Then it disappears for another two years. Currently, this spectacle is happening in even-numbered years.

CANADA

HALIFAX, NOVA SCOTIA
The Halifax Public Gardens began in 1863 under the care of the Nova Scotia Horticultural Society. Today the 5.5-acre site is flush with trees, plants, sculptures, a lake, picturesque bridges, and a bandstand. In the summer, the garden displays dahlias in several large beds.

SAANICH, VANCOUVER ISLAND
For over 100 years, Butchart Gardens has been a mandatory stop on Vancouver Island. The 250-foot (76 m) dahlia wall is blooming in late August and September.

IRELAND

DUBLIN
The National Botanic Gardens is spread over 50 acres and is home to 17,000 different plant species. Their annual beds host an extensive collection of blooming dahlias in the summer.

ITALY

VERBANIA
The Botanical Gardens of Villa Taranto have over 20,000 plant varieties growing yearly. They present the Dahlia Labyrinth between July and October, a winding switchback path leading into a garden of 1,700 dahlia plants.

GERMANY

KONSTANZ
Off the coast of the city of Konstanz is the small island of Mainau, which features spectacular gardens and sculptures that come alive with hordes of visitors in the summer. Over 12,000 dahlia plants bloom in the island gardens from mid-August until October.

THE NETHERLANDS

ZUNDERT
The world's largest parade of floats made from flowers takes place every year on the first Sunday of September. Called the "Corso Zundert," these enormous and elaborate floats are made from thousands of dahlias. Twenty different towns compete in a parade that decides the winning float. While the parade is the grand finale of all this effort, growing and preparing the dahlias used in the floats is mainly a social event. Each town's experienced dahlia growers produce the blooms while younger volunteers sort, organize and build the floats. The construction of these massive (house-size) floats happens under tents all summer

long. In the last days before the parade, there is a flurry of activity as the fresh dahlias are applied to the armatures. Every year about 20 different towns compete in the parade. You cannot just show up if you want to witness this event. Tickets must be purchased in advance and are available at corsozundert.nl.

UNITED KINGDOM

CAMBRIDGE, ENGLAND
The Dahlia Garden at Anglesey Abby was first planted in 1952 by Lord Fairhaven. The sweeping dahlia borders are replanted yearly. With 70 cultivars on display, the thick hedge of color in the formal garden is stunning.

BIDDULPH GRANGE GARDEN
This National Trust garden near Staffordshire has a landscape of distinct spaces, including Chinese and Egyptian gardens. One popular feature in the summer is the "dahlia walk," a series of walled-in dahlias on formal display.

EAST SUSSEX
Ashley Manor Gardens is an English country estate with 11 acres of gardens. Each year they grow over 70 dahlia cultivars and celebrate "Dahlia Days" for one week in mid-September.

HEDDON-ON-THE-WALL
Halls of Heddon grows, hybridizes, and sells dahlias and chrysanthemums. They also sell dahlia tubers and plants. Visitors can view over 15,000 dahlias blooming in August and September at their nursery. They have two nursery locations, about 3 miles apart.

LAPWORTH
Baddesley Clinton is a 16th-century country estate and gardens open to visitors. A moat surrounds the beautiful castle. The "dahlia border," a long planting bed of bright-colored dahlias, is in bloom in August and September.

ROUSHAM
Rousham House & Garden was designed by William Kent 300 years ago. Kent did not grow dahlias, but they were added as a magnificent border later. This garden is unusual as each year they recycle and grow the same 500 varieties in a 150-foot-long (45 m) bed that was first planted in 1946.

UNITED STATES

MENDOCINO, CALIFORNIA
The Mendocino Coast Botanical Gardens were founded in the 1960s by Betty & Ernest Schoefer; the 40-acre gardens are now managed by the Mendocino Coast Recreation and Park District. In the summer months, they have over 400 dahlia plants in bloom. The climate on the foggy and cool Mendocino coast is perfect for growing dahlias.

SAN FRANCISCO, CALIFORNIA
Since the 1940s, members of the California Dahlia Society have grown a beautiful display of over 1,000 dahlias. Called the "Dahlia Dell," this oval garden is located in a turn-around just to the right of the Conservatory of Flowers in Golden Gate Park. Society members keep their oval gardens immaculate and their plants perfectly maintained. Usually, you can find a society member to chat with across the fence.

BRISTOL, INDIANA
The Bonneyville Mill County Park features a historic grist mill and 222 acres of parkland. The Elkhart, Indiana Dahlia Society maintains a dahlia garden next to the pond opposite the mill.

SHELBURNE FALLS, MASSACHUSETTS.
The Bridge of Flowers is unique in the entire world. Built in 1908 for trolley service over The Deerfield River, the bridge was repurposed as a walkable garden in 1983 when trolley service ended. It is tended by a professional gardener and many volunteers. The bridge has various

Triple Wren Farm in Ferndale, Washington.

flower species blooming many months of the year. The dahlias are in bloom from mid-July through September.

MIDLAND, MICHIGAN
Dahlia Hill is a formal terraced garden of 3,000 dahlia plants open to the public every summer. Founded by Charles Breed, the society that cares for the garden grows 29 dahlia forms in their garden. Blooms are best from August through October.

CHASKA, MINNESOTA
The Dahlia Society of Minnesota maintains a changing selection of dahlia cultivars at the University of Minnesota Landscape Arboretum. The arboretum is extensive, with over 1,100 acres of plants, trees, and sculptures.

NORTH HAMPTON, NEW HAMPSHIRE
Fuller Gardens is a beautifully maintained Colonial Revival summer estate from the 1920s that features formal gardens of roses and a dahlia display garden. A nonprofit organization today runs the estate.

CANBY, OREGON

Swan Island Dahlias have been growing and selling dahlias for over 90 years. Their 40-acre farm is open for visitation in August and September. Swan Island is also home to one of the ADS trial gardens, where new dahlia introductions are grown and scored by senior dahlia judges. Most of the ADS trial gardens are open to the public. So if you go to Swan Island Dahlias, see the Trial garden and catch a look at the latest cultivars.

COOS BAY, OREGON

Just southeast of Coos Bay, Oregon, a grand mansion was built in 1921 by lumber baron Luis Simpson. The property included sweeping ocean views, a heated swimming pool, and manicured formal flower gardens. The mansion burned down, and a second home was built, but following the stock market crash of 1929, Simpson lost the property. The house and grounds fell into disrepair until the Oregon State Parks purchased it. Today, in August and September, over 250 dahlias bloom at the park. The rugged land the park is on is home to Sunset Bay State Park and Cape Arago State Park. The Oregon Coast Trail connects all three parks. I recommend walking from Shore Acres to Cape Arago on the walking trail.

BELLEVUE, WASHINGTON

The Bellevue Botanical Garden is home to a dahlia display bed planted and maintained by the Puget Sound Dahlia Society since 1993. The dahlias are in bloom from July through October.

FERNDALE, WASHINGTON

Triple Wren Farm is a 20-acre family-run flower farm that hosts events and workshops between May and October. In addition, they have an annual two-day Dahlia Festival in early September, including U-pick blooms, previews of upcoming cultivars, a food truck, a sunflower patch, and tens of thousands of dahlias in bloom. This festival has become a favorite event for Washington and Oregon residents. There is only a handful of dahlia gardens in the United States this large.

SEATTLE, WASHINGTON

In 1913 the dahlia was made the official flower of Seattle. Volunteer Park in Seattle is home to a dahlia display bed of over 250 plants maintained by the Puget Sound Dahlia Society. The dahlias are in bloom from July through October.

SPOKANE, WASHINGTON

The Inland Empire Dahlia Society operates a Trial Garden in Monito Park in Spokane. The Trial Garden is located in the Rose Garden of W. 21st Avenue. In August and September, the ADS Trial Garden is open to the public. At the same time, be sure to see the Duncan Garden, a formal and manicured display garden full of color and perfectly trimmed hedges. The Duncan Garden is located right in front of the Gaiser Flower Conservatory.

TACOMA, WASHINGTON

The Pacific Northwest Trial Garden, run by Washington State Dahlia Society members, is the largest of seven ADS Trial Gardens, where new dahlia introductions are grown and scored by senior dahlia judges. Most of the ADS Trial Gardens are open to the public. The dahlia garden is in Fort Defiance Park just east of the Zoo on Robert's Garden Road.

Me and my friend Iris, who is an amazing dahlia grower, at Santa Cruz Dahlias.

GLOSSARY

ADS: The American Dahlia Society.

Baling twine: A bright-colored synthetic twine used to bind bales of straw, hay, or alfalfa.

Bench score: The score given to a new cultivar at an ADS-sanctioned show by three senior judges.

CHD: Classification Handbook of Dahlias published by the American Dahlia Society.

Coolbot: An electronic control that allows a standard air conditioner to cool an insulated space below the device's pre-set temperature limit.

Chicken leg: A slang term for a single tuber divided from a large tuber clump.

Crown: The part of a single tuber closest to the plant's main stem.

Cultivar: A plant humans have developed through controlled or selective breeding, then reproduced through vegetative propagation (cuttings, tissue culture, or tubers).

Cutting: A shoot taken from a tuber that will develop roots and grow into a full-size plant. Like tubers, cuttings are clones of the parent plant.

Diploid: A species that has two sets of chromosomes, one set from each parent. Humans are diploids.

Disc center: A dahlia bloom's yellow open central portion, the part the bees visit and where seeds develop.

Disc floret: The individual parts that make up the yellow disc center of the bloom.

Deadhead: To cut off a bloom that has passed its prime.

Double or Fully double bloom: A bloom that has petals in rows stacked on top of each other, creating a bloom that has depth from front to back. The terms are interchangeable.

First-year seedling: A new plant in its first year grown from seed rather than a tuber or cutting.

Germination: The process of sprouting a seed, usually after a period of dormancy.

Herbarium: A collection and repository of dried and preserved plant specimens and descriptions.

Hybrid: A cross between two different varieties or species of plants.

Hybridizing: Cross-breeding seed and pollen parents to develop new cultivars.

Involute: When margins of the ray florets curve upward, toward the face of the bloom, along its length. When fully involute, the margins touch or overlap, appearing quill-like.

Leggy: A plant that has not received enough light. Instead of bushing up and out, a leggy plant will grow abnormally tall and thin as it reaches for more light.

Meristem: The swiftly-growing tip of a plant where undifferentiated cells divide rapidly to build new plant tissue.

Neck: The thinnest part of an individual tuber between the crown and the tuber body.

Octoploid: An organism with eight sets of chromosomes, four sets from each parent. Modern dahlias are octoploids.

Organza bag: A tight weave mesh bag used to protect blooms from pests or exclude pollinators from a bloom for breeding purposes.

Pollen parent: The dahlia bloom that contributes the pollen for sexual reproduction.

Pot root: A miniature tuber clump from a plant grown in a small pot.

Propagation: Growing a new plant from part of a parent plant. Dahlias can be propagated through tubers, cuttings, seeds, and meristem culture.

Pull: A pull is identical to a cutting (see above), except the shoot is pulled from the tuber crown rather than cut from the tuber crown.

Ray floret: Ray florets are what are commonly called petals. These surround the disc center.

Rooted cuttings: See cuttings.

Sausages: A slang term for single tubers divided from a large tuber clump.

Second-year seedling: A plant propagated in its second year from a cutting or a tuber from the original plant that was propagated from seed the previous year.

Seed parent: The dahlia bloom that receives pollen from another bloom and will gestate the seeds in a seed head.

Seedling bench: An evaluation at a select ADS-sanctioned dahlia shows. Three senior judges give scores to new cultivars that have not yet been included in the Classification Handbook of Dahlias.

Single: Single blooms have an open disc center and a single row of (typically eight) petals around that center.

Termination: Cutting down a cover crop to stop it from re-growing while leaving the roots in the soil.

Tetraploid: A species that has four sets of chromosomes, two sets from each parent.

Tissue culture: A laboratory-based process of harvesting meristem cells from fast-growing plant tissue. This process is done to develop virus-free plant stock.

Trial garden: A garden operated by a dahlia society for growing and evaluating new dahlia seedlings.

Variety: A plant that reproduces and grows without human intervention. A breeder produces a new seedling through selective breeding called a cultivar. When a new seedling is generated in the wild without human intervention, it is called a variety. Wild dahlias are also referred to as species dahlias. Note that many dahlia growers interchange the terms cultivar and variety.

BIBLIOGRAPHY

George N. Agrios, *Plant Pathology (Fifth Edition)*, 2005.

Kristine Albrecht & Brion Sprinsock. *Dahlia Breeding for the Farmer-Florist and the Home Gardener.* KDP Publishing. 2020

Benzakein, Erin. *Discovering Dahlias.* Chronicle Books L.L.C. San Francisco, California. 2021.

Buchmann, Stephen. *The Reason For Flowers.* Simon and Schuster, Inc. New York, New York. 2015.

Cook, Ward H. *Guide to Judging Dahlias.* American Dahlia Society. 2002.

Frost, Jessie. *The Living Soil Handbook.* Chelsea Green Publishing. White River Junction, Vermont. 2021.

Gips, Kathleen. *Flora's Dictionary.* T.M. Publishing. Chagrin Falls, Ohio. 1995.

Hammett, Keith. *The World of Dahlias.* Kaye & Ward Ltd. London, England. 1980.

Hodge, Geoff. *Practical Botany for Gardeners.* University of Chicago Press. 2013.

Jahren, Hope. Lab Girl. Alfred A. Knopf. New York, New York. 2016.

Lowenfels, Jeff & Wayne Lewis. *Teaming With Microbes.* Timber Press Inc. Portland, Oregon. 2010.

McClaren, Bill. *Encyclopedia of Dahlias.* Timber Press Inc. Portland, Oregon. 2004.

Mefferd, Andrew. *The Organic No-Till Farming Revolution.* New Society Publishers. Gabriela Island, B.C. Canada. 2019.

Menzel, John. *Dahlias in Australia "The Winkie Way."* Bounty Printing. 2016.

Cristian Olaya, Badri Adhikari, Gaurav Raikhy, Jianlin Cheng & Hanu R. Pappu, *Virology Journal, volume 16, Article number: 7* (2019) Identification and localization of Tospovirus genus-wide conserved residues in 3D models of the nucleocapsid and the silencing suppressor proteins.

Peters, Richard W. M.D. *Raising Beautiful Dahlias the Easy Way.* American Dahlia Society. 2006.

Pollan, Michael. *The Botany of Desire: A Plant's-Eye View of the World.* Random House Publishers. 2001.

Puget Sound Dahlia Society. *Dahlias: A Monthly Guide.* Puget Sound Dahlia Society. 2018.

Rowlands, Gareth. *The Gardener's Guide to Growing Dahlias*. Timber Press Inc. Portland, Oregon. 1999.

Stout, Mrs. Charles H. *The Amateur's Book of the Dahlia*. Doubleday, Page & Company. Garden City, New York. 1922.

M. Tsompana, J.W. Moyer, in *Encyclopedia of Virology (Third Edition)*, 2008.

Massimo Turina, Marina Ciuffo, *Advances in Virus Research*, 2012.

Waite, W. H. *Modern Dahlia Culture*. A. T. DeLa Mare Company, Inc. New York, New York. 1931.

Weaver, Tara Austen & Poole, Emily, *Dahlias: A Little Book of Flowers*, Sasquatch Books, 2022.

My son Riley and me with a giant pumpkin.

Resources

Agdia Inc. At-home virus test kits. agdia.com.

AgroThrive liquid fertilizer. Agrothrive.com

The Amercican Dahlia Society. dahlia.org

Arbico Organics. Organic & biological pest control products. arbico-organics.com

Coolbot controller for building or buying a cool shed. storeitcold.com

EZ Pots. Makers of pin frogs. ezpots.com

Floral Genius pin frogs and pin cups. hhfshop.com/collections/arranging-tools

GopherHawk. Makers of the GopherHawk Trap. gopherhawk.com

Hida Tool Company. Teflon floral scissors. hidatool.com

Hydrodynamics International. Makers of Root Riot plugs. hydrodynamicsintl.com

Johnny's Select Seeds. johnnyseeds.com

Liquid Fence animal repellant. Liquidfence.com

Midco. Makers of corn tassel bags. midcoglobal.com

Monterey Lawn & Garden Products. Makers of Sluggo & Sluggo Plus. montereylawngarden.com

Stanford University Dahlia Project. web.stanford.edu/group/dahlia_genetics

Stuewe & Sons. Suppliers of Rigi Pots. stuewe.com

Trimax. Makers of the BugZooka. trimaxlocks.com/shop/bugzooka/bugzooka

Xtreme Gardening. Makers of Mykos mycorrhizal inoculum. xtreme-gardening.com

Podcasts

<u>The Joe Gardener Podcast.</u> Joe Lamp'l. US. Organic gardening & cut flowers.

<u>The Flower Podcast.</u> Scott Shepherd. US. Cut flowers.

<u>Flower Power Garden Hour Podcast.</u> Marlene Simon. US. Cut flowers & gardening.

<u>Let's Grow Girls Podcast.</u> Sarah & Nicole. UK. Cut flowers.

<u>The No-Till Flowers Podcast.</u> Jennie Love. US. Cut flowers & regenerative farming.

<u>Quince Flowers Podcast.</u> Caitlyn & Peter Mason. Australia. Exclusively dahlias.

<u>Slow Flowers Podcast.</u> Debra Prinzing. US. Cut flowers.

<u>The Sustainable Flowers Podcast.</u> Heather & Clara. Canada. Cut flowers.

Recording the "Let's Grow Girls" podcast with Sarah & Nicole.

INDEX

ABOUT THE AUTHORS

In 2006 Kristine Albrecht reclaimed an urban quarter acre in Santa Cruz, California, that had been weed-choked and fallow for years. She fed the soil and eventually planted over 1,800 dahlias. Kristine's passion has been hybridizing new dahlia varieties. She develops varieties for both exhibition and cut flowers. As of this writing, Kristine has introduced twenty varieties to the market. All of her varieties start with her initials: KA's. In addition to being an award-winning dahlia exhibitor, Kristine is a cut flower farmer working with florists and designers. She has an active Instagram account at @santacruzdahlias, a YouTube channel at Kristine Albrecht, and a website at santacruzdahlias.com.

In 2020 Kristine and her husband Brion authored the popular book *Dahlia Breeding for the Farmer-Florist and the Home Gardener.* This is considered the first and definitive book on dahlia hybridizing.

Kristine was the president of the Monterey Bay Dahlia Society for 13 years and is currently leading the Dahlia Genome Project at the American Dahlia Society.

Kristine has won the American Dahlia Society's Derrill Hart Award for 'KA's Cloud', 'KA's Khaleesi', and 'KA's Papa John'. In addition, she won the American Dahlia Society's Lynn B Dudley Award for 'KA's Cloud'.

Kristine lives in Santa Cruz, California, with her husband. The couple has two grown children.

Brion Sprinsock met Kristine in high school on a backpacking trip to Yosemite National Park. Brion is a photographer, writer, tour guide, product designer, and builder. His primary role at the dahlia farm is as a builder, photographer, and when a book is in the works, writer, designer, and editor. In addition, he maintains a lively Instagram account that explores "behind the scenes" at Kristine's farm at @dahliasplease. His mother claims that his first word was "flower."

ABOUT THE PHOTOGRAPHS
Except where noted, all the photographs in this book were taken by the authors.

Brion and Kristine near Kanab, Utah. Photo by Iris Wallace.

Made in the USA
Middletown, DE
29 September 2023

39772699R00155